Commercial Dance

This is an exploration of the vital and rapidly evolving world of Commercial Dance, tracing the evolution and merging of Hip-Hop, Club and Jazz dance styles from the music videos of the early 1980s, to today's huge influence on pop music and dance in a multi-media culture.

Chapters including 'Iconic Moments' and 'Main Movers' contextualise and analyse culturally significant works and choreographers. With direct contributions from an international array of industry leading dancers, choreographers and creatives – including JaQuel Knight (Beyonce's choreographer), Rich + Tone Talauega (Madonna & Michael Jackson collaborators), Rebbi Rosie (Rihanna's dancer), Dean Lee (Janet Jackson's choreographer) and Kiel Tutin (BLACKPINK's choreographer) – this book shines a light on the creatives in the Commercial Dance industry who have made significant impacts, not just on the world of dance but on popular culture itself. Chapters discussing dance history, copyright law, inclusivity and dance class culture as well as additional contributions from dance scholars enable this book to give credence to Commercial Dance as a legitimate academic area of study.

This is a complete and comprehensive textbook for all dance students at any level of study on college, university or conservatory courses.

Anthony R. Trahearn is currently the Head of Dance and programme leader for the BA (Hons) Commercial Dance course at the Institute of the Arts Barcelona, Spain. He trained at London Studio Centre and subsequently worked as a Commercial dancer and associate choreographer for 17 years, working internationally with some of the industry's most established creatives.

Commercial Dance
An Essential Guide

Anthony R. Trahearn

LONDON AND NEW YORK

Designed cover image: © Cover design by Nekrasova-Studio.com. Credit for "Vogue dancer" cover image: Photography – Nicole Guarino, Dancer – Ida Paulsen. Other three images used with permission from Getty images.

First published 2024
by Routledge
4 Park Square, Milton Park, Abingdon, Oxon OX14 4RN

and by Routledge
605 Third Avenue, New York, NY 10158

Routledge is an imprint of the Taylor & Francis Group, an informa business

© 2024 Anthony R. Trahearn

The right of Anthony R. Trahearn to be identified as author of this work has been asserted in accordance with sections 77 and 78 of the Copyright, Designs and Patents Act 1988.

All rights reserved. No part of this book may be reprinted or reproduced or utilised in any form or by any electronic, mechanical, or other means, now known or hereafter invented, including photocopying and recording, or in any information storage or retrieval system, without permission in writing from the publishers.

Trademark notice: Product or corporate names may be trademarks or registered trademarks, and are used only for identification and explanation without intent to infringe.

British Library Cataloguing-in-Publication Data
A catalogue record for this book is available from the British Library

Library of Congress Cataloging-in-Publication Data
Names: Trahearn, Anthony R., author.
Title: Commercial dance: the essential guide / Anthony R. Trahearn.
Description: Abingdon, Oxon; New York, NY: Routledge, 2024. |
Includes bibliographical references and index.
Identifiers: LCCN 2023014594 (print) | LCCN 2023014595 (ebook) |
ISBN 9780367626006 (hardback) | ISBN 9780367625955 (paperback) |
ISBN 9781003109884 (ebook)
Subjects: LCSH: Dance in motion pictures, television, etc. | Music and dance.
Classification: LCC GV1779 .T73 2024 (print) | LCC GV1779 (ebook) |
DDC 791.43/6578—dc23/eng/20230515
LC record available at https://lccn.loc.gov/2023014594
LC ebook record available at https://lccn.loc.gov/2023014595

ISBN: 9780367626006 (hbk)
ISBN: 9780367625955 (pbk)
ISBN: 9781003109884 (ebk)

DOI: 10.4324/9781003109884

Typeset in Sabon
by codeMantra

"For all the dancers – beginners, advanced or professional. Never forget why you started dancing in the first place…

And also for my parents, who drove me to dance class for the first time when I was 8 years old and have supported my career ever since."

Contents

1	Introduction	1
2	The Definition	7
3	The Ingredients	11
	3a. Hip-Hop & Funk Styles	11
	3b. Jazz Dance	24
	3c. Club Styles	37
	Professional Insight – Barry Lather	47
	Professional Insight – Rebbi Rose	49
4	The People	55
	4a. The Commercial Dancer	55
	4b. The Commercial Choreographer's Assistant/Associate	57
	4c. The Commercial Dance Choreographer	58
	4d. The Creative Director	60
	Professional Insight – Reshma Gajjar	61
	Professional Insight – Jono Kitchens	63
5	The Realisations	67
	5a. Music Video and MTV	67
	5b. Musical Theatre and Dance Theatre	82
	5c. Live Concerts and Televised Events	90
	Professional Insight – Karla Garcia	96
	Professional Insight – Kiel Tutin	98
6	Iconic Moments	103
	Michael Jackson's 'Thriller'	103
	Janet Jackson's 'Rhythm Nation'	105
	Beyonce's 'Single Ladies'	108
	SIA 'Chandelier'	109

Contents

	Pink: What About Us	111
	'The Greatest Showman'	114
	Mary J Blige Live Performance	115
	Rihanna's Savage X Fenty Fashion Show Vol II	117
	'Us Again' Walt Disney Animation Studios	120
7	**Main Movers**	**123**
	Brian Friedman	123
	Charm La'Donna	125
	Christopher Scott	126
	Fatima Robinson	128
	Frank Gatson	130
	Jamie King	132
	JaQuel Knight	133
	Laurieann Gibson	135
	Marty Kudelka	138
	Michael Rooney	140
	Nadine 'Hi-Hat' Ruffin	142
	Paul Roberts	143
	Paula Abdul	145
	Rich + Tone Talauega	147
	Tina Landon	149
	Toni Basil	151
	Vincent Paterson	153
8	**Talking Points**	**157**
	8a. Copyright and Commercial Dance	157
	8b. Commercial Class Culture	162
	8c. Polar Paradigms – Inclusivity and Sexualisation	165
	8d. A Supporting Dancer	168
	8e. Street Dance versus Urban Dance	169
	Professional Insight – Randall Watson	172
	Professional Insight – Xena Gusthart	174
9	**Places to Train**	**179**
	9a. BASE Dance Studios	180
	9b. Broadway Dance Centre	180
	9c. Pineapple Dance Studios	181
	9d. Millennium Dance Complex	182
	Professional Insight – Kashika Arora	183
	Professional Insight – Nathan J Clarke	184

| 10 | Academic Insight | 189 |

10a. Dancing on a Cliff Edge — 190
10b. Collaborations between Early 20th-Century European and American Concert and Commercial Dance: Tamiris and Nagrin — 198
10c. Punkin' and Werkin' It: The Queer Roots of Commercial Dance — 203
10d. A Reflection on Hip-Hop, Hegemony and Appropriation — 209
Professional Insight – Dean Lee — 215

Acknowledgements — 221
Index — 223

Chapter 1

Introduction

Most dance students know that Jerome Robbins choreographed the 1961 movie 'West Side Story.' They also know that Bob Fosse choreographed 'Cabaret.' These are two movies which made a large impression on the trajectory of dance in the 20th century. Michael Jackson's iconic 'Thriller' short film and Beyonce's 'Single Ladies' music video have also made a notable impact, not just on the development of late 20th-century dance genres, but they are also immensely significant moments in global popular culture, just as 'West Side Story' and 'Cabaret' were. So why do so few people know who choreographed these music videos, yet Jerome Robbins and Bob Fosse are widely recognised as performing arts pioneers? Michael Peters choreographed Michael Jackson's 'Thriller' short film and Frank Gatson Jr and JaQuel Knight choreographed Beyonce's 'Single Ladies' music video. Far fewer students know the names of those choreographers. Over the last 40 years, remarkably influential moments of dance in film, television, music video and on the stage have passed without a tip of the hat to the choreographer and the dance creatives involved.

Commercial Dance's further inclusion into academic dance studies is necessary to recognise the impact it has had on popular culture. Working hand in hand with pop music, these two areas of performance art have created a cultural tidal wave, which from the mid-20th century has helped to steer everything from fashion to socio-political movements. 'Thriller' (1983) and 'Single Ladies' (2008) are both cultural outliers, not only because of the immense popularity of the songs but also for the choreography in the short film and music video that accompanied these songs. Accordingly, these visual companions must also be acknowledged as ground-breaking – and they are of course, frequently – the artist's performance, special effects, costume, make-up, styling, photography, film direction are all exhaustively referenced and discussed in documentaries, articles and books. Unfortunately, all too often we find that the choreographer – the person who actually created these dance sequences (which in these two examples are as iconic and as easily recalled as the songs they were created for) – is left off the list of acknowledgements. Google your favourite music video or dance film and see if you can find who the choreographer was and whether they are credited on sites such as IMDB. If they are credited, how far down the list of creatives do they appear? You may be surprised by what you *don't* find!

Introduction

Defining Commercial Dance

I worked in the Commercial Dance industry as a dancer, assistant choreographer and occasional choreographer for 16 years in London. 'What is Commercial Dance?' is a question I have struggled to answer comfortably since I started working in 2001. Whilst researching and writing this book over the last three years, I have asked this same question to many different people. I always had the feeling that they had not been asked this question before and weren't really sure how to answer it. Most people have an idea of what Commercial Dance *looks* like and where we can *find* it… but what actually *is* it? You probably have your own idea of what Commercial Dance is but articulating exactly what it is can be challenging, but for the sake of the academic progression of Commercial Dance itself, absolutely necessary.

During my research I noticed that 'commercial theatre/work/arts' are referenced frequently throughout the archives of dance history – loosely referred to as a form of theatre motivated by making a profit ahead of a purely artistic or creative desire, its purpose is to sell stuff. In this book, I have focused on the term 'Commercial Dance' as both a genre of dance and a sector of industry. Commercial Dance as a dance form is an amalgamation of a number of popular dance styles including Jazz through to Hip-Hop, taking in Voguing, Popping, Locking, Breakin', Krump, House, Waacking, Dancehall and Contemporary along the way. It is performed by dancers in music videos, in movies, on television shows and at concerts supporting music artists. There are many expressions of dance that can be found simmering in the melting pot of Commercial Dance.

Artistic appreciation is subjective and based largely on personal taste, so applying labels and quantifiable dimensions to works of performance art, although imperative for further understanding of the area, can be a dull and unnecessary exercise in academicising and quantifying the creative industries (after all – one person's work of art is another's trash – that's part of the fantastic subjectivity which art encourages). However, this analysis and evaluation is necessary in order to study Commercial Dance effectively and in a way that can be compartmentalised and discussed succinctly.

Expansion in Education

Commercial Dance is everywhere – on TV screens, social media feeds, in our favourite singer's music videos and in nearly every dance centre, yet so few questions have been asked, let alone answered, about the nature and evolutionary path Commercial Dance has taken. How do we evaluate such a diverse area of performing artistry? Is Commercial Dance and the canon of work which it consists of on an artistic par with that of Contemporary dance or is it the shallow art form some consider it to be – just a hallow, dispensable piece of the marketing and branding jigsaw that dominates today's media-driven consumerist societies? As a dance genre, is it capable of growing up, leaving its adolescence and taking a permanent seat at the table of Performing Arts education and academia?

Commercial Dance is increasingly studied in universities and performing arts institutions. Globally, undergraduate courses and programmes which include Commercial Dance elements currently sit alongside historically established areas of performing arts academic study such as Musical Theatre and Contemporary Dance – about which the recommended reading lists are endless. Sondheim, Gershwin, Graham, Bausch – the amount of academic reading, analysis and research material available to students studying these musical theatre and modern dance luminaries is extensive. Their stature is justifiably solidified by a mountain of books, collections and research papers which have been produced over the last 100 years or so. A student of Commercial Dance today hoping to find some solid study support will more than likely leave empty-handed after visiting their local bookshop or college library, unless they want to read a book about Misty Copeland or Darcy Bussell (both great classical artists in their own right, just not related to Commercial Dance). They may find a chapter or two in a Dance Studies Companion from the 1990s dedicated to 'Dance in Music Video' or 'Street Dance' but often the focus is somewhat ambiguous as to what this 'music video/street dance' is and where it actually sits in the world of movement and dance studies. Research into subjects related to Commercial Dance including Dance on Screen, Hip-Hop studies and Music Videos has expanded significantly over the last decade with specialists such as Professor Sherril Dodds, Professor Mary Fogarty and Professor Emily Caston providing solid, insightful analysis, giving credence to areas that have been somewhat overlooked. What is still missing is coverage of how to relate the study of these individual specialisms to the broader content and industry of Commercial Dance.

Widening the Scope of Dance Literature

The validity of Commercial Dance and the popular social dance genres it envelops has still not really been secured within the world of academia. It has not been dismissed, but its development within universities or conservatoires has been at a glacial pace. For decades, scholars have been advocating for an updated, broader and more inclusive approach to dance studies, an approach that recognises the cultural and artistic importance of social and popular dances. Professor of Dance and Performance at New York university, Julie Malnig, acknowledged back in 2001 that '*one of the fascinating aspects of social dance itself is the variety of styles it encompasses and the continually fluid exchange among what we call social, vernacular and popular dances*' and commenting that sometimes these areas of popular entertainment are '*hidden in the recesses of culture where scholars had seldom tread.*' Malnig was fighting Commercial Dance's corner 20 years ago, just calling it by a different name. In 2009, Gay Morris, a dance historian and critic, also urged dance academia to engage further with cultural studies whilst '*broadening conceptions of what constitutes "dance"*' advocating that unless the importance of the social role that dance plays is acknowledged, then dance studies cannot continue to be successful. The intention has long been there to expand the scope of Dance studies to include social and popular dances prevalent in the area of entertainment. Social and popular dances provide the fabric from which Commercial Dance is constructed.

Still, there seems to be a reluctance to take dance in the Commercial arena seriously in some quarters. Perhaps, it is subconsciously dismissed by scholars (those still immersed in European studio based dance genres) as a dubious area of 'art' with no history or repertoire to speak of – not in comparison to modern dance history and the great works of Balanchine, Bausch, Khan, Hofesch, Cunningham et al. This perspective may appear elitist, blinkered and outdated to current students of dance – Commercial Dance deserves the same consideration and intellectualisation afforded to classical and contemporary dance genres. I hope that this book is able to cover some of the areas which have not been sufficiently documented and discussed.

Why I Wrote This Book and Creating Relatable Dance Literature

I have always been a practitioner by trade, not a theorist. Furthermore, I am not a dance historian, academic nor an anthropologist and although I back the idea of intellectualising

Introduction

Commercial Dance and I am wary of *over* intellectualising it. Having had many discussions with current dance students and taking heed from my own experiences of studying dance in an academic sense, I feel that some academic writing can alienate dance students. I have written this book hoping to help bridge the gap between academic and editorial writing in dance. If a student is interested in digging deeper about the past and potential future paths of dance, they can be stifled when presented with disengaging and verbose academic writing so complex that if you are not from a background of academic theorising (as I wasn't), you are left feeling a little lost and disconnected. In reviewing a 1993 book about Madonna, the academic and cultural critic Camille Paglia comments on the pretentious nature of some academic writing which covers popular culture, noting that the consistent use of words like "diegesis," "intertextual," "narrative strata" and "discursive practices" would be "comical except for the ill effect on students." I hope that this book avoids such grandiose words and yet still encourages thoughtful critical reflection about Commercial Dance without hindering the reader's enthusiasm for study and research by offering a relatable and engaging approach to the subject matter.

Throughout this book, I have tied the historical and cultural perspectives directly to relevant practical performance work. It is an attempt to collate, collect, and to an extent, catalogue the components of a young, complex industry. There is a lot of material covered in these pages, it is essentially an oversight of a 40-year-old genre of dance. Collecting this information has been possible only from an enormous amount of research which has included many different modes – journal articles, newspaper reviews, interviews, e-mail exchanges, zoom conversations, documentary footage, academic books and my own experiences have all been utilised. There are areas which I would have loved to have spent more time on – I would have liked to delve a little deeper into some of the topics. I offer that this book is a starting point and I encourage *you*, the reader, to delve deeper and continue the research into many of the areas included in this book.

My Own Experience... and Ignorance

Contained within the text are occasional observations from my own experiences as a professional, working in the Commercial Dance industry. This is not a thinly veiled attempt at a memoir, but I use these personal references as a way of providing relatable human insight into the working practices of the Commercial Dance industry and some of the talented creatives catalogued in these pages. I also believe that in a time when AI software is developing rapidly, real world experience and having been "in the room where it happened" is increasingly valuable for arts education to maintain a sense of authenticity rooted in human observation.

I have learned so much from researching and writing this book. As a dancer and dance educator, some of these things I now realise I should have known and understood as an 18-year-old dance student, I did not. After reflecting on this, I have identified two reasons for this. Firstly, when I was studying dance in London at a pre-professional level (late 1990s) there just wasn't the educational material, nor faculty knowledge about what was thought of as 'street dance in music videos.' Within dance education at this time, there was no acknowledgement that this industry actually existed, very few thought that becoming a full time, specialist "music video or back-up dancer" was a viable and sustainable career choice and certainly not one that had had much artistic merit. There was no YouTube or Vimeo, no social media channels that shared choreography or videos with the world. Any music video or live performance you had heard whispers about had to be sought after, usually by borrowing a VHS or waiting up all night to catch the music video on MTV, so discovering this new and exciting choreography,

Introduction

from a UK perspective anyway, was not easy. Secondly, my own ignorance is to blame. I could and should have asked more questions about the industry I was actually working in, what the origins were and the cultural contexts of the movement I was performing. So perhaps by writing this book, I'm actually trying to compensate for my earlier ignorance.

I must also acknowledge that there are choreographers, dancers and creatives, those working today and those who offered their work decades ago, that have contributed significantly to the growth of Commercial Dance who may not be mentioned in this book. Any omission is simply down to a limited amount of page space and research and writing time. Initiatives such as 'The World Choreography Awards' (USA) and 'Move It' (UK) illuminate just how many exceptional Commercial choreographers are producing noteworthy work. I am sure that in future editions of this book, and other books specialising in Commercial Dance, their artistic endeavours will be captured. The selected 'Main Movers' and 'Iconic Moments' are not intended to be part of a definitive or exhaustive list – as with much within this book, it is a starting point for a catalogue of work which I hope will be continually expanded.

Reflect, Question and Research!

I urge every reader of this book to ask questions about the dances they dance. Who originally choreographed this routine? What actually *is* this style of dance I'm performing and what part of the world did it originate from? I guarantee that learning more about the historical and cultural context of the 5, 6, 7, 8's you are perfecting will open your eyes and enable you to perform the choreography with a greater authenticity, will further your appreciation of its origins and no doubt progress your abilities as a dancer. Hopefully, this book can advance the conversation about Commercial Dance and be a helpful tool for dancers of all ages, whilst also giving Commercial Dance history and its creatives, past and present, the attention, affirmation and acclamation they deserve.

Keep up to date with news and features about this book at
www.commercial-dance.com

The Outline

Commercial Dance: An Essential Guide will take you through the ideas of what Commercial Dance is and discuss its roots, its current state, its pioneers, those currently bringing innovation to the game and the industry's potential future trajectories. It's intended to be informative and interesting – regardless of whether you are a dancer or not. I hope that the features and spotlights included about some of the key personalities and moments in Commercial Dance are engaging for all. I am also optimistic that some of the historical insights might awaken a curiosity to learn more about the steps you see on the screen.

'*The Definition*' chapter opens the book and ponders exactly what Commercial Dance consists of, as a performing art and as an industry, and strives to place a firmer handle on its origins.

'*The Ingredients*' looks at the origins of the individual styles of dance that provide the base material in the complexion of Commercial Dance. Styles have been categorised into three groups: Hip-Hop & Funk Styles, Jazz and Club Styles. Within these broader groups, you will find sub-chapters covering everything from Breakin' to Waacking.

'*The People*' gives a breakdown of the main job roles found within the industry. This section covers the key players in the industry – the dancer, the assistant choreographer, the choreographer and the Creative Director.

Introduction

'*The Realisations*' observes the various channels of entertainment in which Commercial Dance finds its audience: MTV & Music Video, Live Shows & Television and Musical & Dance Theatre.

'*Iconic Moments*' will focus on some of the notable moments in the evolution of this dance form, from Sia's 'Chandelier' music video to Janet Jackson's 'Rhythm Nation.'

'*Main Movers*' puts some of the choreographers and creatives who have helped to shape this industry centre stage, including Fatima Robinson, Marty Kudelka and Rich & Tone Talauega.

'*Talking Points*' is a chance to explore some of the many conversation points pertaining to social and cultural issues which are prevalent throughout the Commercial Dance industry. Areas including copyright law, sexualisation, the term 'Urban Dance' and dance class culture are discussed.

'*Places to Train*' provides information about, and a brief history of, some of the most prominent dance studios offering classes in Commercial Dance internationally.

Academic Insight is a collection of four essays from Dance scholars covering subjects such as the manifestation of queer cultures in Commercial Dance, appropriation and the gig economy.

Throughout the book *Professional Insights* features are included in each chapter, which provide a series of spotlights on creatives working in the Commercial Dance industry. They share their stories, inspirations, philosophies about dance and advice for budding dancers wishing to pursue a career in this eclectic and exciting industry.

References

Malnig, J. (2001). Introduction. *Dance Research Journal*, 33(2), 7–10.
Morris, G. (2009). Dance Studies/Cultural Studies. *Dance Research Journal*, 41(1), 82–100.
Paglia, C. (1993). Review of Madonna: Blonde Ambition, by M. Bego. *Notes*, 50(1), 88–90.

Chapter 2

The Definition

What Is Commercial Dance?

Commercial Dance is a vast area of performance art comprising a multitude of blended dance styles and influences which are delivered via various media and entertainment-based industries. When discussing Commercial Dance, we address two separate entities – Commercial Dance as a dance genre and Commercial Dance as an industry. The content of Commercial Dance as a dance genre embodies steps from many popular and social dance styles. The label also acknowledges that this dance genre was cultivated for, and is embodied in, an industry which strives to commercialise and monetise a product, using entertainment as means to connect with the audience and in turn, convert that engagement into a purchase of the product which the dance has been created to promote. It's a genre and industry of dance interwoven with many different artistic and cultural fabrics, presenting an exact definition is not easy. There is currently no dictionary definition of Commercial Dance but it can be broken it into two parts:

i) The 'Commercial' part….
   Cambridge Dictionary defines **Commercial** as:
   Adjective
1. Related to buying and selling things:
   a commercial organisation/venture/success
2. Used to describe a record, film, book, etc. that has been produced with the aim of making money and as a result has little artistic value

   Using a literal translation of this definition, acknowledges that Commercial Dance sells things – it is… *'produced with the aim of making money and as a result has little artistic value.'*

The Definition

Such a definition unfairly suggests that Commercial Dance has 'little artistic value' but it does give a clear insight into the initial motivations for the creation of Commercial Dance choreography. It explains why it developed in the late 1980s in a prosperous North American economic climate which used advertising and marketing strategies in an increasingly effective way. It identifies what the driving forces are behind most Commercial Dance commissions: To promote and to *sell* a commodity.

Purpose, Product and Promotional Channels

According to this dictionary definition, Commercial Dance refers to movement that is created and performed with the purpose of promoting a product via different promotional channels. At its core, the original purpose of Commercial Dance was, and still is, to sell or endorse commodities or products. This endorsement is often manifested through various promotional channels such as TV commercials, stage productions or music videos. Commercial Dance strives to offer an exciting, instant and culturally relevant way to promote the goods. It engages its audience with exhilarating, energetic choreography and often offers the viewer relatable steps that can be mimicked on the dance floor. It is viewed as exhilarating but fun, avant-garde yet relatable. In an age where the audience's gaze equates to money in the bank, Commercial Dance is a proven marketing asset.

ii) The 'Dance' part....

What are the fundamental Commercial Dance movement characteristics? In many cases, characterising forms of dance in terms of their recognisable somatic traits and

Table 2.1 Table showing avenues of promotion in Commercial Dance

Purpose	*Products include*	*Promotional channels include*
Creating and performing dance to entertain an audience and in the process promoting, selling and monetising a commodity or product.	A music artist and their material	Music videos, tours and live and televised events
	Consumer goods: Cars, watches, phones, fashion brands, etc.	Television advertising, fashion shows, editorials and live events
	A movie or television show	Providing on-screen action to complement and heighten entertainment value of television and cinema releases, helping to increase tickets sold at the box office or viewing figures on streaming platforms.

associated movement has been straightforward. Ballet, for example, has a clear syllabus of technical steps and choreographic phrases which are universally recognised. Pas de Chat's, Chasses and Rond de Jambes all form the fabric of its technique, allowing ballet its own dance structure and clearly identifiable motifs which are recognisable to all.

The definition of Commercial Dance in its physical sense must acknowledge that it is a relatively new dance form that has enveloped and fused together a multitude of different dance styles and sub-genres. This pliable dance genre is driven and shaped by cultural pillars such as fashion, music and media and judging by the content of Commercial Dance seen throughout various promotional channels over the last 30 years, Commercial Dance's melded form consists of elements including:

Hip-Hop & Funk Styles (including Locking, Breakin', New Style, Popping)
Vogue Fem
Jazz dance
Waacking
House
Latin American Styles
Krump
African dance
Contemporary
Dancehall

Commercial Dance has readily engulfed many sub-genres of previously socially niché and popular dance forms, bringing them to the casual mainstream viewer and introducing them to a larger market who are eager to observe and enjoy the infectious flavours and grooves on show. It is possible to analyse nearly any phrase of Commercial Dance, whether taught in a class or seen in a professional music video and tick off most of the styles mentioned above as being referenced in some way, even if only for a few counts.

Image 2.1 Commercial Dance is regularly used to promote fashion brands in TV commercials as seen here in a still from a 2015 'House of Fraser' television commercial, choreographed by Parris Goebel

The Definition

'Commercial' + 'Dance' = a definition:

> *Commercial Dance is a genre of dance composed of a collection of dance sub-varieties including Hip-Hop & Funk styles, Jazz dance and Club styles. Its conception is often commissioned by commercial industries to advertise and consequently monetise the product for which the choreography was created.*

Undoubted Artistry
Despite this definition of Commercial Dance suggesting that artistic creativity comes second to the dance form's innate purpose to sell a product, celebrated works of high artistic value have appeared in all articulations of Commercial Dance since the early 1980s. Commercial Dance has cultivated a rich canon of quality, artistic works, many of which are catalogued throughout the pages of this book. Innovative choreographers and creative teams creating works for production companies, record labels and fashion houses have devised unique and imaginative dance projects which have penetrated popular culture globally.

Chapter 3

The Ingredients

As discussed in the opening chapter 'The Definition,' Commercial Dance as a movement genre is a concoction of different dance styles which are referenced frequently in nearly every eight count sequence of choreography seen in commercial performance channels. In these forthcoming chapters, we will discuss the essential 'Ingredients' that make up the dominant vocabulary of Commercial Dance choreography. The styles of dance included under the Commercial Dance umbrella have been broken into three main categories that form the main architecture of most Commercial Dance – Hip-Hop & Funk Styles, Club Styles and Jazz dance.

Hip-Hop and Funk Styles gives an overview of Hip-Hop culture and explains the various genres which make up what we broadly term 'Hip-Hop' choreography – Breakin', Locking, Popping, Hip-Hop social steps & New Jack Swing and Krump.

Jazz Dance looks at essential elements of Jazz as it is manifested in the commercial industry today and also provides a broad historical journey of the Jazz genre, from its roots to its most notable contributors over the last century.

Club styles have been grouped together as they originated primarily on the dance floor – House, Vogue/Fem, Dancehall and Waacking. New styles within popular and social dance are consistently evolving and integrating into Commercial Dance meaning that this list is one that will be consistently in flux as trends develop.

3a. Hip-Hop & Funk Styles

The Float, Scooby-doo, Boogaloo, Bart Simpson, Glide, Butterfly, Ticking, Threading, Robocop, Stomp, Robot – these are just some of the terms applied to the myriad of steps and styles associated with Hip-Hop & Funk dance styles. Although a patchwork of different styles and expressions, 'Hip-Hop Dance' is succinctly defined as a

> group of related Afro-Diasporic dance forms, characterised by a competitive orientation and a close relationship with Hip-Hop music and culture. Hip-Hop dance generally falls into two categories: dance forms that have been continuously maintained as

cultural traditions since Hip-Hop's birth in the early 1970's, and relatively short-lived social or 'party' dances. As befits a relatively young art form, these dances – and the categories themselves – are very much in flux.

(Miyakawa & Schloss 2015)

Hip-Hop & Funk styles have consistently fertilised the dance ecosystem within which Commercial Dance has flourished, whilst also maintaining distinct historical and social cultures of their own. Perhaps one of the most prominent distinctions between what we see within the Commercial world of dance and Hip-Hop dances in their originate states is that they are "marked by their relationship to industries as opposed to communities" (Fogarty Woehrel, 2019). As Hip-Hop dance dissipates further into the melded Commercial choreography of television and music video, we see a loosening of its link to the culture from which it was born as the demands of a consumerist society (the TV network, the record company, us – the audience) mould its form – simultaneously sanitising whilst also deforming its characteristics. Washed away are some of the original dance narratives and texts from US east and west coast Black and Latino communities as 'commercialised' versions of the movement osmose into combo's taught in Commercial Dance classes the world over. Comparable to when a rapper guests on a pop record, the skills of the rapper aren't diminished (in many cases the guest rappers verse improves the record, there's too many examples to list) but the narrative content of the lyrics – historically one of struggle, social rebellion and defiance – is flipped for wholesome themes which satisfy the pop culture saturated demographic the record is aimed at. Nevertheless, the advancement of Hip-Hop dance styles has contributed significantly to what Commercial Dance actually is and what it looks like.

Hip-Hop Collective Culture – A Brief Overview

Hip-Hop culture is a social and anthropological medium which includes music, dance, language, art and fashion. Its influence on mainstream commerce and culture since the late 1970s and early 1980s has been vast. Considered to have four main elements – MC-ing (creating vocals or rapping over a beat), DJ-ing (using turntables to scratch, sample and create beats), writing (graffiti art) and B-boying/B-girling (dancing to the beats curated by the DJ), each of these slices of Hip-Hop culture are frequently manifested within Commercial Dance.

NY Back-drop

Hip-Hop culture evolved in the impoverished neighbourhoods of New York in the 1970s, against a backdrop of frugal, austere educational and social spending programmes which impoverished communities further. Not only were the poorer New York City boroughs engulfed by a tide of crime and drug-related issues, but the city was also on the verge of bankruptcy. Kim Phillips-Fein's sets out in his book, *Fear City: New York's Fiscal Crisis and the Rise of Austerity Politics*, the stark state the New York economy was in –

> When the national economy went into recession in the early 1970s, the loss of jobs turned into a flood: between the late 1960s and the mid 1970s, half a million jobs disappeared from the city. Job loss and the attendant deepening poverty (especially severe for Black and Latino New Yorkers) meant that more and more people were in need of city services.

A destitute housing situation and a lack of social building initiatives pushed the young black and Latino residents onto the streets of their barrios where the four primary pillars of Hip-Hop culture were cultivated and practised. A competitive flare within Hip-Hop sub-culture helped evolve the community rapidly – MCs battled MCs, B-boys and B-Girls danced off against other Breakers, Graffiti artists fought for neighbourhood notoriety and DJ's pushed each other to provide the slickest and most seamless break beats and sample loops. These key Hip-Hop aspects began to intertwine and merge into a social urban collective.

DJ Afrika Bambaataa is credited as a leading early advocate of Hip-Hop culture's positive societal energy. His creation of the Zulu Nation offered community support and artistic outlets for the youth who were often tempted by the more financially lucrative criminal opportunities in their neighbourhood. Bambaataa was a key force in turning the youth of the NY boroughs away from 'gang culture' and encouraging the growth of a Hip-Hop culture based on positive virtues. It was this positivity energy that facilitated Hip-Hop's rapid increase in exposure to the mainstream media during the 1980s. Dance scholar Susan Leigh Foster maintains that the *"immense appeal of Hip-Hop's vitality and physical articulateness and the sense of empowerment that the movement sequencing communicated reached across class and racial lines, hailing a youth population of many backgrounds."*

From Breakbeat to Breakin'

Whilst dance was only one of four plinths of Hip-Hop culture, being part of a Breakin' crew was a galvanising movement amongst the struggling underclasses in New York city in the late 1970s and early 1980s. DJ's such as DJ Kool Herc, Grandmaster Flash and DJ Afrika Bambaataa were key technicians who created the beats and pushed Hip-Hop dance culture to flourish. Developing the use of dual turntables, they made an art of sampling bars from Jazz and Funk records. Not only did this sampling and looping of Jazz and drum solos catalyse Breakin' as a dance style, but it also provided the basis from which Hip-Hop music would grow. The samples and loops not only gave opportunity for dancers to express themselves but also provided a meter for MC's to speak rhyming, poetic couplets over the beat – creating rapping.

Tied to the Music

Hip-Hop, Funk and other associated dance styles covered in this chapter have followed the ascending trajectory taken by their associated musical genres. During the late 1980s and 1990s, Hip-Hop music started to heavily re-shape the sound of Pop music. Visionary Hip-Hop producers such as J Dilla, Rick Rubin, DJ Premier, Q-Tip, Rodney Jerkins, Pharrell Williams and Kanye West have provided media outlets with a version of Hip-Hop music that has commercially crossed over to global audiences. Producers Timbaland and will.i.am have mixed 1990s House beats with Hip-Hop rhymes and Bruno Mars has brought James Brown's funk back to life. The flagrant choreography which accompanies these tracks in live performance and music videos matches the flavour of the music. As the music has morphed and infiltrated mass markets, so has the multitude of social Hip-Hop dance steps and trends that accompany these addictive rhymes and beats which are now seen on an endless loop on TikTok, Instagram and YouTube.

Covered in this chapter are a selection of the main Hip-Hop and Funk Styles commonly embodied in the genre of Commercial Dance: Breakin', Locking, Popping, Hip-Hop social steps & New Jack Swing and Krump.

The Ingredients

Breakin'

What Is It?

The prime dance element to emanate directly from original Hip-Hop culture. Breakin' flourished on the gritty streets of New York neighbourhoods such as The Bronx, Brooklyn and Queens in the 1970s, a few years later making its way to the US west coast. As with MCing, Graffiti and DJing, Breakin' is a product of the larger Hip-Hop ecosystem. Breakin' has completed a remarkable arc of growth, beginning in the pauperised and violent streets of New York city in the 1970s and culminating in the ultimate societal endorsement by being featured in the 2024 Paris Olympic games as a competitive pursuit for the first time. Mary Fogarty, a b-girl and Associate Professor of Dance at York University, Toronto is actively developing the dance form into a sport which can be judged fairly and have a wide reaching cultural impact during its debut at the Olympics in Paris. Fogarty speaks on Breakin' as an Olympic sport:

> I hope there is a fruitful synergy and we can present the form for what it is – one of the most exciting dance artforms of our times – and through presenting it to ask questions about decolonizing art, speaking from the margins of society, and questioning everything to make a better world.

Breakin' is a physical, acrobatic, competitive, stylised and increasingly gymnastic form of dance. As with many styles of dance, the origin story of Breakdancing, or Breakin' to give it its original and correct moniker, is bound to the parallel development of a musical nuance – the breakbeat. The breakbeat existed so dancers could get down, battle and 'break.' The combative element of Breakin' reflected the gang culture which was prevalent in New York in the 1970s. Crews would challenge each other on the street corners of their barrios to earn respect and notoriety in the boroughs. Jeff Chang's expansive book, *Can't Stop Won't Stop*, details the extensive gang networks that controlled the Bronx between in the late 1960s/early 1970s, a key time in Breakin's early development:

> Other gangs (along with the Javelins) kept Third Avenue hot -the Chingalings and the Savage Nomads to the west, the Black Falcons to the north. Below Crotona Park, in the heart of the burnt-out South Bronx, were the turfs the Ghetto Brothers, the Turbans, the Peacemakers, the Mongols, the Roman Kings, the Seven Immortals and the Dirty Dozens. Most of these gangs were predominately Puerto Rican. East of the Bronx River, the Black Spades consolidated the youths of the mostly African-American communities (43).… In three years, the gangs colonised the borough. Gang colours transformed the bombed out city grid into a matrix of beefs. 'If you went thought someones neighbourhood, you were a target. Or you had to take off your jacket,' Carlos Suarez, the president of the Ghetto Brothers, recalls,' If you got caught they beat the hell out of you' (50)

This social obligation to pledge allegiance to a gang from their block influenced the formation of and loyalty shown to Breakdance crews at that time.

The Steps

Breakin' is generally performed as an improvised freestyle and sometimes inside of a circle, or cypher, made by other Breakers (often from opposing battling crews) and spectators. There are four main dance elements: Top Rock/Up-Rock, Floor work, Power moves and Freezes.

The Ingredients

The *Up-Rock* element derives from a popular Latino style of dance (Rockin') which evolved in the 1960s and 1970s in New York, using footwork set to Latin drum rhythms – this element is used as an initial challenge to the dancers 'opponent.' It is performed standing up and has a 'throw down' feel to it, similar to when two boxers take the first minute or so of the first round to size each other up and gauge their opponents' skills and potential weaknesses. The 'Brooklyn Rock' for example sees the dancer lunge forward onto one foot before scooting backwards on the same foot, followed by an "Ali Shuffle"-esque switch of feet as the dancer's body drops to the floor (in a manner influenced by Ukrainian Hopak or Cossak dances). Scholars Miyakawa & Schloss explain the embattled nature of Rockin' in their 2015 research paper on the origins and development of Hip-Hop:

> Partially due to this directly confrontational orientation, the dance became associated with New York City gang culture and it's early development, although this association is now more historical than contemporary…. Conceptually, 'Rocking', resembles a kind of sparring in which dancers are trying to outdo each other in real time through a combination of superior dance technique, physical intimidation and specific burns.

There are a bunch of different Up-Rocks, all used as prep before *Floor work* – when the B-boy or B-Girl drops to the floor and executes rapid, fluid leg and foot movements, keeping their weight central as their legs perform intricate moves like the Six-Step, CCs and Threads.

Next comes the *'Powermove,'* the impressive, showpiece element of the dancers' work. Often gymnastic and requiring a lot of physical dexterity, there are a whole arsenal of Powermoves including Windmills, Suicides, Air-Flares, Turtle Spins, Kick the Moon, Headspins and Backspins.

Freezes are the fourth part of Breakin' essentials and consist of a dancer ending a phrase of movement by 'freezing' on the floor in a cartoon-ish yet physically skilled, tableaux or 'Freeze.' This often requires a lot of upper body strength and creates an illusion of a defiance of gravity. As with most elements of Breakin', the Freeze looks effortlessly cool.

Commercial Impact

In the early 1980s Breakdancing was abruptly launched into commercial mainstream media after the documentary 'Breakin' N' Enterin' and the budget movie 'Wild Style' (which in

Image 3.1 'The Rock Steady Crew' made one of their first international appearances in the movie 'Flashdance' (1983)

The Ingredients

2020 Vulture magazine called one of *"the most momentous portraits of hip-hop culture committed to film"*) captured the Hip-Hop movement's curious and charismatic nature, lifting the curtain internationally on an entirely new American subculture. These were followed with breakdance showcases in Malcom Mclaren's 'Buffalo Gals' music video (1982) and international box office movies such as 'Flashdance' (1983), 'Beat Street' (1984) and 'Breakin' (1984) (or in Europe – 'Breakdance') as well as the TV pilot 'Graffiti Rock' (1984). B-boys from the 'Rock Steady Crew' who featured in these projects, such as Frosty Freeze (Wayne Frost) and Crazy Legs (Richard Colón), found a celebrity status of their own after their memorable features on the big screen. Unsure of exactly how to describe this branch of Hip-Hop culture, the media branded it as 'Breakdancing' or 'Street Dance' – a term which was applied to any kind of dance that wasn't taught in a traditional dance studio. Street Dance was a term which was coined to include emerging west coast Funk styles such as Locking, Boogaloo and Popping as well as east coast Hip-Hop styles, inaccurately putting them all into the same pot.

By 1984, Breakin's authentic beginnings were already changing into a diluted, commercialised version of itself. Jeff Chang explains that

> After 'Beat Street', every kid wanted to breakdance and every city council and shopping mall official wanted to ban it. But the only thing that put a stop to the dance was its marketing overkill.
>
> (Chang 2005, 203)

Hip-Hop had been reduced to a kid-friendly Broadway production, scrubbed clean for primetime, force-fitted into one-size fits all…Hollywood had broadcast hip-hop onto tiny islands in the Pacific and into teeming working class ethnic suburbs in Europe but the spit-shined thing only increased the craving for the real thing.

(Chang 2005, 194)

Image 3.2 Check out some of the Breakers from the 2022 Red Bull finals in New York city

Locking

What Is It?

Locking is a dance style born out of the Funk era in Los Angeles in the 1970s and was traditionally danced to funk or disco music such as Earth, Wind and Fire, Herbie Hancock or James Brown. It was created by merging and developing a number of social dances and melding them into stylised, often cartoonish, stops or 'locks.' Locking has evolved to include a whole movement vocabulary of its own, containing distinctive mimetic steps and sequences of movement danced by Lockers from all over the world.

The style is attributed to Don Campbell (1951–2020) who patched the staccato 'locked' positions together from popular social dances of the early 1970s, creating a unique and almost caricatured volume of movement. Nods to traditional mime acts, clowning, numerous social dances and Campbell's own intuitive way of moving form the basis of what he initially coined as the 'Campbellock.' As its popularity grew, it became known as 'Locking.' Locking has been, and continues to be, used extensively in the world of Commercial Dance – Michael and Janet Jackson infused it regularly into their routines in the 1990s and it's also featured in much of the Commercial Dance choreography of the early 2000s – the work of Travis Payne, Wade Robson, Tina Landon et al show inflections of this distinctive style. Campbell explained in his own words what Locking was and is:

> Sometimes, I would stop, freeze, and lock it up! Or sometimes, it would be just one continuous motion. It wasn't a specific move that I practiced.... And I wasn't trying to name things. I wasn't trying to break things down. I was just doing me. It was my dance. And it's what made me "Campbellock".

Campbell was featured as a dancer on the television show 'Soul Train' from 1971 to 1973 and continued to refine his style of 'Campbellock' at popular dance contests. He formed the icon dance group 'The Lockers' with Toni Basil, Shabba Doo (star of the movies Breakin' & Breakin' 2) and Fred Berry, amongst others. The Lockers had a significant impact on the advancement of what had been termed 'Street Dance,' arguably becoming the first group to begin to codify dances of this style. Locking and 'The Lockers' not only influenced the dance landscape of the US in the 1970s but also defined a fashion movement with their unique ways of dressing which incorporated luminescent flat caps, striped knee-length socks, jodhpur-style trousers and oversized shirt collars.

The Steps

Locking as a dance dialect is incomparable to any other and easy to spot. It is a mix of dance, mime, comedy, acrobatics and most importantly flavour. A good Locker projects character and playfulness in their performance which is laid over a set of dynamic angular pictures created by the dancer as they fluidly travel through a range of well-versed steps, personifying the funk in the music they are dancing to. Snapped finger points, jagged arm breaks and knee drops are some of the striking visuals you may take away with you after watching a few 8's of Locking. Foundational steps include 'The Up-Lock,' 'The Muscle Man,' 'The Scooby-Doo,' 'The Stop n Go' and 'The Skeeter Rabbit.' The animated names of these steps indicate the light-hearted nature of Locking and the fun eccentricity of its performance traits – referencing popular cultural interests of the 1970s such as Bruce Lee martial arts movies and ground breaking animations from Disney as well as Hanna-Barbera cartoons like Scooby-Do.

The Ingredients

Image 3.3 Don Campbell and his group, 'The Lockers' in a 1974 feature for Esquire magazine (US). Don Campbell is on his hands while Toni Basil kicks in the yellow and red socks. The image displays the athleticism of this performance oriented dance, whilst also showing their signature fashion style.'

Commercial Impact

Locking was given a prominent national platform on the culturally iconic US TV show 'Soul Train.' 'Soul Train' was created by Don Cornelius, it first aired in 1971 and its goal was to specifically showcase music from black artists. The sound of R&B, Disco and Funk (performed live by artists such as The Jackson 5, Gladys Knight & the Pips and The Temptations) played out alongside the new dance steps which would infect every dance floor in the US as viewers would mimic their musical idols. The show would also feature a group of regular dancers who would take part in 'The Dance Line' at the end of each episode – the dancers would stand in two lines and filter down the centre one or two at a time, improvising and giving life to the popular dance fads that were 'in' that week.

In one episode of Soul Train, influential dancer of the time, Damita Jo Freeman, explained what kind of style she was dancing with her partner, Don Campbell. Her answer, "*It's a combination of the 'Breakdown,' the 'Rubberband,' the 'Campbellock' and many other things,*" illustrates the large number of popular social dances and how they were melded into new and exciting steps with street-cool names. Locking had a large impact on the advancement of what was being termed 'Street Dance,' arguably becoming the first street sub-style to label and partially codify its steps.

The improvised and sub-cultured origins of the dances displayed on Soul Train suggest that the show was one of the most important vehicles for the development of early Commercial Dance. Entertainer Nick Cannon remarks on the impact of the dances featured on Soul Train in Questlove's 2013 book *Soul Train: The Music, Dance, and Style of a Generation*:

> My earliest memories of Soul Train are dancing in front of the television as a toddler.…
> As I got older, I would see different dance moves take off after being showcased on Soul

Train. It was an amazing vehicle for dance culture in it's very early days. And it was huge deal for me watching a lot of the dancers start in Soul Train and then, from there, begin to dance for a lot of the major artists of the day.

Popping

What Is It?

Popping is a dance style performed by specialist dancers (Poppers) who create illusions with their body. Whether this illusion is created by mimicking the mechanical movement of a robot (The Robot) or moving their body with such fluidity that it appears it's made of water (The Wave, The Boogaloo), the dancer punctuates their performance with 'hits' or 'pops' to the beat of the music by using sharp micro contractions of muscle groups, which gives the dance this distinctive 'pop.' Showing complete control over their body by contracting whilst simultaneously tranquillising other muscles in their body, Poppers create an animated, illusionary way of moving similar to that of great mime artists like Marcel Marceau. Danced originally to Funk music, Popping matched well with the futuristic, electronically synthesised sounds of the 1980s. The ethereal, science fiction sound on 1980s records by bands like Kraftwerk combined with a sharp prominent snare drum provided Poppers with music that complemented the unique movement and accentuated their 'hit.' It's a dance that is mesmerising to watch and enraptures audiences of all ages.

Born in neighbourhoods of California in the late 1960s, Popping was developed during the Funk era at a similar time to Locking. It graduated from another street dance style subset called the 'Boogaloo' (from the James Brown record) – an improvised and free way of moving which demonstrates a specific fluidity and funk in the movement. The Soloman brothers (Sam and younger brother Timothy a.k.a. Popin' Pete) were founding members of The Electric Boogaloos, a pioneering group of dancers formed in the mid-1970s who experimented with this new way of moving. The group provided a starting point from which Popping as a dance art could grow from. Thomas Guzman-Sanchez documents and re-traces the roots of Boogaloo and Popping in his book *Underground Dance Masters*. Popping began to evolve organically from this west coast Boogaloo style, specifically from an element known as the Freeze:

> A key movement within Funk Boogaloo was the Freeze. The Freeze was basically an abrupt stop or hesitation during a broad movement. This Freeze was not a jerk or a jiggle but simply a momentary stop of motion to the beat…. This was not called Popping but it was the precursor movement to what may years later would be referred to as Popping or Hitting.
>
> (Guzman-Sanchez 2012, 15)

During the writing of this book, one of the original masters of this art form passed away – Bruno Falcon aka, 'Pop n' Taco.' In the early 1980s, he was a prominent figure in Boogaloo and Popping styles. Anyone who has marvelled at how Michael Jackson integrated elements of Popping into his own movement repertoire must watch Pop n' Taco's work in the 1980s. Falcon's swagger, his styling, all of his animation work (the lateral slide, the Snake, the 360 Float) are all watermarked in Jackson's performances. A very influential individual. With other masters like Shabbado (Adolfo Gutierrez Quiñones), Boogaloo Shrimp (Michael Chambers) and Popin' Pete (Timothy Soloman), Pop n' Taco brought the magic of Popping to millions of people with their work in the 1984 movies *Breakin'* & *Breakin 2: Electric Boogaloo* and in the documentary *Breakin' and Enterin'*. These guys were originals at the front

The Ingredients

Image 3.4 Renowned Popper Bruno 'Pop n Taco' Falcon performs in the 1984 movie Breakin'

of a cultural movement – the fashions, the music and the movement were exhilarating for audiences. No one had moved like that before or expressed themselves through dance with such freedom.

The Steps

Performed primarily to amaze and awe an audience, Popping strives to create illusions and stretch the spectators' assumptions about what the human body's rhythmic movement capabilities are. A loose vocabulary has developed which include steps such as Ticking (creating a strobe like effect with your body), The Robot, Slides (similar to a Moonwalk), Glides, Floats, Tutting (making shapes with hands and arms that resemble Egyptian hieroglyphics) and Waving (creating the illusion of an electrical impulse which travels through your body via individual muscle and joint isolations).

Nuria Beltran, an accomplished Popper from Barcelona, competes in competitions worldwide and in 2019 reached the semi-finals of the Juste Debout World Finals in Paris. She believes that dedication and discipline are the central tenets required of a Popping specialist:

> If we talk about Popping, we talk about patience, constancy, and perseverance. A Popping dancer knows that quality is much more valuable than quantity of movement, so one of the "secrets" in the evolution in this style is to repeat, repeat and repeat the same movement and/or technique to achieve perfection. Under the same foundation, a good Popping dancer will distinguish themselves when the technique is so assimilated, that they can express it naturally and creatively with the music, reaching the point of creating a unique identity within the style. Fortunately (or unfortunately), this is a very long road (perhaps never-ending), and that's why enjoying the process is key to the dancer's growth. And all of this without forgetting the history and the great references of the style, knowing the why and the how will give more meaning and solidity to the dance.

The Ingredients

Commercial Impact

Dancers such as Popin' Pete have ensured that Popping remains true to its original codes whilst also securing its place in modern popular culture. His appearance in Chris Brown's 'Yeah 3x' video (2011) is a great marker as to how Popping is used within the realms of Commercial Dance vocabulary, Chris Brown being a master of this dance form himself. Perhaps more so than Locking vocabulary, key Popping elements such as animations and glides are seen frequently in choreographies seen on screen in the 2020s. Choreographer Ian Eastwood displays significant influences from Funk styles in his work, particularly Popping – using waves and hits to enhance his innate musicality. Some of Marty Kudelka's precise movement has a meticulous animatronic feel to it and Christopher Scott's work regularly features hits, waves and glides as a foil to the numerous other styles he works with.

Hip-Hop Social Steps & New Jack Swing

What Are They?

Towards the end of the 1980s and early 1990s, Hip-Hop music developed further, becoming more sophisticated and digitalised in its production. Using disco samples and combining R&B vocals over Hip-Hop beats, it grew slicker and broader in its appeal. In tandem with this, more dances were created in social environments where Hip-Hop music was played such as house parties and nightclubs. These fun dances offered bite-size sequences of movement which could be enjoyed by anyone, regardless of age or dance ability. Social Hip-Hop steps such as the Roger Rabbit, the Reebok, the Cabbage Patch, the Kid n' Play and the Harlem Shake made a notable impact on popular dances seen on screen. Between the late 1980s and mid-1990s, the Hip-Hop and R&B musical landscape was also marked by the appearance of a prominent new musical and social dance style – 'New Jack Swing.'

New Jack Swing was a particular style that was engineered and cultivated by music producer Teddy Riley and his writing partner Bernhard Belle, which combined elements of Hip-Hop, Funk, Pop, Rap and R&B. Producers working with artists such as TLC, Salt n Pepa, Bobby Brown, Jodeci, Heavy D, Michael Jackson, Boyz II Men, Whitney Houston, Big Daddy Kane, Keith Sweat, Madonna and Mary J Blige all used the production traits of Riley to create this unique sound of the early 1990s – soulful, harmonised vocals over a 808 drum machine engineered beat, with a sharp snare, often with guest rap verses appearing after the second chorus, marrying R&B and Hip-Hop elements for the first time. Teddy Riley explained his sound:

> New Jack Swing is a sound of music that doesn't have a colour line. And it doesn't have an expression, it fits the occasion. But it's a collaboration of rap and singing together. It's a collaboration of different genres of music and styles that is put together all in one bag. I would say New Jack Swing is heavy R&B, heavy rhythm and blues, all stuck in one bag.

A new dance style evolved, building on foundational social Hip-Hop steps to complement this style of music. The music videos for Bobby Brown's 'Every Little Step' (1989), Heavy D and the Boyz, 'Now That We've Found Love' (1991) and Salt N' Pepa's, 'Shoop!' (1994) are clear examples of the vocabulary of steps associated with the New Jack Swing style.

The Ingredients

Image 3.5 Hip-Hop social steps and elements of New Jack Swing were featured in the 1990 cult classic movie 'Houseparty'

The Steps

Although the musical styles from which they originate may differ slightly, both Hip-Hop social dance steps and New Jack Swing steps use many of the same traits and much of the vocabulary is interchangeable. There are a large variety of steps but they generally all consist of relatively simple and fun movements which match the bounce and 'into the floor' groove of the music and are rarely more than two to four counts in length. Rocking movements (the Reebok) and knee dips (the Roger Rabbit) form the basis of many of the steps. New Jack Swing is marked by its longer choreographic phrases and an energetic and cardio-taxing style, it features a flurry of dynamic steps which have a criss-cross 'hop-scotch' quality – simple kick ball changes, shuffles and two-steps were accentuated with a deep knee bounce, giving them a heavy and distinctive funk groove which aligned with the sharp signature snare sound of the 2/4 rhythm phrasing of the music. The famous 'Running Man' step forms the basis of much of New Jack Swing influenced choreography, also seen in the popular videos from MC Hammer and Vanilla Ice in 1989 – 'U Can't Touch This' and 'Ice Ice Baby' respectively.

Commercial Impact

Original Hip-Hop social steps are still used consistently in Commercial Dance projects, providing an essential ingredient in the make-up of many choreographies. The Superbowl LVI (2022) halftime show and The Grammy's 2023 '50 Years of Hip-Hop,' performance (both choreographed by Fatima Robinson) attests to this, using notes from old school Hip-Hop party steps throughout both sets.

New Jack Swing also still influences movement today. The emergence of 'Shuffle Dance' (see 'Party Rock Anthem' by LMFAO, 2011) in the early 2010s used many characteristics from New Jack Swing but increasing the tempo of the steps and performing them to electronic dance music altered the feel and Hip-Hop tinged dynamics of the original steps. Bruno Mars and Cardi B created an homage to New Jack Swing with 2018s throwback hit 'Finesse,' complete with a video which referenced New Jack Swing steps and the original 'In Living Colour' set (where 'The Fly Girls' would perform dance routines on each show), showcasing the dance style and fashions which accompanied the music of the early 1990s.

Krump

What Is It?

A relatively recent dance form which originated on the streets of south Los Angeles in the early 1990s. Evolving from a hybrid form of mime and Hip-Hop dance called 'Clowning,' it was David LaChapelle's documentary Rize in 2005, which gave Krump a platform with an international audience. The word 'Krump' is often cited as being an acronym of 'Kingdom Radically Uplifting Mighty Praise,' suggesting that the dance form also has a spiritual and religious basis. Thomas 'Tommy the Clown' Johnson is regarded as the originator who developed his extrovert 'clowning' performances into Krump. The genre developed further through a crew of dancers such Christopher 'Lil C' Toler, Ceasare 'Tight Eyez' Willis and Marquisa 'Miss Prissy' Gardner. Broad in its improvised nature yet distinctive with unique traits, Associate Professor Robeson Taj Frazier and journalist Jessica Koslow classify Krump as "*hybridised Hip Hop dancing that fuses west African, Latin, b-boy/b-girl and other vernacular dance forms.*" They describe a Krump session in a parking lot in Los Angeles vividly:

> The dancing ignites. A male Krumper assertively stomps the asphalt. He snakes in and out of the Toyota's driver side window with his upper body. His arms whip at the aired, his ankles twist side to side, rolling him up onto his tiptoes. His torso undulates, then his chest pops out and contracts back repeatedly, powered by the push of this hand resting lightly on his heart. The lights that surround the dancer create a leviathan outline of his shadow. He looks at the crowd with a tasteful smirk and then his face morphs into an expression of anger and anguish. The groups converge tightly around him as if to keep his body warm. They push him when he comes close, yelling, "That's buck!" and "It's your world!" What prompts the krumper to initiate this session? Maybe he was guided by the beat, a challenge by a fellow dancer, or a sudden rush of adrenaline.
>
> (Frazier & Koslow, 2013, 2)

Image 3.6 Krumper 'Tight Eyez' performs in the David LaChappelle directed documentary Rize (2005)

The Ingredients

The Steps

Like many sub-genres of Hip Hop dance, Krump has developed its own lexicon of steps and vocabulary. Watching Krumpers battle highlights what an intense, sporadic, energised and sometimes possessed nature it has, it is rarely choreographed and serves as a cathartic vessel enabling dancers to cut loose. 'Stomps' and 'Chest Pops' form much of the dance's content. Kick stomp, slide stomp and lift stomp are the most common 'Stomps' whilst 'Chest Pops' are isolations which are furiously performed, using all of the upper torso/rib cage and often incorporating the hips and pelvis. Arm swings are also important, at times resembling a frenzied boxer – jabs, wild hooks and crosses create a hyped yet carefully articulated phrase of dance movement. The harsh piston-like foot stomps contrast feverishly with the whipped and arced lines the arms create.

Commercial Impact

Beginning in the early 2000s, Krump has appeared in many commercialised areas of dance. Music videos including Christina Aguilera's – Dirrty (2003) (where director David LaChapelle was introduced to the underground Krumping scene whilst looking for dancers for the clip). The Chemical Brothers – Galvanise (2005) and FKA Twigs' – Wet Wipez (2014) have all heavily featured Krumping in their video. Krumping has also featured in dance movies like Stomp the Yard (2007), in multiple episodes of the international franchises of TV show 'So You Think You Can Dance' and in theatrical performances by UK Hip-Hop theatre collectives 'Boy Blue' and 'Zoonation: The Kate Prince Dance Company.'

Unlike some other Hip-Hop and Funk styles which were also originally improvisational forms of dance but are now predominantly performed in choreographed sequences, Krumping is rarely tamed and included in '5,6,7,8' combinations with other choreographed styles – it remains a freestyled form of dance. Perhaps its virile and potent nature makes it an uneasy fit with some sanitised and commercialised styles. In many ways, the rawness of the Krumping seen in works such as FKA Twigs' 'Wet Wipez' video (featuring the Wet Wipez dance collective) is a welcome antithesis to the clean, tightly choreographed routines that have become prevalent in many music videos. A dance form that has not been 'cleansed' of its foundationary spirituality and maintains its original street born purpose is a breakthrough in a commercialised industry which sometimes sacrifices authenticity for palatability.

3b. Jazz Dance

Jazz dance is a genre of dance which became culturally prominent in the mid-20th century and is synonymous with cultural beacons including the movies 'Fame' (1980), 'Flashdance' (1983) and 'A Chorus Line' (1985), the choreographer Bob Fosse and Broadway shows such as 'Cats.' It is a style which requires tough technical training to master and is embedded with Commercial dance styles globally. The following chapter breaks down Jazz into its base components, summarises it's key contributors and also provides a brief overview of its pre-20th-century origins, exploring the forces which have moulded this genre of dance – from the shores of 18th century West Africa to the lycra-clad Jazz classes of 1980s New York.

What Is It?

Jazz dance makes up a large part of the movement vocabulary of what we consider to be 'Commercial Dance.' The influence of Jazz dance within the sphere of Commercial Dance is

Image 3.7 Jazz dance became synonymous with movies such as 'A Chorus Line,' choreographed by Jeffrey Hornaday (1985)

extensive. Its impact on the shaping of phrases, the different textures it offers to the movement and the adhesive it provides which binds these multitude of styles together, illustrates how Commercial Dance as a movement genre is a direct derivative of Jazz dance.

Jazz technique is considered imperative for a dancer hoping to enjoy a long, sustainable career in the Commercial Dance industry. In much the same way, classical ballet aids dancers of all specialisations, Jazz also assists dancers in their understanding of placement which elongates the body, enabling the creation of clear silhouettes within choreographic sequences. A strong grounding in Jazz allows a dancer to contrast clean and precise lines with other Hip-Hop and Club styles that often utilise a softer fluidity, making use of a less edged set of movements – forging a dancer who is able to offer a range of alternating aesthetics and dynamics. Graeme Pickering, a Jazz choreographer and international casting associate for Celebrity Cruises, believes that:

> Commercial Dance today has strong roots and connections to the fundamentals of traditional Jazz Dance. The use of isolation, a lower centre of gravity and strong dynamics are key within all aspects of Jazz Dance and this has paved the way for the style we see today across all genres of Commercial based performance.

Jazz originator Gus Giordano offered his opinion about the importance of Jazz dance technique for a student in a 1992 publication recording his work:

> Jazz dance as an art form is the perfect blend of mind and body founded on a firm technical base…. Discipline is as inescapable in Jazz as it is in any other art form. Flexibility, centre placement, clean lines, multiple turns, leaps and the ability to quickly submit combinations from the brain to the body are the nuts and bolts of technique. A student seeking a career in dance learns very quickly, by failure at auditions, how important technique is.

The Steps

Jazz is generally taught in a similar manner to classical ballet in that a class will consist of a series of exercises which are compiled to improve core strength, enable full articulation of limbs, feet and hands, understand alignment and harness the ability to isolate various parts of the body. Plie and tendu exercises progress through to pirouettes and corner work which focus on travelling steps and jumps such as jetes, barrel jumps and stag leaps. The class will usually finish with a freer dance combination.

The discipline required in class and simple repetition of many of these exercises enable a student to master the fundamental details of Jazz dance as it is known today. Much like ballet, Jazz classes are encouraged to be taken a number of times a week to accelerate technical progress and strengthening. This progressive class structure and codified dance syllabus can be attributed to a number of practitioners including Eugene Louis Faccuito (known as Luigi), Gus Giordano and Matt Mattox. Each of these codifying choreographers complimented each other stylistically – Luigi created a flowing, fluid syllabus which grew out of his quest to find a type of dance movement which would aid his recovery from a near-fatal car crash. Giordano built on Katherine Dunham's foundations, creating dance exercises which emanated from the pelvis and paid attention to the classical lineage. Mattox created a unique and angular style, concentrating on isolations of the body and precise placement of the limbs. My own education in Jazz dance was invaluable and became an essential skill which continually aided me during my time working as a Commercial Dancer. I was fortunate to have a strong local dance school in my hometown in the UK, where the Jazz classes laid a foundation for me to learn codified exercises and strengthen my overall dance technique. Being taught by pillars of the London Jazz community in my late teens (including Molly Molloy, Alison Desbois, Daniel Crossley and Dollie Henry) was invaluable for my progression as a dancer. Jazz taught me how to isolate and identify movement, how to keep simplicity in expression and the importance of underpinning movement with a core strength.

Commercial Impact

Many of the lines, the presence and the precision of physical sequences observed within Commercial Dance have a tangible link to Jazz dance born in the US in the 1950s and 1960s. The work of the Jazz pioneers of the 20th century such as Jack Cole, Susan Stroman, Matt Mattox, Gillian Lynne, Jerome Robbins, Katherine Dunham, Arlene Phillips, Michael Kidd, Jojo Smith, Frank Hatchett, Bob Fosse, Debbie Allen and Michael Peters is interwoven within the movements of Commercial choreographers such as RJ Durell & Nick Florez, Brian Friedman, Frank Gatson, Tina Landon and Michael Rooney. Durell & Florez's work on the US version of 'So You Think You Can Dance' (check out their piece 'Zodiac') is a great example of Commercial Dance heavily underpinned with a strong Jazz base. Brian Friedman's work also incorporates many Jazz based technical aspects which require a high level of dexterity to perform convincingly (see his early work with Britney Spears for evidence of this).

The performance style of many Jazz choreographic combinations hark to a golden era of prominent mid-20th-century Hollywood film and musical releases which are still significant today. Performers including Chita Rivera, Gene Kelly, Cyd Charisse, Fred Astaire, The Nicholas Brothers and Gwen Verdon glided across the silver cinema screens of the day, exuding a style and sensuality that still moves us today. Much is referenced from this rich period of Jazz dance in current day musical trends and Commercial Dance performances. Madonna's 1984 'Material Girl' video (choreographed by Kenny Ortega) re-imagines Marilyn Monroes' 1953 'Diamonds are a Girls Best Friend' sequence from 'Gentleman Prefer Blondes' (choreographed by Jack Cole) and Mandy Moore's movement style in 2016s 'La La Land' movie emits flagrant notes of Jerome Robbins and Michael Kidd from the rich mid-20th-century Jazz dance era. Harry Styles' 2020 video for 'Treat People with Kindness' gave choreographer Paul Roberts' the opportunity to create a whole sequence which used the many Jazz-tinged duets of Fred Astaire and Ginger Rogers/Cyd Charisse as a reference point for Styles and Phoebe Waller-Bridge's cheerful duo.

Jazz dance performance carries a particular air of nonchalance/sass/coolness which has a timeless quality – Bob Fosse's 'Steam Heat' from 'The Pyjama Game' looked as cool in 1957 as it does today. This may well be a prominent reason why Jazz dance is still so prolifically prevalent within Commercial Dance choreography today.

Historical Overview of Jazz Dance

Origins

A more immersive look at Jazz dance reveals an art form that was conceived much earlier than the golden age of Hollywood movies from the mid-20th century such as 'West Side Story,' 'Damn Yankees' and 'Seven Brides for Seven Brothers.' As influential as Jack Cole's choreography for the screen was and as pioneering as the ordered exercises of Mattox, Giordano and Luigi were, the story does not start with the creations or the codified exercises of these well-known dancers. Jazz dance's origins are intertwined with African American social history. Kadifa Wong's 2021 documentary 'Uprooted' (HBO) is an expansive examination of the deepest origins of Jazz dance and is an essential watch for any student of dance.

The slave trade and the forceful displacement of West African families, resulted in estimated figures of around 10.7 million slaves landing in the Caribbean, South America and North America over the course of 250 years before the 13th Amendment of the U.S. Constitution banned slavery in the US in 1865. The harrowing and barbaric journeys from Africa to the New World, made by millions of those enslaved also carried African culture and dance to different shores. The genesis for the development of many north American social and popular dances, including Jazz, Rock n' Roll and Hip-Hop styles lies in this mass West African displacement. Dance theorist Carla Stalling-Huntington recognises the African diaspora as a key effector in the development of America's dance history:

> Between their launch from the coast of Africa and their arrival to the Americas, it was common practice for slaves 'to be taken first to the West Indies and the islands of the Caribbean' (Emery, 1989, 9) where Africans picked up ways of writing dances and theorising their existence. This trajectory from Africa to the West Indies and the Caribbean influenced the text of African American dances from early enslavement and continues to do so today.

The link from the African diaspora to American Jazz dance has long been noted in academia but there has been a slower acknowledgement in the wider dance community that the essence of Jazz dance goes back further than the lexicon of steps performed by the likes of Cyd Charisse and Bob Fosse. In her 1970 paper 'The Origins of Modern Jazz Dance,' author Dolores Kirton Cayou observed that key characteristics of rooted African movement included *"(1) Bent knees, with the body close to the earth, (2) tendency towards use of the whole foot, immediate transference of weight, (3) isolation of body parts in movement, (4) rhythmically complex and syncopated rhythm."* Cayou's description could also be used to succinctly describe the characteristics of movement in a Matt Mattox warm-up exercise – the lineage of movement is tangible.

For those enslaved in the US, dance was used as a mode of rebellion and emotive cultural expression. Restrictive laws which further infringed rights of African slaves, such as the 1740 law passed in South Carolina which forbid slaves to play or own drums, did not stop those displaced from expressing their cultural roots. Dance was still free and rhythms were transmitted by using the body – clapping, stomping and slapping of arms and legs as well as using instrumentation such as banjo's or bone clappers ensured expressive movement continued in southern towns like New Orleans and Charleston, South Carolina. 'Juba' or the 'Pattin' Juba' was a dance form developed by African slaves expressing themselves socially and emotionally using these improvised dances emanating from African culture. Foot shuffles, rhythm stomps and free expression were at the heart of much of this movement. The America of the 19th century was a conflation of different migrant cultures, each absorbing influences from the other. A cross pollination between steps from eastern European, Anglican and Celtic clog and jig dances with west African movement and rhythms would gradually meld to make the Vaudevillian Tap dance of the mid- to late 19th and early 20th centuries.

Lane, Robinson and Bubbles

William Henry Lane (also known as Master Juba) was an African American who in the 1840s, with his lightning-fast feet, performed such steps as the 'walk around' or 'cake walk' for white audiences in New York and London. This satirising of the popular and formal white social dances (which would have been performed in front of the white masters of the enslaved) became a common part of stage and musical productions in the 19th century and developed further the stylisation of these steps as they started to resemble inflections of future popular Tap and Jazz dances.

Bill 'Bojangles' Robinson (1878–1949) and John W Bubbles (1902–1986), also both black American artists, brought Tap into the 20th century and demonstrated complex rhythms driven through heel taps and scuffs but also with an elegance and freedom displayed in the upper torso and arms – a characteristic which would provide the template for the effortless 'coolness' we associate with Jazz dance today. They created an inspirational blue print which successful song and dance men, Fred Astaire and Gene Kelly, would base their own Jazz and Tap dance styles on. A concoction of dance continued to develop in the early to mid-20th century – classical 'Balanchine-esque' leg movements and lines – plies/tendus/pirouettes, began to fuse with the bowler hat-chic and effortless cool of performers such as Bubbles and Bojangles.

Jazz Progressions in the Early 20th Century

Initially, a predominately African American dance trend, Lindy-Hop was a cultural craze of the 1920s and 1930s which influenced Jazz dance's progression as well as being a predecessor to rock n' roll and swing dances. It flourished firstly in Harlem, New York and caught the eye of the larger dance community. The Savoy Ballroom in New York city hosted big band nights and dance marathons that would see an integrated crowd of blacks and whites dancing together (something unprecedented for the 1930s) as they showed off new steps and acrobatic partner work. The Savoy was the place to watch and learn from the best Lindy Hoppers around such as George 'Shorty' Snowden and Dean Collins. The energy of Lindy Hop was something not seen before. It encouraged dancers to cut loose, improvise and play with the rhythms of the band.

Emerging dance artists such as Jack Cole, Katherine Dunham and Jerome Robbins encouraged this hybridisation of multi-cultural dance genres and choreographed entire works mixing all of these unique styles with their other influences from India, Europe and the Caribbean and in the process slowly created a new vocabulary of dance. A dance which relied on rhythm and aplomb whilst also creating a connection between Euro-centric classical ballet technique and world dance flavours. Sharing the same philosophy as Jazz music (also an art form forged by predominately African Americans) – a dancer could express themselves through emotive, improvised and ever increasingly difficult technical dance steps. This new variety of dance also became referred to as Jazz. In the essay, 'Where's the Jazz?,' Lindsey Guarino eloquently sums up the vivacity and eventual separation of Jazz music and dance. She describes Jazz in the early 20th century as being

> the pulse of African American culture, the spirit moving in conversation with swinging rhythms and the soulful sounds resulting in a distinct energy known as "Jazz".... The symbiotic relationship between Jazz music and Jazz dancing, once a defining characteristic of the form, fractured when popular social dance music shifted away from Jazz and towards rock n' roll, rhythm and blues, funk and latin music forms in the years before and after World War II.

1940s Onwards

By 1940, Jazz dance, still in a relatively embryonic state, had gradually emerged as the dance that reflected the music and mood of the time in the US. Bounding advances in television and cinema led to an increased demand for dancers and choreographers from film studios and theatre audiences alike. Collaborations between composers such as Leonard Bernstein, Cole Porter, Stephen Sondheim and George Gershwin and budding choreographers including Jack Cole, Jerome Robbins and Michael Kidd, created a rich vein of Musical Theatre based performance, each film or show bursting with numbers perfectly composed to be filled with the high energy, excited and acrobatic nature of Jazz dance.

New musical works that were crossing over from Broadway to the cinema screen (or vice versa) were the order of the decade – 'Showboat' (1951), 'Guys and Dolls' (1952), 'Gentlemen Prefer Blondes' (1953), 'Singin' in the Rain' (1955) and 'Damn Yankees' (1958) are just a few of the many dance laden films of the 50s. New York and Los Angeles were such rich, fertile fields of theatrical talent at this time that it is no wonder that the names we now associate with being the guiding hands of Jazz dance were cultivated in this era.

Pioneers of 20th-Century Jazz Dance

Katherine Dunham (1909–2006)

Katherine Dunham continually pushed artistic, social and intellectual boundaries. She left a multi-faceted legacy and demonstrated that the intellectualisation of dance was as important as performing it. Born in Illinois, US, to a father from West African descendancy and a mother with French Canadian heritage, Dunham studied anthropology at the University of Chicago in the early 1930s and married this academic study with the development of her dance career. She travelled to Jamaica, Trinidad and Haiti during her study of what she would term 'Dance Anthropology,' fascinated by different cultures and their unique dance practices:

> You can't learn about dances until you learn about people. In my mind, it's the most fascinating thing in the world to learn.

The Ingredients

Choosing to finally pursue a life in dance over academia, Dunham lead her own dance company and one of the first all-black dance companies in the US (as her company developed, it would become truly international, featuring dancers from many different countries and creeds). She focused on Caribbean, Asian and Latin flavours of dance and melded them with European influences, her work sensual and fluid.

In 1940, after the critical success of her company's performance works such as 'Woman with a Cigar' and her staging of the musical 'Pins and Needles,' Dunham and her company were contracted to work on Broadway in a production of 'Cabin in the Sky,' with George Balanchine at the helm. No doubt collaborating with the neo-classical master would have further influenced her canon of movement vocabulary. Balanchine was known to let his choreographic collaborators have a large degree of creative scope, especially when the style of dance was outside of his own neo-classical movement. According to the Katherine Dunham Collection at the Library of Congress, *"Dunham found this method of collaboration quite agreeable, and she and Balanchine enjoyed a particularly amicable working relationship."*

Dunham would continue to have mainstream success in films such as 'Stormy Weather' (1943) and 'Casbah' (1948). Katherine Dunham and Her Company would tour globally until 1960, as word spread of the uniqueness and inter-culturality of her choreography.

Dunham technique was developed and taught in a similar way to other modern dance artists of the time such as Martha Graham – barre work, breathing exercises, walks etc. What made Dunham's work unique was the union between so many different cultural dance influences and the different uses of body and rhythms that this combination brings. Although Dunham could be termed as a 'modern dance' pioneer, she also influenced Jazz dance greatly – the use of isolation in the body, undulations through the torso, the intertwined African rhythms and the study of classical techniques via Balanchine and the European dance scene resulted in her work directly steering the direction of Jazz dance in this era. Other dancers of the time, such as Jack Cole, were moving in a similar direction to Dunham.

Jack Cole (1911–1974)

Jack Cole was colossal in his contribution to formulating the essence of Jazz dance technique and choreography for the screen. He provided the original playbook for future choreographers to work from in terms of movement vocabulary to fill the film frames of Hollywood in the 1950s and 1960s. Like Dunham, he was an explorer of cultures – studying, welding and disseminating the movements he developed to every member of his cinema or nightclub audience.

His physical style pulled from East Indian and Afro-Cuban influences on top of the Lindy Hop social dances that were in vogue at the time. The duet caught on film between Cole and Rita Hayworth in 1945s 'Tonight and Every Night' illustrate what a low centre of gravity Cole had, his wide, plié stance and lunges harking to the East Indian dance he had trained in and exposed audiences to in his earlier works such as 'Hindu Swing' from 1937. In this duet, the imprint of Lindy-Hop can be seen in Cole's interaction with Hayworth and also in the chorus dancer's movement in the background. In Cole's 1950s performance of 'Sing, Sing, Sing!' on the Perry Como Show one can see the early Jazz technique that he was creating (much of the feeling of this performance can also be felt in Bob Fosse's later version of 'Sing, Sing, Sing!' in the late 1970s).

The Ingredients

Image 3.8 Jack Cole choreographed Marylyn Monroe and her dancers in the famous 'Diamonds are a girl's best friend' number from the movie 'Gentleman Prefer Blondes' (1953)

Not only an important contributor to the evolution of Jazz dance technique, Cole was a coach to the female Hollywood stars of this period. Before Laurieann Gibson trained Lady Gaga and JaQuel Knight coached Beyonce, Jack Cole paved the way to on-screen prominence for female stars including Gwen Verdon, Rita Hayworth, Betty Grable and Marilyn Monroe, giving them the confidence and panache to hold the camera's focus through not only their natural charm but also the dance technique they had worked hard to achieve under his tuition. His work with Marilyn Monroe on 'Gentleman Prefer Blondes' (1953) was iconic, the choreography for 'Diamonds are a Girl's Best Friend' depicts Monroe as the star with a horde of tuxedo trimmed male dancers gravitating towards her, to lift and support her. Coaching this kind of assured performance to camera and staging the supporting dancers with such subtlety was not easy to do and it set the benchmark for the choreographers that followed such as Jerome Robbins and Michael Kidd. The scene's influence can be seen directly in a number from Gene Kelly's 'It's Always Fair Weather' (1955) as well as in Madonna's 'Material Girl' (1984) music video, the TV show 'Glee' and the movie Harley Quinn: Birds of Prey (2020). All of these examples have distinct directorial and thematic similarities to the Cole choreographed 'Diamonds Are a Girl's Best Friend.' The Jazz dance choreographer, teacher and historian Bob Boross talks eloquently about Cole's legacy in his book *Comments on Jazz Dance 1996–2004*:

> His work transcends Jazz dance. It gives the dancers such precise and exacting control over their movements that they will feel better at any technique. Cole's work brings clarity, strength, and very importantly presence.... As for Jazz dance, Cole's application of motivation for movement brings the Jazz dancer arguably into the realm of artistic expression – something that Jazz dance is still not known for.
>
> Jack Cole is the prime innovator of our theatrical Jazz dance heritage, and his work should be valued not only by Jazz dancers, but by anyone seriously interested in dance as an art form.

The Ingredients

Image 3.9 Link to dance critic Debra Levine discussing Jack Cole and his work on 'Gentleman Prefer Blondes'

Michael Kidd (1915–2007)

If there is one choreographer from this era of New York and Hollywood musical theatre who's work could be directly transferred to a piece of Commercial Dance theatre today, then it is Michael Kidd's. Some of his work could comfortably sit in a musical number from a new Lin Manuel Miranda production or Netflix movie. His choreography and staging still feel so relevant.

From a Jewish Russian family who immigrated to New York in the 1920s, he changed his name from Milton Greenwald to Michael Kidd in 1942 after his stage career as a ballet soloist began to take off. However, as a choreographer on New York's Broadway is where Kidd really flourished. Winning a total of five Tony Awards, it was after his second win for the Broadway show 'Guys and Dolls' (1950) that he became synonymous with the big and brash acrobatic style of Jazz dance. In 1953 he followed with the movie 'The Band Wagon' (the Fred Astaire vehicle that Michael Jackson's Smooth Criminal video would later borrow from) and in 1954s 'Seven Brides For Seven Brothers,' Kidd created some spectacularly acrobatic dance scenes and cast talented dancers such Matt Mattox and Russ Tamblyn in prominent roles (Tamblyn would later play Riff in Jerome Robbin's West Side Story). His career continued to ascend and some of his most memorable work is seen in the Hollywood hit adaption of 'Guys and Dolls' (1955) which starred Marlon Brando and Frank Sinatra.

Kidd would later stage scenes for Janet Jackson in the 'When I Think of You' (1986) and 'Alright' (1990) music videos, two influential videos in the early development of Commercial Dance work. In 1997, he received an honorary Oscar for his services to the art of dance on screen. His work is remembered as being spirited and high powered, developing the acrobatic and dynamic possibilities within Jazz dance. Kidd's acceptance speech at the 1997 Academy Awards gave an idea of where his motivation came from to consistently create such positive work:

> So many of today's films stress the terrors that await us, perhaps this award signifies an awareness that we have been missing something, namely the vitality and the joy of living that movie musicals can express in song and dance…. I accept this award in the name of all choreographers and especially the dancers, who made it all possible.

Jerome Robbins (1918–1998)

Jerome Robbins is perhaps the name most synonymous with choreography from the mid-20th-century American musicals. His works have been hugely influential for choreographers working in all areas of dance, particularly Jazz, despite his work being of a classical nature. In 1948, Robbins' became associate director of the New York City ballet after performing as a dancer and choreographer under George Balanchine. After this, he focused more on choreographing works on Broadway. He wrote and directed much of his own work and his collaboration with composer Leonard Bernstein was a commercial success.

Although Robbins used classical ballet as a choreographic base, he helped to steer Jazz dance's evolution due to his dynamic staging (both for the stage and camera) and via his ability to tell a story through movement. Using improvisation as a method of creation with his dancers and never being fearful of breaking the classical mould, Robbins created work that moved narrative forward. Applying the mimetic elements of storytelling seen mainly in classical ballet theatre, Robbins's used movement not just as a punctuation mark to excite the audience but as a narrative tool. His work on the show 'On the Town' (based on Robbin's and Bernsteins's 'Fancy Free') and the film adaption of 'West Side Story' (1960) are fine examples of this.

The opening 9 minutes of West Side Story display a blend of movement – a ballet in Levi's & Converse – aggression, joy, camaraderie, anger, all communicated with a clear intention through movement. Robbin's frequently directed his filmic work – such an important part of ensuring that a project creates dance scenes that follow the through line of action that drives the movement/narrative/emotion from the start to the finish of the scene. The direction of the camera in this opening scene of West Side Story (co-directed by Robert Wise) gives punch to the choreography at the correct moments and allows dance lines to be extended just that little bit further due to favourable shooting angles being selected. A director with a dancer's intuition can ensure that the camera moves in this way – a skill that Bob Fosse would also later come to finesse.

By creating a precedent for breaking the classical lines of ballet in dance film and incorporating a way of storytelling through movement, Robbin's marched beside Dunham, Cole and Kidd in the advancement of Jazz dance.

Robbins' reflected in a short documentary 'Jerome Robbins in His Own Words':

> I know that one of the things I worked on so hard was to find the best way to communicate the clearest thing to the audience, so that the audience will receive the strongest impact, whether it's a comedy point or a nuance, if it's not clear to them then why all this bother? Its no good doing it for yourself.
>
> I enjoy making ballets. I like to see bodies in movement, in time and space and to see the relationships between them – to see what happens between people together. And there is a joy for me to be able to build something, to be able to create something, starting from the empty volume of a room or a stage and putting movement into it and seeing what happens as you develop that movement.

Matt Mattox (1921–2013)

Matt Mattox created one of the first and most widely read, syllabi for Jazz dance. He wanted to establish exactly what Jazz dance was and how to teach it in a free yet disciplined way. He created a class pedagogy that would enable dancers to train in Jazz dance in a similar manner to how classical dancers trained. His classes consisted of a number of exercises, each concentrating on a different aspect of the body: pliés, tendus, pirouettes, etc. He would call it 'Freestyle Dance.'

The Ingredients

As a performer, Mattox was a regular dancer on Jack Cole and Michael Kidd projects including his most recognisable role as Caleb Pontipee in 1954s 'Seven Brides for Seven Brothers' (the guy doing the impossible split jumps on the workbench is Mattox). His work in creating a system for teaching Jazz dance created a connection between the exciting and fluid work of Cole and Kidd to a classroom methodology which is still used today. Mattox developed his style of teaching in the 1960s and taught regularly in New York city before moving to Europe in the 1970s. There he created a Jazz dance company in London called 'Jazz Art' before moving to France in the 1980s where he continued to teach his method.

Bob Borross is a former student of Mattox's and defines his teacher's teaching philosophy in his article 'The "Freestyle Style" Jazz Dance of Matt Mattox':

> The guiding principle of Mattox's Freestyle tradition is that once a dancer desires to express a thought in dance form, the dancer will then draw from his mastery of an eclectic range of dance techniques. The dancer is 'free' to express what is in his soul and also 'free' of allegiance to any one particular style of dance.

Boross goes on to describe the class structure of a typical Mattox class:

> The Mattox class techniques is crafted in the progression of a ballet class but is performed standing at centre floor. The class design includes exercises for demi-plié, plié, tendu, dégagé, ronde jambe, piqué and so on. However these exercises are often performed with a parallel hip alignment, in a plié level and peppered with body isolations for the head, shoulders, rib cage, and hips…
>
> The culmination of his class is a unique, extended combination set to a variety of music styles – swing, pop, densely textured instruments, and even new age classical. Each combination demands attention to design, rhythm, attack, nuance, feeling, and drive to achieve perfection in execution.

Image 3.10 See Matt Mattox in action at the 1990 World Dance Congress

Bob Fosse (1927–1987)

A turned-in stance, hunched shoulders, a bowler hat slanted downward covering the eyes and both hands cocked, resting on the hip bones – the distinct silhouette of a Bob Fosse dancer. Bob Fosse created one of the most unique and distinctive languages of movement. Angular, quirky, sexual, ugly and yet beautifully poised – his style is easily recognisable. Fosse created his own Jazz dance vocabulary, which he communicated through his choreography. Hip swings, Back Bumps, the Broken Doll, Durantes, Leg Hooks, Sugars and Lola's are just some of the names given to Fosse's steps (see Debra McWater's book *The Fosse Style* – McWaters was a frequent collaborator of Gwen Verdon and Ann Reinking). His work covered a large spectrum, from light and comical (DamnYankees's 'Who's Got the Pain') to dark and carnal (Sweet Charity's 'Big Spender'). Fosse explained some of the influences on his choreography to *The New York Times* in 1959:

> I have taken more from old time Vaudeville than anything else…and I have frankly based many movements on Charlie Chaplin – the way he walks and the way he turns a corner. I used to see every vaudeville show that came to Chicago two or three times. When I was 17 I worked in strip joints, I was the thing between the acts….

Born in Chicago in 1927 to an Irish American mother and a Norwegian American father, Fosse was interested in dance from an early age, beginning to work professionally at 13. Following his three brothers who had all served in the military during the war, Fosse signed up to the Navy in 1946 where he served in the entertainment branch before signing to MGM Studios as an actor and dancer in 1953.

In 1954, he choreographed his first Broadway show, 'The Pyjama Game' which was directed by Jerome Robbins and featured one of his most notorious pieces 'Steamed Heat.' He followed this in 1955 with the hit 'Damn Yankees.' Both of these successful Broadway shows would be made into films in 1957 and 1958, starring Doris Day and Gwen Verdon. 'Damn Yankees' was the start of a long professional and personal relationship with Gwen Verdon. One of his most successful partnerships with Verdon was in the 1966 Broadway show 'Sweet Charity,' which he directed and choreographed and was followed in 1969 with the film adaption starring Shirley MacLaine.

Fosse created some of his most iconic works in the 1970s – the movie 'Cabaret' and the show 'Pippin' in 1972 and perhaps his seminal work, the show 'Chicago' in 1975 (particularly in terms of posthumous revival and acclaim). It was in these works that his choreographic style became noticed and appreciated for the rare dance text that it is. As Robbins had done, Fosse directed and choreographed many of his projects including Cabaret and his 1979 semi-autobiographical movie 'All That Jazz' in which he cast Ann Reinking as the female lead 1.[1]

He won a plethora of awards throughout his career including winning the Academy Award for 'Best Director' for 'Cabaret' over Francis Ford Coppola and his work on 'Godfather' in 1973. He also won an Emmy (for the TV special 'Liza with a 'Z'') and two Tony Awards for 'Pippin' in the same year. Sometimes considered a cantankerous task master by the people that he worked with, Fosse was a choreographer that strived for perfection through repetition, until his dancers really understood the language of the text he was writing. An unstoppable appetite for work combined with a clear and pronounced creative vision, his choreography has embedded 'the Bob Fosse style' in our popular cultural consciousness.

The Ingredients

Image 3.11 From the movie 'Damn Yankees' (1958). Bob Fosse performing with wife and long term artistic collaborator Gwen Verdon in their athletic duet 'Who Got the Pain?'

He was an architect of Jazz dance like no other, before or since and his impact on the fabric of Commercial Dance is consistently evident. Beyonce's 2006 'Get Me Bodied' music video references the 'Rich Mans Frug' from Sweet Charity and much of Michael Jackson's styling and movement lexicon was inspired by Fosse.

Frank Hatchett (1935–2013)

A popular Jazz teacher and choreographer from New York and creator of his much loved 'VOP!' style of Jazz dance, Frank Hatchett was an important figure in the evolution of the phenomenally popular Jazz forms of the 1970s and 1980s to the styles that emerged in the late 1980s and 1990s which ultimately constitute what we consider to be 'Commercial Dance' today.

A student of Katherine Dunham, Hatchett's training consisted of a number of styles – East Indian, African and Caribbean dance were all important parts of his dance education. As a Jazz dance educator, he became synonymous with the noun 'VOP!' which evolved from vocal punctuation marks Hatchett would use in class to help his students accent different movements or hits in the music. His style was one that encouraged freedom of musical and emotive expression without disregarding the underlying technique that was being taught.

Jazz dance in the mid-1970s and early 1980s was culturally very prominent in America and gaining traction by being featured in films like 'Stayin' Alive,' 'Flashdance' and 'Footloose.' Jo-Jo Smith and Sue Samuels (both very influential Jazz teachers in their own right) were also teaching classes at the popular New York dance school 'Jo-Jo's Dance Factory' and invited Hatchett to teach classes there. By 1984, the school would become 'Broadway Dance Centre'), the first dance studios of its kind, a place where different teachers, specialising in all different styles of dance were able to hold their own classes on a daily basis (see the chapter on 'Places to Train' for more on BDC). It gave dancers in New York, whether professional or beginner, the opportunity to take a Ballet, Jazz or Salsa class at the same place, on the same day. Hatchett became a permanent figure there, teaching three Jazz classes a day.

The fashion, music and positive mentality found in these classes taught by teachers such as Hatchett, Smith and Samuels, at the now famous Broadway Dance Centre were fundamental in catalysing the cultural wave of popularity which Jazz dance surfed during the 1980s. Acknowledging new street styles of dance and bringing them into technical Jazz classes made Hatchett's sessions very popular and also makes him one of the important players in the early years of the development of what would boom to be known as Commercial Dance. His students included Madonna, Olivia Newton-John and Naomi Campbell. A friend and student of Frank Hatchett, the actress Brooke Shields described her experiences of taking his class:

> His unique style runs the gamut in sensibility. VOP incorporates everything from lyrical to funk, from primal African and sensual Latin to raw Hip-Hop. VOP is a groove that combines technique and style infused with personal flavour. I used to fear technique because I lacked training, but Frank said that while technique without style lacked emotional quality, style without the control, intrinsic to technique, lacked value.

Moving Jazz Forward

Jazz in the 21st century is being led by a host of dynamic and energised choreographic contributors. Andy Blankenbuehler, Drew McOnie, Stephen Mear, Karla Garcia, Bob Borross, Mandy Moore, Brian Friedman, Ashley Andrews and John DeLuca to name a few. Musical theatre has realigned itself by showing a willingness to move away from Jazz in its traditional sense and embrace a more Commercial version of the dance form (see 'Hamilton,' 'Six the Musical,' '& Juliet' and 'Moulin Rouge'). As dance develops commercially, more frequently the traditional Jazz steps of the mid-20th century are becoming infused with the à la mode dance trends of our day, in a similar way they were in Frank Hatchett's Jazz classes in New York during the explosive time of the early 1980s.

These choreographers are preserving the work of Bubbles, Robinson, Dunham, Cole, Kidd, Mattox, Robbins, Fosse and Hatchett whilst also allowing Jazz dance to inhale fresh movement and inspiration from the multitude of styles it rests alongside, as it continues to provide a foundational structure for Commercial Dance vocabulary to build on.

3c. Club Styles

Grouped together in acknowledgement of where these styles emanated from, House, Vogue Fem, Waacking and Dancehall each have distinct histories and stories whilst all sharing a common thread – that the House beats on a communal dancefloor forged these styles. All four styles feature recurrently in Commercial Dance choreographies.

House

What Is It?

House music developed predominately in the clubs of Chicago during the mid-1980s. Coming in on the heels of the dominate 1970s disco era, it was a musical revolution which saw DJ's and music producers such as Steve 'Silk' Hurley, Todd Terry, David Morales and Frankie Knuckles quickly catapult House music to other international hubs such as

The Ingredients

Tokyo, Ibiza, New York and London. The live instrumentation recorded for many disco tracks was substituted for electronic sounds made on advanced music production equipment such as Roland's TR 808 drum machine, which gave a deep bass drum sound and a steady BPM (typically 120 or higher). The extended, long playing tracks were formulated to keep club goers dancing all night. The nature of this affordable and space minimising electronic equipment meant that much of the music could be made at home – hence the term 'House' music, although there are some differing ideas as to the origins of the term 'House' music. Respected House dancer Caleaf Sellers believes that the term 'House' music is a truncated version of the word 'Warehouse' – 'The Warehouse' being a popular dance club in Chicago in the 1980s. People began to refer to the music Frankie Knuckles played there as 'House music.' Regardless of the origins of the phrase, House music was created to make people dance, providing a heavy 4/4 beat which people could lose themselves in. Dance historian and critic, Sally R Sommers, paints a vibrant picture of experiencing an underground House club:

> Once inside (the club), the body vibrates as the bass resonates in the bones. On the floor, strobe lights pixelate space and action, light cones probe the darkness, and whirling light-flecks reflect off the mirrored balls to produce visual and physical disorientation. Perceptual modes shift – sensing with the skin and seeing in the dark. Everything is in motion. The only way to get balanced and centred is to move your feet. House music is 'produced so that it must be listened to with the body' (Rietveld 1998, 10).
>
> (Sommer 2001, 80)

House dance styles developed in tandem with the musical progression, creating a dance style characterised by fast and distinctive footwork which melded Latin flavours like salsa with floor work and up-rocks from Breakin', and cross pollinating them with a fresh way of feeling the music known as 'Jackin'.' House choreography diversified as it mirrored the splicing of House music into sub-genres such as Electro House, Latin House and Funky House, each encouraging a slightly different movement texture in each. House dance is improvisational in nature however the footwork based movement does lend itself to four or eight count phrasing as many of the fundamental footwork steps follow the musical compartmentalisation of a regular 4/4 beat.

The Steps

Although House evolved as a social dance, one with a free spirited and improvised nature, followers have scribed their own codification over the last three decades. The 2010 Sommers directed documentary 'Check Your Body at the Door' gives an insight to the styles and steps House dancers were compounding in the early 1990s. Ignoring any type of 'armogrpahy,' often the only movement in the arms is a natural swing initiated because of the groove in the hips and the rapidity of the feet. Acrobatics and floor work sometimes feature, as do smooth turns and spirals as the dancers glide over the floor, as if performing a soft-shoe sand dance. The commonality throughout the phrases are the effortless footwork based grooves. Weight shifts from one leg to the other as the torso follows in a rag doll manner, reflecting the laid-back yet pulsing rhythms of the House tracks which drive the dance.

As House dance has largely emigrated from the club floor to the dance studio and House classes have multiplied, three key elements – Jackin', Footwork and Lofting, are outlined as essential components of the dance:

- *Jackin'* is a base step which gives House its unmistakeable 'bounce.' As dancers bend their knees to the tempo of the track, a ripple works up through their body from the legs, through the hips and to the chest. This is the basic idea but fails to really describe the fluidity or flavour of the movement, especially with the high BPM rate which the dancers are matching. Each dancer Jacks differently, according to their individual feel, groove and interpretation of the music.
- The dominant *Footwork* element consists of a plethora of different steps such as Loose Legs (a descendent of various Latin footwork patterns), Heel Step (similar to a 'heel tap' exercise in Tap dancing) and the Cross Step (similar to a 'ball-change step' pattern in Jazz). As with many relatively new dance styles, there are variations taught for each step depending on the dancer's individual style and background. For example, the integral 'Loose Legs' phrase is sometimes taught with a heel tap on the two count, sometimes not, but what remains consistent is the 'rolling' feel added from the hips, giving the step a universal groove.
- The Third House element of *Lofting* is a mix of different dance dynamics and levels as dancers spiral and glide before dropping to the floor and integrating floor work reminiscent of dance vocabulary commonly seen in Breakin' or Capoeira.

Commercial Impact

House dance has expanded rapidly and seamlessly integrated into many Commercial Dance choreographies over the last 30 years. Mainstream Commercial choreographers such as Tina Landon promoted notable House influences in music videos such as Janet Jackson's 'Together Again' and in the 'Throb' dance number from Jackson's The Velvet Rope Tour in the late 1990s (see Tina Landon's 'Main Mover' feature for more on this). Justin Timberlake's freestyle sections in his live performances from the 20/20 Experience Tour in the mid-2010s show inflections of lofting and footwork elements which compliment his fluid, 'Kudulkian' dance style.

The House dance community has maintained an inclusive and acquiescent nature, providing a place for dancers to reflect with their feet the uplifting grooves which House music delivers. Jojo Diggs is a prominent House dancer, instructor (representing Steezy) and Jabbawockees member. Her methodical breakdown of House steps and the calm philosophies she advocates illustrate what a nourishing and plenary climate House dance has matured into – a dance that still flourishes in social cyphers in the club whilst continuing to embody the carefree messages embedded in House music. Commercial Dance content can sometimes appear saturated by aggressive and sometimes overtly sexualised choreography. When House is implemented into Commercial Dance well, it adds a welcome antidote to this roughness – House brings a softer flow, a subtlety and calm neutrality to this coarse commercial movement. In a promo clip for her House classes, Diggs advocates what House culture has offered her:

> When I first found House music, or sometimes I'll say 'when House music found me', I was so, so introverted…. When I was in that club, I would look around and everyone was just free…It was just a natural 'letting their guard down', it was like reading everybody's journal and it was just amazing. So I slowly let my guard down and figured out who I was. House has given me a place to find myself and express it and I love everything about the culture – the music doesn't downgrade women, it's just beautiful.
>
> I love everything about House. I support it and I believe in it.

The Ingredients

Image 3.12 Jojo Diggs performing in the US at the Bay area World of Dance convention (2015)

Image 3.13 Watch Jojo Diggs perform in 2015 at the World of Dance Bay Area competition

Vogue

What Is It?

Vogue Fem (or 'Femme' depending on which part of the world you are in) has been very influential on what we now consider to be generic Commercial Dance. Its impact can be seen distinctly in several styles which have developed to emanate feminacy – mostly labelled along the lines of 'Heels Technique' or as New York based dancer and choreographer Danielle Polanco has eloquently called her classes – 'Femmology.' As a sub-style of the broader dance known as Voguing, the energy of Vogue Fem and its movement quality contrasts with that of Hip-Hop styles, one of the other main contributors to the fabric of Commercial Dance.

It is this dynamic and visually alluring juxtaposition of movement qualities – the perceived masculinity of some Hip-Hop styles spliced with the femininity of Vogue Fem, which gives Commercial Dance its signature traits. Vogue Fem is the youngest incarnation of the dance form known as 'Voguing.'

Developed in Harlem, New York, during the mid-1980s, Vogue dance was cultivated in the Ballroom culture which is

> sometimes referred to as the House/Ball community, (and) is a community and network of black and latina/o, women, men and transgender women and men who are lesbian, gay, bisexual, straight and queer. The black and latina/o members of this community use performance to create an alternative discursive terrain and a kinship structure that critiques and revises dominant notions of gender, sexuality, family and community.
>
> (Bailey 2011, 367)

The ballroom scene in the 1980s New York not only provided a regular performance outlet for those in the LGBTQ+ community but also gave support and a safe space to many Blacks and Latina/o's who were battling with social challenges of the era. Living in a racially discriminate and broadly homophobic society during the beginning of the AIDS/HIV pandemic left many in this community disenfranchised and ostracised from society. The surrogacy offered by the 'Houses' in the Ballroom community provided an important support network to members. As ballroom culture became less underground and more commercialised throughout the 1990s and 2000s, Houses and communities appeared in cities internationally. Many of the Balls are now focused specifically upon Vogue dance battles. Competing in Houses, competitors at the Balls dance against each other in different categories to win prizes and respect in the community.

The Steps

Vogue dance's movement vocabulary often consists of a series of poses – mimicking a catwalk fashion model or replicating the pose of a model on the cover of a fashion magazine such as 'Vogue.' The angular lines created with the hands and arms also allude to the regality of Egyptian hieroglyphics. The shapes created may frame the face, as if a photographer is experimenting though the viewfinder as they look for the perfect shot.

As Voguing has advanced, three styles can be identified: 'Old Way,' 'New Way' and 'Vogue Fem.' The Smithsonian National Museum of African American History and Culture defines the differences:

> With time, Vogue changed from the "Old Way" (which emphasized hard angles and straight lines) to the "New Way" in the late 1980's (which added elements like the catwalk, the duckwalk, spinning, bussey and enhanced hand performance).... Vogue Fem uses similar "New Way" elements but focuses on speed, flow and stunts. Regardless of the style, voguing shows the courage of black and Latino LGBTQ+ communities to make an art form that goes beyond creative expression.

Vogue Fem is the form that is now found in generic Commercial Dance phrases – this fluid style has incorporated theatrical elements including contortion, acrobatics, elements of Jazz dance and Tutting. Dips, Catwalk, Spins and the Duckwalk are some of the key steps. The essence of Commercial Dance has been shaped prominently by its amalgamation with Voguing, and as with Dancehall, a diluted form of Vogue Fem's traits are used frequently in Commercial choreography for music artists or in choreography that is required to be sexual or sensual in nature.

The Ingredients

Image 3.14 Madonna's iconic 'Vogue' video (1990) brought the Vogue dance style to an international audience. The video was choreographed by Jose Gutierez Xtravaganza, Luis Xtravaganza and Vincent Paterson and was directed by David Fincher.

Commercial Impact

The 1990 documentary, 'Paris is Burning,' directed by Jennie Livingston is a prominent reference point in the study of the history of LGBTQ+ communities in America and the evolution of Vogue dance. It offered an illuminating look at the ballroom scene in New York and featured many eminent members of the House community including Willie Ninja, a leading Voguer in the early 1990s. He started the renowned House of Ninja and worked as dancer in many commercial projects around this time, he also released his own single in 1994. Also in 1990, Madonna's 'Vogue' song and music video were released. The video, directed by David Fincher and choreographed by Jose Gutierez Xtravaganza and Luis Xtravaganza, from the acclaimed House of Extravaganza, had a monumental impact on this previously ostracised sub-culture. Instigating the commercialisation of Vogue dance, Madonna gave the LGBTQ+ Ballroom culture an international, mainstream audience. Her 1990 'Blonde Ambition' tour would continue to put Vogue influences at the centre of its choreographic style and featured contributions from dancer Jose Gutierez Xtravaganza and Luis Camacho under the co-direction of Vincent Paterson.

Vogue dance and ballroom culture has continued to garner interest and has become increasingly celebrated in popular culture. Mainstream TV shows such as the Vogue dance competition series 'Legendary' (HBO, 2022) and the drama series 'Pose' (FX, 2018), which covers the New York ballroom scene in the 1990s, have both achieved considerable success. In a 30-year commemorative editorial piece for Madonna's 'Vogue' music video, Liam Hess wrote a piece for Vogue magazine which debates the effect the almost instant commercialisation of the ballroom scene had upon members of its community:

> It's a topic (commercialisation) that was grappled with thoughtfully in Ryan Murphy's award-winning show Pose, premiering in 2018 to retell the birth of the Harlem ballroom scene with an authenticity that can only be arrived at through meticulous research. Its second season took the moment of Madonna's "Vogue" hitting the charts as its starting point. While some of its characters met the news with excitement, as underground queer culture was repackaged into something the public could respect

and appreciate, others, like Billy Porter's Pray Tell, approached it with scepticism, recognising that the dilution of their culture into a series of dance moves would see it remembered merely as a fad.

Both perspectives are valid, but the irony now is that "Vogue" is remembered as neither of those things—instead, it's looked at with hindsight as a seismic shift for queer culture in the broadest sense, as it hit the mainstream for the very first time. Yes, there are valid questions around Madonna profiting off a movement that was spearheaded by a marginalized community she was not a part of, but, in her own way, she gave back. Even the year before "Vogue" was released, the liner notes for her album Like a Prayer came not with a series of thank yous to those who had helped her with the record, but an urgent message describing the "Facts About AIDS" to encourage safe sex, the most visible step yet in her efforts to promote AIDS/HIV awareness. And while she might occasionally miss the mark, who knows the number of young, queer people of color who saw Madonna's video playing on MTV and recognized within it a community that promised a lifeline.

For a further look at the manifestation of Vogue Fem in Commercial Dance, see Joseph Mercier's essay in the Academic Insights chapter.

Waacking

What Is It?

Waacking (also historically spelt 'Whacking' in some instances) is a dance style which evolved from Los Angeles and was inspired by the disco music played in the LGBTQ club scene in the 1970s and early 1980s. Initially known as 'Punking' (a 'Punk' was a derogatory term for a gay man), the dance style later changed its name to Waacking after the dance form was further adopted by a straight, mainstream demographic. The dance's recognisable traits involve a 'whacking' of the arms as they make rapid circular, whipped movements which rotate around the head and torso. The style shares some common characteristics with 'Locking,' with both styles finding initial inspiration in the disco and funk records of the 1970s and also using frequent, accelerated wrist rolls as a main part of their movement lexicon.

Tyrone 'the Bone' Proctor is credited with much of the development of Waacking, as a regular dancer on 'Soul Train' in the 1970s, he worked regularly with other originators such as Don Campbell from The Lockers and formed the 'Outrageous Waack Dancers' with Jeffrey Daniel. After moving to New York in the 1980s he also collaborated with Willie Ninja and Archie Burnett, two early dignitaries from the Vogue community, to form the dance creative 'Breed of Motion,' which took these underground dance styles to international audiences. Proctor's multi-faceted involvement in the dance community perhaps clarifies the various different flavours (Locking and Vogue) manifested in Waacking dance. Singer Jody Watley, a friend and collaborator of Proctor's, defines his early involvement with moulding Waacking as a dance form:

> We had a dance group at one point called "The Outrageous Waack Dancers" profiled in Ebony Magazine at the time… Waacking was a west coast style of dance to the east coasts Voguing. Tyrone helped bring the dance from the underground black and Latino gay clubs to the show – a dance style that was originally to disco music with strings, horns and accents for days and about your dance movements and attitude showing and making people 'see' the music. The term 'Waacking' was coined by those early Waacking pioneers Tyrone speaks of as his mentors.

The Ingredients

The Steps

The defining armography of Waacking consists of 'Lines,' 'Overheads' and 'Rolls.' 'Lines' involve using the arms to create sharp shapes and lines, usually flicking out from the elbow. 'Overheads' occur when the hands flick over the head of the dancer and appear to 'whack' or bounce off the top of the back and shoulder. Often an 'overhead' repeats in reverse, creating a rotational movement which is usually combined with a 'roll.' Combining the 'overhead' with an arm which 'rolls' from the elbow either towards or away from the body creates the recognisable flurrying arm movement seen in Waacking. Dancers who specialise in Waacking also incorporate movement from other genres such as Jazz, House, Hip-Hop and Vogue which they then lay the mercurial Waacking armography over the top of.

Another important part of Waacking is demonstrating an acute sense of musicality and translating the subtleties and multi layered rhythm sections of the disco or House music the dancer is jamming to. As with Vogue dance, creating dynamic tableaux's and snapping into shapes with the arms and body is also a prominent feature of the dance's fabric. Movement influences from the cartoons and martial arts movies of the 1970s are also evident.

Commercial Impact

Waacking lost visibility in the mainstream dance community from the mid-1980s through to the early 2000s. Similar to the tragedy which decimated the ballroom and Vogue dance community, many of the original pioneers of Punking or Waacking had passed away in the AIDS/ HIV pandemic which began in 1981, leaving very few to carry on and teach the original principles of the dance's culture. Elements of Waacking occasionally surfaced in blended choreography on projects such as the movie 'Staying Alive' (1983) and 'Breakin' (1984) but it is credited to the choreographer Brian Green who made a concerted effort to teach and include Waacking again as a mainstay Commercial Dance style in the early 2000s. Green used Waacking and Locking as two of the main dance styles in Mya's 'Free' (2000) video, helping to bring both genres back into the spotlight for a new generation of dancers and choreographers. In the 2020s, Waacking has re-established itself as a popular dance genre, featuring in international competitions such as Juste Deboute and Red Bulls 'Dance Your Style.' Traces of Waacking can regularly be seen in current performance and video choreographies made by K-Pop choreographers such as Bae Yoon-jung and Lip J.

Image 3.15 Waacking is used in many K-Pop choreographies such as in this dance video by Dreamcatcher for the song 'Fly High' (2017)

Dancehall

What Is It?

Dancehall is a music and dance style which derives from Jamaica. A sub-genre of reggae, Dancehall evolved in the 1970s. Originally enjoyed in Jamaican dance halls as an expressive and energetic musical and dance style, Dancehall is now celebrated the world over, with strong followings in the UK and the US. Musically, the differences between Reggae and Dancehall lie in traits such as the BPM and production values of the songs – music journalist Elias Leight clarifies the differences between these two varieties of music:

> Dancehall is effectively a sleeker, rowdier descendant (of reggae), with electronic programming in place of reggae's live instrumentation and a more declarative vocal style relative to reggae's laidback, melodic singing. Together, the two forms have shaped wide swathes of modern pop, starting with hip-hop – reggae helped popularize "toasting" over a rhythm-heavy backing track – but extending far beyond. Several of the biggest Top 40 hits of the last five years have a Jamaican foundation, including Justin Bieber's "Sorry," Sia's "Cheap Thrills" and Ed Sheeran's "Shape of You."

As explained earlier in this chapter, the content of Commercial Dance has often followed the trends already initiated by high charting popular music. As global Hip-Hop artists such as Rihanna, Drake, Beenie Man, Shaggy and Sean Paul have used Dancehall as a sonic base for much of their music, the choreography associated with Dancehall has also been incorporated into the broader vernacular of Commercial Dance, appearing in the music videos and live performances which promotes these records (see the music videos for Beyonce's' Baby Boy,' 2003, and Rihanna's 'Rude Boy,' 2010, both choreographed by Tanisha Scott).

The Steps

A myriad of Dancehall dance steps are consistent condiments to the energetic and vivid music which it accompanies. The nature of the movement is low, grounded and often consists of winding the hips, booty, back and torso. Zenina Rashed demonstrates clearly a number of Dancehall steps on the dance class website www.hipshakefitness.com. Steps such as the Butterfly, Chop da Grass, Row da Boat and the Tick Tock are seen frequently as components of Commercial Dance choreographies created to many music styles outside of Dancehall such as Hip-Hop, R&B, Pop and Reggaeton.

Commercial Impact

Dancehall has courted scrutiny as a culture closely tied to Jamaican social and political issues including class, sexuality and race. Opinions about the cultural and social impact of Dancehall lifestyle vary. As well as being associated with fun and lively musical celebrations at Jamaican dance halls it is also *"known for its bawdy, sexual lyrics, which can be considered misogynistic; its violent content, which at times glorifies the gangster persona; and its reference to drug use, in particular marijuana"* (Galvin 2014, 76). Elena Monteiro contends that *"Dancehall thus expresses the oppression experienced by the black Jamaican urban youth, and their resistance to this situation"* (Monteiro 2018, 237). Sometimes referred to as a way of life, Dancehall artist Beenie Man deftly attests that *"Dancehall is the lifestyle that the reggae lovers live."*

The Ingredients

Image 3.16 Dancer and choreographer Tanisha Scott performing with Drake in his 2015 video for 'Hotline Bling'

Image 3.17 Learn more about Tanisha Scott

Regarding the stylistic advancement of Commercial Dance over the last ten years, Dancehall could be regarded as having an indelible influence on the observable kinetic qualities of the dance's form. Infectious and impossible to ignore, the commercialised Dancehall rhythms underpinning songs like Drakes's 'Hotline Bling' and Justin Bieber's 'Sorry' have sold Dancehall and its dance vocabulary to millions over the world. Tanisha Scott is a Canadian born dancer and choreographer with Jamaican heritage who has contributed greatly to authenticating Dancehall movement in US artists music videos. She has been nominated for an MTV VMA for 'Best Choreography' three times (Sean Paul's 'Like Glue' 2003, 'Temperature' 2006, and Eve's 'Tambourine' 2007) and also provided movement for Rihanna and Drakes 'Work' (2016) video. Choreographers including Parris Goebel and

Keil Tutin have also integrated Dancehall movement dialect into their broader commercial choreographic constructions to great effect. Bieber's 'Sorry' video includes choreography influenced by popular Dancehall steps like the Willie Bounce and the Butterfly, executed in perfect synchronistic group formations with dynamic spatial placement, a recurrent aspect of Goebel's work. The colourful Hip-Hop flavoured styling of the dancers, Goebel's drilled Dancehall influenced steps, Bieber's simple vocal and the Jamaican rhythms laced throughout the track's production are a fitting example of how opulent the commercialisation of Dancehall culture has been.

PROFESSIONAL INSIGHT – BARRY LATHER

Location: Los Angeles

Barry Lather is an American Creative Director and choreographer. He has directed world tours and television performances for some of the biggest artists in the world including Mariah Carey, Miguel, Katy Perry, Justin Bieber, Usher, Rihanna, Robbie Williams, The Pussycat Dolls and Carrie Underwood. Barry began his career as a dancer and then choreographer in the mid-1980s, creating steps for Prince's 'Batdance' music video, Michael Jackson's 'Ghost' short film and Janet Jackson's VMA winning 'Pleasure Principle' music video. His work is also covered in the chapter, 'Music Video and MTV.'

Prince was such a brilliant artist and musician.
Just working with him and being in his presence was very inspiring to me. He was a genius and he knew what he wanted for that theatrical video ('Batdance'). That is a memorable moment for me in my choreography career. Usher was another artist that worked extremely hard, was very focused and put in the time to rehearse the movement so it was perfect. He always strived to leave a mark with his work and was pushing himself for a new flavour all the time. I directed two tours with Usher and many award show performances – he always delivered and pushed his limits. I love that dedication and determination.

My style has always been a mixture of Jazz with street flavour or some funk sprinkled in.
That was my foundation and what I was attracted to as a young dancer. It became a part of me. I was not aware in the mid-1980s that choreography was specifically changing – it felt normal to me to blend Jazz with influences of street dancing at the time. It was a hybrid style, and it seemed to push its way through. Times had changed, music and dance were changing in the early 1980s, especially with music videos, it was inevitable it would evolve and new styles would develop and show up. It was a great time for music videos and dance to join forces…the energies would feed off of each other.

I feel Commercial Dance has been around for a long time, although that phrase may not have been coined years or decades ago.
It is the style that is very current and reflective of the mainstream dance that the audience sees in film, commercials, video, stage and television. It is always evolving and changing – as trends, styles, fashion and music are always changing every year. It has its hand on the pulse of movement, and leads the way of new creativity with the influences of each generation. The new flavour, the new feel, what is happening in the clubs, all contributes to Commercial Dance.

The Ingredients

I worked with Michael Jackson a few times through the years.
The first time as a dancer in 'Captain EO' the 3D film for Disney at The Epcot Centre. That experience was amazing and I witnessed how on point and intense Michael was. Then I choreographed for him years later for an HBO special that eventually got cancelled but some of the choreography was featured in the short film 'Ghost' in 1996. Michael's execution of choreography, the power and attention to detail was incredible to be around. He strived for absolute perfection and wouldn't settle for anything less.

I worked with Prince on the 'Batdance' video and Janet Jackson for 'The Pleasure Principle' video, they are two other artists that inspired me. Janet was very dedicated and put in the hard work at rehearsals. She pushed herself and strived for perfection as well – that dedication I respect.

I was an MTV video generation teen. I watched videos all the time and when little moments of street dancing were featured, I would go crazy!
I grew up watching Soul Train and American Bandstand on TV in the 1970s. The legendary dance group 'The Lockers' had a huge influence on me, they were always performing on Soul Train. They were so different at the time and so funky. I was inspired by them and would emulate some of their moves and style. I loved Locking, Poppin', The Robot – and then breakdancing blew up. I was obsessed with any kind of 'street dancing' at that time. The movies 'Breakin'' and 'Beat Street' had a big influence on me as well as the famous Rock Steady Crew of New York City. Of course Michael Jackson and his iconic videos also had an impact on me. I would actually teach street dance classes when I was 17 and 18. Everyone wanted to learn it at the time. My Mom was a dance teacher and I was encouraged by her as well. I had been dancing since I was 5. Dance and music was always a part of my life growing up.

I was a dancer first then transitioned to a choreographer. That was always my dream when I moved to Los Angeles.
I always knew I wanted to choreograph. I feel blessed to have had all the experiences that happened during the 1980s, 1990s and 2000 to now. You always learn from projects, even if it's just a little gem to take away with you. The pressure of delivering on time, striving to present new style and movement, the creative process, not to repeat yourself, being able to adapt on the spot and communicate well are all part of it.

The discipline of dance and the constant attention to detail with choreography have both helped me with directing projects.
That foundation and base grooms you to excel at other levels. With directing, there is a more leadership role along with the creativity. Following through on the complete vision and all the production elements fall on your shoulders. I love that adrenaline rush, the pressure, and seeing all the creativity come together, it's very rewarding. Understanding dance, staging, camera angles, lighting have all contributed to the directing responsibilities.

Time management and communicating with the team are key factors. Being a positive leader, keeping the energy up and pushing yourself during long hours are all traits that come with directing. That hard work and dedication all comes back to the hard work you do as are a dancer – being focused both physically and mentally.

I still feel like the 18-year-old dancer that moved to Los Angeles years ago.
That energy, passion and love of music and dance is always with me...it has never left.

The Ingredients

Image 3.18 Barry Lather with Michael Jackson on the 1986 short film 'Captain EO,' choreographed by Jeffrey Hornaday

PROFESSIONAL INSIGHT – REBBI ROSE

Location: Los Angeles, USA

Originally from London, UK, Rebbi left her home town in 2014 and travelled to LA to live out her ambitions of dancing for the biggest artists on the largest stages in the world. She toured with Rihanna on her ANTI World Tour in 2016 and performed at the 2023 Superbowl, also with Rihanna. Rebbi danced alongside Beyonce for her iconic 2018 Coachella performance. Also on her CV are gigs with Missy Elliot, JLo and Pharrell Williams. Rebbi also plays the role of 'Angel' in the Starz's produced TV series 'Step Up,' alongside Ne-Yo and Christina Milian.

Working with Beyonce was a huge teaching moment for me even after dancing professionally for more than 10 years already.
You need a certain kind of discipline to be on that team, you have to push harder than you ever have because you are sharing the stage with literal greatness! Everyday you are expected to show up at 100%. The process is long and meticulous sometimes painful but the result is always FLAWLESS. I will forever be grateful for having the honour to share the stage with her.

Rihanna has always been a favourite of mine even before I worked with her. Touring with her was definitely one the most incredible experiences in my career. She taught me how to own my individuality and be braver and more confident. Not that I lacked confidence before but I was stepping into a newer version of myself and I didn't really know it. Watching her take risks creatively and having fun whilst doing it, not caring what the world thinks of her is something I really do respect. It was contagious to me and she has definitely had a very positive influence on me.

The Ingredients

During my career as a dancer in London, I rarely worked with other BIPOC.
I was mostly the token black girl. On very rare occasions I had the pleasure to work with other BIPOC but it did not happen very often for me. Now, since being in the US almost 9 years, I can say that the majority of my career here has been spent working on Black projects, with BIPOC dancers and teams.

I have noticed from afar how much the industry has changed in the UK. I think more BIPOC dancers are being hired on the same gigs that existed in my time as a dancer there and I love to see it too!

Stay focused, train as much as you can, wherever you can.
DO NOT QUIT (the most important thing). When you keep training, you are always at your very best. It's important to be as versatile as possible so as not to limit the types of jobs you can do. Get an agent, start auditioning when you can. Make a bucket list, when you check everything off, make another. Having something to work towards helps to not get complacent. Do your research and make a list of choreographers you want to work for, if they teach classes then make sure you are there.

Take care of your mental health, the industry can be brutal and yet we must still push on but you gotta get your mind right to fight another day. Being a part of a dance community is so important because they will support you when you need. I did not do any of this alone.

Dancers in the US have support from the union that we have never had in the UK.
Although there is always work to be done, the industry in America is miles ahead than that of the UK. Award shows, TV shows, music videos and anything on camera is typically union work and there are contracts for each type of gig. I never really had to sign much paperwork/contracts when I was in London, but here in the US, the majority of my work requires me to sign contracts and/or paperwork.

The contracts/paperwork cover several aspects of the job. Rates, buyouts/usage fees, overtime, days/hours contracted. Tax deductions, hazard pay (when applicable) agency fees (which are usually on top of your pay and not a deduction) plus more. When working

Image 3.19 Rebbi performing with Rihanna on the ANTI World Tour (2016), choreographed by Tanisha Scott

on any union job, the union reps are always available for additional support. Sometimes they are even present on the job and provide immediate support by working with the production teams. I think overall as dancers, we are more protected in the US than we are in the UK.

During the pandemic, I booked a role as a series regular on Step Up Season 3.
Acting was never on my radar so this entire experience felt like a dream. I was so scared of doing it that I knew that I really had to! I had the best time filming this show and I can't wait for the world to see it!

References

3a. Hip-Hop & Funk Styles

https://historyofthehiphop.wordpress.com/hip-hop-cultures/break-dancingdance/ [accessed: 11/2021].

https://www.vulture.com/2020/09/the-timeless-honesty-of-wild-style-the-first-hip-hop-movie.html [accessed: 20/11/2021].

Breaking in the Olympics. https://www.worlddancesport.org/News/WDSF/New_WDSF_Appointments_Advance_Olympic_Breaking_Goals-3190 [accessed: 30/06/2022].

Chang, J. (2005). Can't Stop Won't Stop. *Picador*, https://campbellock.dance [accessed: 10/12/2021].

Damita Jo Freeman. https://www.youtube.com/watch?v=RoH1VGA9-oE&t=10s [accessed: 27/12/2021].

Demonstration of Dancehall steps by Zenina Rashed. https://www.youtube.com/watch?v=VCj454t1UZM&t=4s [accessed: 10/08/2020].

Elias Leight on Dancehall in the US. https://www.rollingstone.com/music/music-features/dancehall-reggae-jamaica-breakthrough-704969/ [accessed: 10/08/2020].

Fogarty Woehrel, M. (2019). On Popular Dance Aesthetics: Why Backup Dancers. Matter to Hip Hop History. *Performance Matters*, 5(1), 116–131.

Frazier, R.T. and J. Koslow (2013). Krumpin' in North Hollywood: Public Moves in Private Spaces. *Boom: A Journal of California*, 3(1), 1–16. https://doi.org/10.1525/boom.2013.3.1.1

Galvin, A.M. (2014). *Sounds of the Citizens: Dancehall and Community in Jamaica* (pp. 76–110). Vanderbilt University Press. https://dokumen.pub/sounds-of-the-citizens-dancehall-and-community-in-jamaica-0826519784-9780826519788.html

Guzman-Sanchez, T. (2012). *Underground Dance Masters: Final History of a Forgotten Era*. Westport, CT: Preager.

Leigh Foster, S. (2019). *Valuing Dance: Commodities and Gifts in Motion*. Oxford: Oxford Publishing.

Miyakawa, F. and J.G. Schloss (2015). *Hip-Hop and Hip-Hop Dance: Groove Music Essentials*. Oxford: Oxford University Press.

Monteiro, C. (2018). The International Dancehall Queen Competition. In S. Dodds (Ed.), *The Oxford Handbook of Dance and Competition* (p. 237). Oxford: Oxford University Press.

Phillips-Fein, K. (2017). *Fear City: New York's Fiscal Crisis and the Rise of Austerity Politics*. New York, NY: Metropolitan Books/Henry Holt & Company.

Questlove. (2013). *Soul Train: The Music, Dance, and Style of a Generation*. New York, NY: HarperCollins.

Zeze Mills interviews Beenie Man. https://www.nycaribnews.com/articles/beenie-man-breaks-down-dancehall-ragga-and-bashment/ [accessed: 10/08/2020].

3b. Jazz Dance

https://www.britannica.com/art/cueca [accessed: 03/08/2021].
http://www.streetswing.com/histmain/z3cake1.htm [accessed: 02/08/2021].
https://www.youtube.com/watch?v=7vyx6ue7K6o [accessed: 17/07/2021].
Cayou, D.K. (1970). The Origins of Modern jazz Dance. *The Black Scholar*, 1(8), 26–31.
George, M. (2022). Considering Jazz Choreography. In L. Guarino, C.R.A. Jones, & W. Oliver (Eds.), *Rooted Jazz Dance: Africanist Aesthetics and Equity in the Twenty-First Century* (1st ed., pp. 163–176). Gainesville: University Press of Florida. https://doi.org/10.2307/j.ctv28m3hd6.24
Giordano, G. (1992). *Jazz Dance Class: Beginning Thru Advanced*. Princeton, NJ: Princeton Book Company.
Guarino, L. (2022). Where's the Jazz?: A Multi-layered Approach for Viewing and Discussing Jazz Dance. In L. Guarino, C.R.A. Jones, & W. Oliver (Eds.), *Rooted Jazz Dance: Africanist Aesthetics and Equity in the Twenty-First Century* (1st ed., pp. 103–118). Gainesville: University Press of Florida. https://doi.org/10.2307/j.ctv28m3hd6.16
Oliver, W. (2022). Professional Jazz Dance in North America. In L. Guarino, C.R.A. Jones, & W. Oliver (Eds.), *Rooted Jazz Dance: Africanist Aesthetics and Equity in the Twenty-First Century* (1st ed., pp. 34–47). Gainesville: University Press of Florida. https://doi.org/10.2307/j.ctv28m3hd6.11
Stalling-Huntingdon, C. (2007). *Hip-Hop Dance: Meanings and Messages*. Jefferson, NC: McFrakand & Company.

Katherine Dunham

https://memory.loc.gov/diglib/ihas/html/dunham/dunham-notes-cabininthesky.html [accessed: 20/08/2021].
Aschenbrenner, J. (2002). *Katherine Dunham: Dancing a Life* (p. 32). Champaign: University of Illinois Press.

Jack Cole & Matt Mattox

Boross, B. (2015). *Comments on Jazz Dance 1996–2014*. Amazon, US.

Michael Kidd

https://www.nytimes.com/2007/12/25/arts/dance/25kidd.html [accessed: 18/08/2021].

Jerome Robbins

https://www.youtube.com/watch?v=9ChbvQGSedw [accessed: 10/08/2021].
'Jerome Robbin in his own words.' The Jerome Robbins Foundation & The Robbins Rights Trust.

Bob Fosse

https://www.nytimes.com/1954/05/14/archives/theatre-in-review-pajama-game-musical-comedy-has-debut-at-st-james.html?searchResultPosition=4 [accessed: 08/08/2021].
Mcwaters, D. (2008). *The Fosse Style*. Gainesville: University Press of Florida.
Wasson, S. (2014). *Fosse*. First Mariner Books.

Frank Hatchett

Hatchett, F. and N. Myers Gitlin (2000). *Frank Hatchett's Jazz Dance*. Champaign: Human Kinetics.

3c. Club Styles

www.jodywatley.net/2020/06/08/in-celebration-of-tyrone-proctor/ [accessed: 26/08/2022].
www.nmaahc.si.edu/explore/stories/brief-history-voguing [accessed: 24/08/2022].
Bailey, M.M. (2011). Gender/Racial Realness: Theorizing the Gender System in Ballroom Culture. *Feminist Studies*, 37(2), 365–386. https://www.jstor.org/stable/23069907
Hess, L. (2020). Strike a Pose! Why Madonna's "Vogue" Is Still Relevant 30 Years Later. Vogue magazine. www.vogue.com/article/madonna-vogue-video-30th-anniversary [accessed: 25/08/2022].
Jojo Diggs interview for Steezy – https://youtu.be/XuNX000xG-0 [accessed: 16/08/2022].
Sommer, S.R. (2001). "C'mon to My House": Underground-House Dancing. *Dance Research Journal*, 33(2), 72–86. https://doi.org/10.2307/1477805

Chapter 4

The People

This chapter gives a brief overview of the most common roles found in the Commercial Dance industry – The Dancer/The Assistant/ The Associate/The Choreographer and the Creative Director.

4a. The Commercial Dancer

A Commercial Dancer is a movement artist who specialises in seeking work in various areas of popular entertainment including music videos, tours with music artists, cruise-ships, film and television work, live theatrical events and various types of advertising. They are often required to display a high level of versatility and need to execute professional levels of performance in several of the dance styles which Commercial Dance consists of. Being adaptable to their environment and potential last minute choreography and production changes are essential virtues for a Commercial Dancer to refine. Being able to thrive in high-pressure environments where rehearsal time is limited and expectations are high is also an essential characteristic for any dancer wishing to work consistently in the Commercial industry.

Often referred to as a 'back-up' or 'background' dancer, the actual job description of a Commercial Dancer can be a lot broader and more difficult to articulate than that of a company dancer or a Musical Theatre performer due to the vast spectrum of projects Commercial Dancers are required for. The term 'back-up dancer' is one that undervalues the efficacy of a dancer in Commercial performance, using the title 'Supporting Dancer' could be viewed as a more apt approach. Read about this more in the Talking Point! essay.

Highs and Lows

Having worked as a Commercial Dancer myself in London and managing to sustain a career for 16 years, I can attest that it is a career of contradictions and contrasts. Exhilarating performances in front of 10,000s of people, painful disappointment when a third audition call-back for a dream job results in rejection, 5 am taxi's to the airport, hours spent waiting in a freezing cold dressing room on a 15-hour video shoot, pre-show nerves and last-minute rehearsals, a lot of jokes, drinks in the Green-Room, meeting and working with people you see on TV, adrenaline-fuelled live television performances and only having 3 hours in the studio to learn a 3-minute routine are just a few of the memorable peaks and troughs in a typical Commercial Dancer's career.

Despite these varied sentiments, being a working dancer always made me feel that the years I spent training and sweating in a dance studio from the age of 8 years old were all worth it in order to be just a small, ephemeral part of an exciting and celestial industry. Being a professional dancer afforded me to travel the world and also work with some of the most talented and creative people in it. That was my experience and it was largely very positive, but each person's own experience as a professional in the dance world will vary. As many experience in the artistic industries, it is a world of complexities, with no barometer of what is considered to be 'fair' and offering very little security or protection, neither financially nor artistically.

Pentathletes of the Dance World

Within the arts, studying a technique until the point of mastery is often the long view goal of students when starting out. Sport science research has suggested that around 10,0000 hours practice over 10 years of quality, committed study of any craft, artistic or sporting, is what is required to become a 'master' in that particular technique (see Malcolm Gladwell's book *Outliers*, 2008 and Matthew Syed's *Bounce*, 2011). Many dancers will spend time from the age of 5–18 studying only one discipline – this is very common in Ballet and Ballroom dance for example. Commercial Dancers have to split their time between different styles, something that they are sometimes slighted for. They do not spend years locked into studying the nuances of a single dance genre and for this, a dismissiveness – an unfair 'jack of all trades, master of none' view of Commercial Dancers is sometimes pedalled by dance educators, even if only sub-consciously. A more equitable and astute perspective is that *Commercial Dancers are the pentathletes of the dance world*. Commercial Dancers make it their business to perform at a very high level in many different genres – operating at a highly dexterous level in a multitude of disciplines is a mastery in itself.

Versatility

Television and its Saturday night 'prime-time' schedule is one of the main entertainment faucets in which Commercial Dance is prevalent. An international television franchise, such as The X-Factor, which may hire a dozen or so dancers for each episode, illustrates the heavy expectations regarding their skill set which are placed upon a professional Commercial Dancer. The choreographer will often require the same dancers to perform a number of different styles in one show. A typical episode of The X-Factor, for example, may feature a 1970s Disco section, followed by a Hip-Hop number, then a Vogue inspired section and conclude with a Salsa-infused Jazz dance finale. The dancers who are hired are expected to switch styles quickly and seamlessly. They must have, at the very least, a sound understanding of the defining principles of each genre of dance. The underlying attribute of a Commercial Dancer is more often than not – versatility.

Litza Bixler, an established US- and UK-based commercial and film choreographer with a background in Contemporary dance (credits include choreographing the movies 'Shaun of the Dead' (2004) and 'Scott Pilgrim v The World' (2014)), remarked that:

The Commercial dancers that I think in many respects have been most successful are the ones that have trained across a wide variety of forms and can basically 'shape-shift' between those different forms without watering them down and the same goes for a Commercial choreographer…

Dance Captain

The role of dance captain offers a dancer the opportunity to step up and engage more with the creative team as well as taking on the role as the dancers' representative. A dance captain's role can range from taking rehearsals when the choreographer or assistant/associate is not available, watching dance rehearsals to offer feedback and give notes, whilst also being a point person for the creative team to communicate with the dancers. If the project goes on tour, the Dance Captain can be responsible for re-staging and cleaning the choreography as it moves into different venues.

4b. The Commercial Choreographer's Assistant/Associate

An invaluable and increasingly important aide to the Commercial choreographer is the choreographer's assistant and/or associate. These job titles are often used interchangeably, but since the early 2010s, the distinctions between an assistant and associate have become more noted and financially respected in the Commercial industry.

An assistant helps the choreographer in a number of ways, including taking cleaning calls with the dancers, organising rehearsals or liaising with other members of the project such as the record label rep or the director on the choreographer's behalf.

An associate is sometimes charged with similar tasks as an assistant but has a larger creative input, often contributing sizeable chunks of their own choreography to the project, something an assistant should not be required to do. If working in a theatre or a touring production, an associate may also visit the production to re-stage, give cleaning calls and make sure that the original qualities of the choreography are not lost.

There are now very few choreographers who work with neither an assistant nor an associate. The increasing scale of productions, time pressure and different choreographic demands in commercial work in TV commercials, stadium tours, films and music videos make an assistant/associate all but essential. The actual job description of these roles differs depending on the working practices of each choreographer. Some assistant/associates are brought onto the job to help translate the choreographer's innovative minds-eye concepts and movement ideas into a physical form, with the choreographer guiding the assistants movements as they create. They help solidify counts, work with the company of dancers and aid the choreographer to overcome any stylistic dance limitations they may have. It is not necessarily a choreographer's job to be able to physically demonstrate the movements they conceive, as long as they can verbally articulate what they want, an assistant can bring those steps to life.

Assistant/Associates can be required to ensure the dancers are clear on the precise form and counts of the choreographers steps. For example, if a Commercial choreographer is booked to create a TV Commercial featuring a hybrid of dance styles such as Ballroom and Voguing, it is common practice for the choreographer to employ both a specialist Ballroom dancer and also a Vogue dancer as assistants or associates to help ensure that movement is kept as authentic as possible. Conversely, the choreographer may create and physically demonstrate all of the steps themselves, using their assistant only as a constructive critic to flag up any phrases that appear out of place or in need of work. Of course, the number of assistants/associates and how many days they are booked for, differs according to the budget of the project.

Be Great All the Time!

During my time working in the Commercial industry, I observed the relationship between many UK and US choreographers and their assistants and associates. It's fair to say that the job requires a different approach depending on which choreographer you are working with, but the skill set needed is usually the same. A Commercial choreographer's assistant is generally expected to be versatile, creative, friendly, well versed in the style they specialise in and also have a good sense of humour – often the most important characteristic given the high-pressured nature of some jobs. They are occasionally used as the middle person between the choreographer, director and the dancers. They must be great observers and astute at reading a room, able to soothe egos and know how to communicate with everyone from the runner to the executive producer. Assistants may not be involved as heavily in the creative process, but are used as consultants or an ear to confide in. Associates are often required to also fulfil all of these duties, as well as offering creative material of their own. How much material associates are required to create will again depend on the needs of the choreographer – with some it could be minimal, perhaps a few 8s, with others, they may be asked to choreograph entire sections of the show.

Madonna and Michael Jackson collaborator Rich Talauega describes what he and his brother, Tone Talauega (see the Main Mover feature on Rich & Tone) expect of the assistants who they book to work with them:

> Firstly, an assistant needs to be able to administer and help delegate our vision as choreographers. Secondly, they need to be able to take in the style of choreography, and of the choreographer, and be able to teach it with the style intact. Thirdly, and this has something to do with anything that we do in life, there are certain tenets that we should always follow as a human beings. Be on time. Work hard. Pay attention. Be fucking great all the time! And the reason I say 'be great all the time' is that your boss is always looking at you – your mannerisms, how you work, how you take things in. Be a good person and work with honour.

4c. The Commercial Dance Choreographer

Commercial Dance choreographers are multifaceted practitioners, sometimes honing their craft in a specific area of dance such as contemporary or hip-hop freestyle before finding their niche as a choreographer on broader Commercial Dance projects. Choreographers such as Hi-Hat, Rich & Tone Talauega, Fatima Robinson and Marty Kudelka all came up with freestyle at the centre of their dance development and creatives including Brian Friedman, Laurie Ann Gibson and Ashley Wallen focused on studio-based training. Some choreographers make the natural graduation from working as a dancer, to dance captain, to assistant, to associate and finally to then taking on the responsibility of creating and overseeing all of the choreography. Some concentrate on choreography from early on, recognising their ability to create interesting movement phrases. The skill set required of a Commercial Dance choreographer includes not just an ability to put dynamic steps together but also have a highly tuned, creatively analytical eye that can see interesting patterns, camera-tracking opportunities and engaging geometric transitions. They are collaborators on a creative team, working closely with the record label, creative director, wardrobe, cinematographer and executive producers. They are ultimately responsible for creating and overseeing all of the choreography on the production.

Coping with Pressure and Management Acumen

Challenges which Commercial Dance choreographers face include: rehearsing huge production numbers in an extremely short amount of time, managing a large number of dancers on set (sometimes 100s), rehearsing with dancers who perhaps they did not personally cast and have been chosen not for their dance ability but for their 'look', working with an artist who wants to do all of the choreography but maybe has very limited dance experience, staying calm in the face of angry directors and short-tempered 1st ADs, being asked by the artist to fire a dancer because they are not fitting in with the overall 'feel' of the project or being told that the track you have choreographed to for the last three days has been changed or drastically edited a few hours before the live show. It's not a job for the fainthearted. All of these are real issues that I have personally witnessed being dealt with while rehearsing and working on television, film and video shoots.

And It's Not Just about the 5, 6, 7, 8…

A common assumption by young dance creatives is that being a successful working Commercial choreographer is all about piecing together slick, innovative dance steps into choreography using highly rhythmical, lyrical and/or technical phraseology. This is no doubt an important part of the skill set required but the real test that working choreographers face is being able to manage the other work-related elements (such as those listed above) which are common place on high pressured and often time-limited projects. Young choreographers showcasing their talents on Instagram and Tik-Tok can become frustrated that the choreography they see on TV and in new music videos is not as slick as theirs. Perhaps they are unaware that the smooth steps they took three weeks to create and perfect and choreographed on their friends, to a song that they chose and love, is only a small part of the puzzle. The real test is in creating the same mesmerising choreography to a track you did not choose and which may not inspire you at all. In creating the same synchronicity with dancers you have never met, who may not know your style and only rehearsing with them for a very short period of time. The dexterity is in being able to make quick, last minute changes to a piece of work because the director has asked you to – adding another chorus, putting another eight bars into the introduction or cutting your favourite part of the dance break without losing your cool. These are some of the things working choreographers deal with frequently, fluently and without fuss on nearly every job they take. If some choreography on a TV show does not appear quite as cutting edge as what you see on Instagram, remember that there is a whole host of other aspects a choreographer has to deal with when working on a professional commercial job – it's not just about the steps.

Money Challenges

The challenges posed when artistic goals are hindered by budget or conceptual limitations from the advertising agency, record company or client (effectively the choreographer's bosses) can make a Commercial choreographer feel like they are at the centre of a tug-of-war contest – on one side they are pulled by their own creative, sometimes experimental ambitions and on the other side they must cater for what works for the artist, the product and (often most importantly) the budget they are working with. Finding that compromise between the various factors of the creative and production team is a skill in itself. Litza Bixler speaks of her experiences balancing artistic and commercial demands:

> It's really challenging as a choreographer because you want to please and you want to do your job - you want to do your job well and you don't want to get in fights constantly. So it's a challenge as you get so used to being compromising (in the Commercial world) that then sometimes when you're given a job where you can have a bit more artistic carte blanche it's like you have forgotten how to really let your creative muscles expand again! That's the challenge, when you're crossing back and forth between the commercial world and what might be perceived as the art world (which allows for experimentation and is often government-funded), it doesn't have those commercial pressures and so there's this interesting tension that always exists between the two worlds.

Expectations: What's Hot Is What Sells

Commercial choreographers are also pressured by knowing that much of their work is required to reflect 'what's hot today'. Which dance styles are on trend in the clubs? What type of music and fashions are relevant in today's popular culture? Is there a sub-genre of dance that is gaining traction, could it be utilised to give a fresh feel to a project or artist's campaign?

A top-end Commercial Dance choreographer does not have the luxury to sit back and rely on an established movement vocabulary that has existed for 60 years, in the same way a traditional Musical Theatre or classical Ballet choreographer may be able to. The language of Commercial Dance is constantly in flux, evolving in close tandem with music and fashion. A choreographer who wishes to have a sustainable career must stay fresh and continually research the styles of tomorrow, expanding and further finessing their own choreographic movement style. What's hot is what sells and a working choreographer needs to sell their product by offering creatively new and innovative ways of moving. When you take into consideration all of these expectations, it's no wonder that day rates for Commercial choreographers are substantially higher than in other fields of dance.

4d. The Creative Director

The job description of a Commercial choreographer has become increasingly blurred as their work frequently crosses over into Creative Director territory: offering artistic options for the overall project, not just creating counts of 8. Moving into Creative Direction has become a natural advancement for many choreographers as their concepts define the television shows and live performances which they oversee. Just as Bob Fosse oversaw entire bodies of work from both the director's and choreographer's chair (Sweet Charity, Cabaret), Creative Directors with a background in Commercial choreography are providing a 'one stop shop' of innovative production ideas, advice on movement and overall creative concept. Established Creative Directors such as Brian Friedman (Dancing with the Stars, American Idol), Kim Gavin (Adele, Take That), Barry Lather (Mariah Carey, Miguel), Gil Duldulao (Janet Jackson), Christian Storm (UEFA Euro's final 2020), Nappy Tabs a.k.a. Napoleon and Tabitha D'Umo (Superbowls 2012, 2018) and Elizabeth Honan (Little Mix, One Direction) all honed their craft as dancers and choreographers first before taking on the heavier burden of Creative Directorial duties.

Barry Lather, who has served as Creative Director for tours with Mariah Carey, Carrie Underwood and Usher, speaks about how he approaches his work as a Creative Director:

> On certain projects I still contribute to the choreography, it really depends on the job. Sometimes I suggest the vision, all the staging ideas and help steer the choreographer I am working with. I see the performance in my head and the special moments that need to happen – making sure those come to life is important.

PROFESSIONAL INSIGHT – RESHMA GAJJAR

Location: Los Angeles, USA

Reshma Gajjar is a first-generation South Asian American performing artist currently living in Los Angeles. Her dance credits include – opening the film 'La La Land' (the girl in the yellow dress), Madonna's World Tours 'Reinvention' and 'Confessions,' touring with Ricky Martin and sharing the stage with Katy Perry, Hozier, Selena Gomez and Dua Lipa.

Madonna is my boss.
The idea of working for Madonna made me equally nervous and excited (you can see this on my face in the audition, as captured in the documentary, 'I'm Going to Tell You a Secret'). So much had been leading up to that moment, I was finally going to do the work that I was born to do! Madonna has an incredible work ethic and is a perfectionist. Rehearsal days of ten hours for months. There was no room for error; we would run the show multiple times a day. Every moment was calculated. She saw my mistakes even when she was in front of me; I swear she has eyes on the back of her head. I always found myself really impressed by her.

Representation matters.
When I look back at my youth, watching performances of Michael Jackson, films like 'Newsies,' and seeing dance on television, it all left an impression on me. However, I never thought that I, Reshma, this little Indian girl could be one of 'them.' I didn't see anybody that looked like me in those realms, therefore I thought it wasn't a profession for me. Also, when I was growing up, generally speaking, first-generation Americans were not encouraged to be artists. I was certainly the black sheep of my family and community. It took a lot of convincing, compromises, and a college degree back-up plan for my parents to support my decision to dance professionally.

I was auditioning but I wasn't booking.
When I moved to Hollywood and started auditioning, the industry was not ready to cast someone of my ethnicity. I could only assume so, because I was talented enough to make it to the end of auditions, but then wouldn't book. I auditioned a lot – the 5'2" brown kid that would show up to every and any audition, even when they were looking for 5'10" white girls. I was super eager, thinking, "I'll just treat auditions like a dance class. If anything, I'm going to meet new people." Wanting a breakthrough, I kept showing up. I'm really good at showing up. I find that's 90% of the work.

I was literally the only one for years.
There were no other Indians in LA pursing Commercial Dance when I moved here. I was literally the only one. Until very recently, I could count on one hand the others I crossed paths with. I didn't realise I was paving a path for future generations. I'm so happy to see more of us now.

In the beginning, it often it felt like I wasn't being hired because I was Indian, or I was only being hired because I was Indian: cast as the token Indian girl, put in Indian outfits, or hired when there was a Bollywood number. I love representing my people, but when your racial identity overshadows your skill set or contribution as an artist, it can be infuriating. And being boxed out of representing your own people is maddening…. I auditioned for the ensemble of the Broadway musical 'Bombay Dreams.' I was capable enough to make it to the end of the auditions, and then was cut. When I saw the show, they'd cast an ensemble of mostly white girls to play Indian. There's still a lot of work to do, but I have hope. I have experienced the progression from tokenism towards being cast as a part of the fabric of America.

In 'La La Land' my ethnicity was not a factor that I am aware of – just an American girl opening a film. Of course, the little brown girl inside me thinks it is incredible that an Indian girl is featured in a Hollywood film. The fact that it is still something to celebrate speaks to where we are culturally: not quite there yet, but closer and definitely moving in the right direction.

If I'm dancing, then I'm a dancer.
There was a moment when I stopped. I quit pursuing dance as a career. The 'business' and lack of booking was getting in the way of my love for the art form that was my best friend.

I moved to India to do social work and volunteered for a non-profit that works with disadvantaged children in Mumbai, helping put together a bilingual musical with the kids. As I was working with these incredibly talented, brilliant young people, the notion of my privilege as an American with so much more opportunity available to me really settled in. My ideas around success were redefined. Work was no longer the measure. Dancing daily and improving my craft, this became the new definition of success.

Soon after returning to LA, I booked the Madonna tour. The world was finally ready for me, but more importantly, I was ready for the world.

The first time I saw myself in La La Land….
After working in the film and television industry for years, I've developed a level of unattachment that comes with experience. It's a constant feeling of duality that you're balancing. As an actor or dancer, you never know if you will end up on the cutting room floor. When it happens, it can be crushing and humbling! We feel so integral to these scenes and yet at the same time, we can suddenly be made to feel not that important after all. Sometimes the whole scene gets trashed… for weeks leading up to the release of La La Land there were rumours that the entire Another Day of Sun sequence was going to be cut from the film, even after they had spent all that money and time developing it. Fortunately, it wasn't. At the screening, it was surreal to see myself. And, that the camera stayed on me, that I got to be the one to tell the story. Forever part of movie history!

Dance for you.
Being a dancer is a hard job. Rejection is frequent; there is a reason why they say it requires a thick skin. One must figure out quickly how to deal with rejection. For me, after an audition,

The People

Image 4.1 Reshma as 'the girl in the yellow dress' in the memorable opening sequence from the movie La La Land (2016), choreographed by Mandy Moore

I move on immediately. I've also learned that even though it feels it – it's not personal. Don't compare yourself with anybody else, know that you are on your own unique path. Trust your life has its own divine timing. It may not make sense now, but it will later. Build a community of people that inspire and celebrate the person that you are. Being healthy mentally, spiritually and physically is what gets us through the process of being a dancer which is good because a lot of the time you will find, the process is what we remember more than the product.

PROFESSIONAL INSIGHT – JONO KITCHENS

Location: Barcelona, Spain & London, UK

Jono Kitchens is a unique Commercial Dancer and choreographer, specialising in Feminine Style and Drag work. He has choreographed for Melanie C's world tour as well as regularly creating work for 'Sink the Pink,' an LGBTQ+ collective specialising in live productions and immersive events, a place where 'everyone is welcome and everyone is celebrated.'

The challenges are often the industry itself.
Despite LGBTQ+ people being a huge part of the arts and entertainment industry forever, it hasn't always been fashionable (or profitable) to have these people in the spotlight. Drag traditionally has a reputation of being about lip-syncing or doing stand-up comedy, so it perhaps isn't the first thing that jumps to mind when planning an artist's live show or tour. However, in recent years with the rise in popularity of shows such as Ru Pauls Drag Race, the world has been able to see that the drag queen community is incredibly diverse and talented.

It was very bold of Melanie C to put drag queens not just on stage behind her but also beside her, collaborating in 2012 with Jodie Harsh (a famous UK drag queen, DJ and music producer) and eventually writing a song dedicated to a whole drag collective 'Sink The Pink' and then taking those artists with her on a world tour in 2019. Thankfully, we are seeing much more LGBTQ+ representation on stage not just as back-up singers/dancers but as fully-rounded, respected, successful artists.

It's really liberating once you understand that you can be both masculine and feminine at the same time, in all situations.

There are of course some obvious visual differences because wearing wigs and heels will automatically change the way in which you carry yourself and move your body but when it comes to performance and artistic expression, I find the gap between the two personas has grown ever closer. As the world continues to evolve and accept all types of gender identity and gender expression, there is much less need to differentiate between what is traditionally seen as masculine or feminine and these attributes can, and should be tapped into whenever the need arises.

There have been times on and off stage when I have asked myself how I would behave or react if I were experiencing the same situation whilst in drag and this has helped me to overcome nerves in everyday life or perform more confidently in a casting. Likewise, my drag persona has also benefited from accessing my masculine energy when performing to add interesting layers and dimension to the way I perform the choreography.

I loved my training and had a wonderful and fulfilling career as a professional Commercial Dancer BUT….

I was often told I was 'too short,' 'too feminine,' 'too skinny,' 'too this' or 'too that' for certain jobs. I got the opportunity to teach classes and found that this was where I could express myself in my own way on my own terms. I stopped thinking about things being 'too girly' and just doing what I wanted to do. Whilst I was enjoying a new-found career as a teacher and choreographer my professional career was also flourishing, but there was always the feeling of unease and I know retrospectively that it was because at that time, I was conforming to the industry's preconceived notions of gender/sexuality and not able to fully authentically exist as a queer performer. The shift in gear to channel my power and energy into drag came in 2010 when I had co-created a dance group called The Breakfast Club. We performed at many LGBTQ+ underground events in the East End and met talented drag cabaret performers such as Johnny Woo, Scottee, Gateaux Chocolat, John Sizzle and of course Sink the Pink. Exposed to this much creative energy, I lost myself in the magic and mayhem of the East London club scene distancing myself from the cold rigidity of the professional dance industry, where I no longer felt I belonged.

I was inspired to explore something that had been within me my whole life – my femininity – and finally I had an outlet for that, where it was not only appreciated but celebrated. 'Sink the Pink' founders, Amy Redmond and Glyn Fussel, already had a small community of drag performers but they welcomed me into their family and generously allowed me to create material which we would trial out to live audiences at their monthly club nights. As the performances became more elaborate, the drag family started to grow and more and more talented performers were joining us, meaning we could be even more ambitious with our shows. Suddenly, UK drag queens were getting a lot of attention and popping up in fashion editorials, in music videos, on TV shows, and at festivals, it was the start of a movement which has led to a 10-year-long career for me as a drag queen and drag choreographer, which shows no signs of slowing down yet.

Like almost everyone on the planet in the 1980s/1990s, I was obsessed with Madonna.

Her presence as a performer and her defiance as an unashamed and confident woman was unmissable. She also was an open advocate for LGBTQ+ rights and victims of AIDS long before many others. I was also inspired by the choreography and musical career of Paula Abdul who was responsible for some of the most iconic choreography in music videos and Hollywood movies of that era. Vincent Paterson was another big influence, unmistakably choreographing Michael Jackson's Smooth Criminal music video and Madonna's Blonde Ambition tour. As a young professional, I owe many of my choreographic influences to the incredible dancers I was exposed to and able to take workshops and classes with whilst training in London including: Brian Friedman, Blake McGrath, Jojo Diggs, Shirlene Quigley, Javier Ninja, Sisco Gomez, Shaun Niles, Benjamin Milan, Rai Quartley, Laura Fletcher. I also owe so much of my success as a dancer and choreographer to David Leighton. Today I find it can be hard to get inspired when there is so much content to wade through especially with apps like TikTok, etc., but I find Parris Goebel the most exciting and consistent choreographer who always seems to keep surprising and delivering!

Image 4.2 Jono performing with Melanie C on the Graham Norton Show in 2019

Chapter 5

The Realisations

To gain an oversight of the advancement of Commercial Dance since the early 1980s, it is helpful to analyse the channels of performance in which it is most commonly manifested: *Music Video & MTV, Musical Theatre & Dance Theatre* and *Live & Televised Events*. The following chapters aim to give Commercial Dance, both as a dance genre and an industry, some social context as well as tracking its journey chronologically and cataloguing important works.

5a. Music Video and MTV

Music videos have shaped the development of Commercial Dance more than any other medium, providing a rich and reliable incubatory vehicle for its development. Music Television, or MTV as it's known, has provided the showroom. It was through music videos and MTV that dancers and choreographers were first able to showcase their work to worldwide audiences. Following the story of music video and MTV offers a way for us to document the journey of dance on screen and the Commercial Dance industry over the last 40 years.

Music Video: A Short Introduction

A contender for title of the 'first music video,' that being a short film clip made with the intention of aiding the promotion and therefore boosting the sales and commercial viability of the song it accompanies, is Bob Dylan's 1965 promotional clip for 'Subterranean Homesick Blues.' It's a simple yet effective video shot in black and white (just on the cusp of universal colour TV broadcasting) and shows Dylan holding up various cue cards which correspond with the iconic song's rap-like lyrics. It's a great example of what a music video *is* and what its *objectives* are – it's a *visual accompaniment* to a piece of music, created to help *promote* the song by *entertaining* its viewers. Memorable and short, Dylan's video offers a visual aesthetic to a song that was ahead of its time, as did Queen's infamous accompanying promotional clip for 'Bohemian Rhapsody' in 1975, at a time when music videos started to become an integral part of the marketing toolkit for leading singles from the biggest artists. In his 1994 paper, 'Postmodernism and Music Video,' author John Mundy describes the raison d'être of a music video as being 'predominately commercial.' He goes on to succinctly define music video and its place in popular culture:

> Commercial in origin, the development of music video as a commodity was paralleled by its development as a specific cultural form…. Like TV Commercials, music video is concerned to exploit the rich, dense, often nostalgic, economy of meanings implicit within the contemporary visual landscape. In it's ability to entertain and sell simultaneously, to collapse, fragment and mutate spatial and temporal geography, to plunder and pillage both esoteric and popular culture, to elevate surface and sensation at the expense of depth and analysis, to reinvent and problematise meaning, and to refuse any sense of textual authority, music video, it has been argued, represents the triumph of postmodern cultural form.

An artist appearing in a high-production music video, flanked by a group of dancers has become a staple of modern musical performance. The 3–4-minute duration of most clips gives the artist, director and choreographer a chance to unashamedly create something engaging and immediate for its audience whilst, as Munday notes, 'elevating surface and sensation.' As with Commercial Dance, music videos are paramountly concerned with two aspects: creative ingenuity and effective marketing. The academic and music critic, Gina Arnold reinforces this idea, professing that music videos operate in a space in-between two worlds, those of art and commerce "…*the music video therefore represents a world of technical and creative passage, situated between art and commerce, the mere illustration and documentation of musical performance and visual creativity and imagination*" *(Arnold et al. 2017).*

MTV: A Short Introduction

MTV was a revolutionary television channel and the first to specialise in one particular subject matter – Music Videos. In the pre-internet world of the 1980s and 1990s, MTV was a phenomenon, offering an instant taste of the music, dance and fashion styles which were trending globally. In this era, a music video premiere could be bigger than the release of the song itself. MTV provided a space for powerhouse icons such as Madonna, Michael Jackson, Missy Elliot, En Vogue, N'Sync, Britney Spears and Janet Jackson to showcase their dance abilities and lead their dancers through exciting choreography, sublime costume design and budget-crushing special effects.

A Revolutionary Way to Watch TV

Music Television first broadcast in the US in August 1981 and was one of the primary offerings on America's cable TV package. For the first time, audiences were offered 24-hour programming on a multitude of channels for a monthly fee. MTV was key in selling this new idea of television as a subscription package. Previously, all programming had been free but with limited schedules and broadcast hours – many channels would stop broadcasting at 11 pm. MTV was a revolution in a pre-internet era. By offering a 24-hour channel that broadcast music videos in the same way that the radio played songs, it became an essential way for the youth of the early 1980s to scope out the current trends. After initially offering a radio show style format in which Video Jockey's (VJ's) introduced clips and conversed in much the same way a radio DJ would, MTV started to offer genre-specific programmes, such as 'Yo! MTV Raps' and 'The Headbangers Ball,' allowing viewers to enjoy videos by category.

Following the early success of MTV, television corporations began to provide much more programming to cater specifically for music videos. In the UK, Top of the Pops, which had been a staple of BBC broadcasting since 1964, started to divert much more of its 30-minute airtime to broadcasting music videos instead of just solely live music performance and Channel 4 also offered their own music video programme with 'The Chart Show' (1986). In the US, Video Hits One (VH-1) launched in 1985 to compliment its sister channel MTV, offering video selections for an older demographic. Globally, MTV franchises in countries including Japan and Australia gave music video an international audience. A shallow pool of music videos grew rapidly deeper to aid the format's meteoric rise in popularity and by the time MTV had arrived in Europe in 1987, artists and bands like Prince, Queen, Madonna, Tina Turner, George Michael, Dire Straits, David Bowie, Whitney Houston, New Order and RUN DMC had made the music video an essential part of promoting any new record release and accordingly, the music videos in rotation grew considerably.

Natricia Bernard, an MTV VMA nominated choreographer for her work on Ed Sheeran's 2021 video 'Bad Habits,' choreographer of Katy Perry's 'Firework' video and Kanye West collaborator, remembers how watching the latest videos on MTV and copying the styles she saw had a huge influence on her development as a dancer and choreographer:

> We were broke and didn't have cable so I used to go around to my friends house to see the first showing of a new video. Salt n' Pepa, MC Hammer, Kylie Minogue were all so influential, what they wore and how they danced. MTV changed how we dressed, before you had to see the dancer's body in class but we started wearing the Spice Girl's Buffalo shoes and MC Hammer's baggy trousers. It opened up so many new avenues for dance, it made everything a lot 'cooler'. We started to see breakdance infused with contemporary dance, which is a beautiful thing. We began to incorporate these styles and steps we saw into our freestyle.

The MTV Video Music Awards

In 1984, MTV hosted the first MTV Video Music Awards, offering an annual 'Oscars style' award ceremony for Music Video. Its stature grew to become one of the most entertaining and eventful award ceremonies in the television calendar. Being nominated for an MTV Video Music Award for Best Choreography in a Music Video has become a highly valued addition to any choreographers CV. It's an event that has lurched from kitsch (Britney Spears, Madonna and Christina Aguilera's kiss in 2003), to surreal (Lady Gaga's Meat-Dress in 2010), to displaying artistic excellence (Michael Jackson's performance in 1995). From a dance creative's point of view, the VMA's in the US, the European VMA's and the Asian VMA's is an opportunity to create memorable dance centred performances, becoming an annual big budget showcase for artists, creative directors and their choreographers to demonstrate their skills to a global audience.

The inaugural 1984 ceremony featured a live performance by Madonna performing 'Like a Virgin' in a revealing white wedding dress whilst dancing provocatively on the floor – it was a performance which caused much controversy in the press. It gave the world an early taste of the daring and cutting edge live performances the show would offer annually in the future – Nirvana's chaotic rendition of 'Lithum' (1992) and Miley Cyrus's twerking with

Robin Thicke (2013) to name a few. Madonna's 1984 performance was a precursor of the indelible impact MTV would have on the world of Pop culture and Commercial Dance.

1980–1990: The Birth of a Genre

If we are seeking a place and a time in which 'Commercial Dance' emerged as a genre in its own right, then there is a strong argument that this period of heavy music video production, from 1983 to 1987 in Los Angeles, USA was the catalyst that took choreography on a different pathway. An intersection was created by choreographers such as Michael Peters, Vincent Paterson, Jeffrey Hornaday, Barry Lather and Paula Abdul who were using the highly technical principles of Jazz dance, previously seen mainly on the Broadway or West End stage, and melding them with new 'street' styles such as Boogaloo, Popping, Breakin' and Locking that were being developed outside of dance studios and on the streets of many American communities, particularly those in marginalised, low-income environments. For the first time, choreography was being created that was principally being used to make a video which would sell a product (the record and the artist). These early music video choreographers used previous dance forms developed by earlier masters such as Michael Kidd and Jerome Robbins and spliced it with new elements of youth and inner city dance culture to create a unique brand of dance. Commercial Dance is the creative and industrial offspring of this marriage of styles.

The Early Influence of Michael and Janet Jackson on Music Video and MTV

In the early 1980s, The Eurythmics, David Bowie, Talking Heads, Duran Duran and Queen were a few of the music artists and bands creating commendable and artistically progressive music videos. From a dance perspective though, Michael and Janet Jackson were immeasurably influential from 1983 through to the late 1990s. The siblings' contribution to dance and choreography in music video format is unparalleled and their work (along with that of their directors, creative teams and choreographers) was hugely inspirational for the dance community globally. Exploring the body of work from these two Jackson siblings is an imperative part of analysing Commercial Dance's advancement in music video.

Michael

Michael Jackson's career was filled with many memorable 'dance-on-screen' moments spanning four decades, but it is the trio of videos released in 1983, which as a collective, mark a moment of genesis in the history of Commercial Dance. Jackson cemented 1983 as a definitive year in the evolution of dance in music video. It was no accident that Jackson was at the centre of this dance revolution.

After breaking away from his family group, 'The Jacksons,' in the early 1980s, Jackson was keen to establish himself as a solo force, one not dependent on his family group's success. It was an era of profound creativity for Jackson, in which he grabbed the reins of his career, taking total artistic autonomy – something that had previously been denied, either by his father and manager or record labels which controlled his and his brothers creative output. His previous album, 1979s 'Off the Wall,' had been well received and he was eager to elevate his artistry further. The three videos from his sophomore solo album 'Thriller' are enormously important regarding the progression of Commercial Dance, these being Billie Jean, Beat It and Thriller.

The first music video from Thriller was the striking 'Billie Jean' (1983). The electric video featured Michael in a satin dinner suit, walking on paving stones that lit up as he walked and danced along a path in an ethereal city scape. A loose narrative strings the clip together – a member of the paparazzi is stalking Michael and his elusive lover (presumably Billie Jean) – the theme of being hunted by the press would become a regular thread in his later music and the accompanying video clips.

Jackson had been training hard behind closed doors to develop his signature movement and idiosyncratic style. Sharp finger points, hip isolations, jumping onto his toes and fast triple pencil turns that he would later become synonymous with, were all displayed in the Billie Jean video for the first time. The movement was free-styled yet deliberate, every finger snap appearing choreographed and every glance full of intention. Within his movement are shades of Bob Fosse, James Brown, Fred Astaire and Sammy Davis Jnr, combined with Jackson's own experience of the Funk styles which he had performed frequently with The Jacksons on shows such as Soul Train in the 1970s. Using his dance as exclamation and punctuation points for this staccato vocals, the resulting movement was a unique conception only Jackson could create. He was demonstrating an innate ability to observe and absorb from dance greats who preceded him as well as digest new dance styles coming through. This sensitivity to, and awareness of, other performer's skills gave his dance performances intense dynamism and a broad cross-generational appeal. This quality of solo dance performance had not been seen before in a music video before.

The 'Billie Jean' video was regarded as unique and became one of the first videos by a black music artist to go into heavy rotation on MTV. Black artists including Prince, Musical Youth and Grace Jones had previously been given air time on the channel in 1981 and 1982, but the Billie Jean video was the first to be shown with frequency on a par with that of a white rock or pop act, opening the door for Soul, R&B and Hip-Hop videos to be exhibited on the channel more regularly. Initially, there was resistance from MTV in playing the video, citing that they didn't think the video was for 'their audience.' A stand-off allegedly ensued, with Jackson's record company CBS (whose signings also included white Rock & Pop tentpole artists such as Kate Bush and Aerosmith) threatening to pull all of their artists from MTV's video playlists unless they played Jackson's video. Steve Barron, the director of the Billie Jean video, commented in 2018:

> I presumed MTV would play what was a really great pop song, and so I was really surprised when I heard it might not go on MTV after we finished it. I was confused as to why, because this video felt different—it felt extraordinary when I was making it, like beyond anything else that was out there, or beyond anything I'd ever seen in terms of movement and style and instinct. I thought it was going to be enormous, that everyone would have the reaction that we were having, and that all we had to do was show them. I thought it would definitely be seen everywhere.

It was only the fact that 'Billie Jean' went to number one on The Billboard Hot 100, which forced the video into high rotation on MTV. The clip's inclusion on their high rotation playlist altered the content of the channel, it increased MTV's viewership and gave an avenue for black artists to promote their records in the same way a white rock band could. The follow-up video to 'Billie Jean' was 'Beat It.'

The Realisations

Image 5.1 Michael Jackson in the Beat It video (1983). On the left (in the white jacket) is Beat It and Thriller choreographer Michael Peters. To the right is the choreographer Vincent Paterson (see his Main Movers feature for more information). Beat It was a seminal moment for Commercial Dance. Mixing dance styles and performing synchronised group choreography in a music video was revolutionary

The video for 'Beat It' changed the game in terms of an audience's experience of dance in music videos.

'Beat It' premiered on MTV on March 31st, 1983 and the final third of the video focused solely on group choreography. 'Billie Jean' had featured Jackson freestyling alone to the music and showcasing his unique signature movement style. 'Beat It' is the first of many Michael Jackson videos where the choreography is as well known as the musical chorus hook, the video featured a group of 18 dancers and culminated in two street gangs performing collective choreography in unison, led by a masterful Jackson. The dance sequences were devised by Michael Peters and the video also features Jackson's future choreographic collaborator Vincent Paterson, who played one of the two gang leaders in the video, opposite Peters.

The Beat It video featured dancers who could be considered to be among the first 'Commercial Dancers' (those earning money as freelance dance artists, not attached to, or on a hiatus from, a Broadway show or dance theatre company) arguably performing the first piece of Commercial Dance in a music video. Featuring elements of Popping, real gang members and integrating a 'worm' like body ripple into its iconic routine, Jackson and Peters took large-scale, synchronised group choreography to the forefront of a music video for the first time. Incorporating moves from the best street dancers of the 1980s, such as Dane 'Robot' Parker (the Popper in the cap), with Peter's Jazz base, the video was ground-breaking in its multiplicity of genres – combining Jazz dance, fresh street dance styles and the guitar rock of Eddie Van Halen meant the video reached a multitude of different demographies. It could not be ignored. Blogger DJ Robb writes about the impact of the choreographed segments of 'Beat It' on his popular music blog site:

> It was that dance sequence during the video's final one minute and one second that revolutionised music videos for ever. Before then, syncopated dance moves featuring

the principle artist had hardly been used in promotional videos…Unified dancing akin to that seen in the movie West Side Story? That was unheard of…. The end result took MTV, America and the world by storm.

Jackson and Peters would collaborate again on the very next project, the seminal 'Thriller' video. The 'Thriller' video would set the benchmark which Jackson strived to rise to on every one of his subsequent choreography-based videos for the next 25 years. It not only altered the music video landscape, but it changed the rules of the game for any other pop artist wanting to include choreography in their music video. Expectations had heightened and Jackson had elevated the quality of dance in music video to an almost unattainable level for many. See the 'Iconic Moment' feature on the Thriller video for a more in-depth look.

Jackson regularly added videos featuring exceptional dance moments to his repertoire, highlights include – 'The Way You Make Me Feel' & 'Smooth Criminal (1987 & 1988 respectively, both choreographed by Vincent Paterson), 'Remember the Time' (1993, choreographed by Fatima Robinson and Buddha Stretch) and 'You Rock My World' (2001, choreographed by Michael Rooney and Rich + Tone Talauega). His influence on dance in music video is immense and has accordingly been recognised by MTV, who in 1991 renamed their 'Video Vanguard' award – The Michael Jackson Video Vanguard Award, which is awarded to artists who have had a significant impact on the medium of music video. Michael Jackson's contribution to dance in music videos and the forging of Commercial Dance as a dance style and industry is arguably matched by only one other person – his sister, Janet.

Janet

In the years after the Thriller campaign, whilst in the studio writing new material for his follow-up album 'Bad,' it was Michael's sister, Janet Jackson, who continued to provide a rapidly expanding Music Video industry with engaging choreography laden music videos. Janet's 1986 album 'Control' wielded four music videos in the same year – 'What Have You Done For Me Lately,' 'Nasty,' 'When I Think of You' and 'Control,' all spotlighting dance and synchronised group choreography. These videos also followed her brother's lead by presenting each clip as a mini-movie, or 'Short Film,' as they began to be referred to. Shot with a cinematic feel and a loose narrative, these theatrical clips continued to move away from the idea that it was sufficient for a music video to be just a recorded live performance of the song.

Janet Jackson's videos in this era, in particular 'The Pleasure Principle' (choreographed by Barry Lather) in which Janet dances solo with a chair in a disused warehouse, show her strength as a technical Jazz dancer and gave inspiration to an entire generation of dancers. Aside from 'The Pleasure Principle,' Paula Abdul choreographed all of the clips for this campaign, winning an MTV Award for Best Choreography in 1987 for 'Nasty.' Janet Jackson's execution of synchronised group choreography in videos such as 'When I Think of You' was unparalleled by any other leading artist at this time, she appears to be capable of matching any professional dancer of that era. Abdul provided strong technical choreography and according to Jet magazine in 1990 she *combined sexual energy with classy, alluring moves.* This suited Jackson's natural style and matched the sharp percussive, synthesised sounds associated with Janet, created by her long-term musical production team, Jimmy Jam and Terry Lewis. The choreography was largely very technique based – high-level Jazz and classical principles, usually suited to a musical theatre production, were included alongside 'Street' elements, such as Locking, Popping and Hip-Hop social steps.

In the 'Nasty' clip, Jackson fronts a group of male dancers whose technical ability could have seen them as comfortable on stage with the Alvin Ailey Dance Company as in a music video. Pas de Chats, Jetes and a dancer nailing eight flawless pirouettes feature alongside snippets of new 'street dance' elements. The 'Nasty' video delivers choreography in which the stylistic ingredients aren't quite blended yet, rather they are performed in different sections by a detached group of dancers, similar to how the street dance performers appear in segregated groups or separate shots in her brother Michael's 'Beat It' and 'Thriller' videos. Styles such as Locking are separated for most of the chorus sections, showcasing their segments as an aside to the main Jazz-based, group action (see the Locking sections in 'Nasty' and 'When I Think of You').

Janet's next creative venture was the critically acclaimed 'Rhythm Nation 1814' album. The accompanying videos put her on an equal footing with her brother regarding her impact on, and quality of, dance and choreography in music video. The choreography used in the Rhythm Nation era saw varied elements of dance such as Locking and New Jack Swing, become a seamless blend of Commercial Dance movement – constructed by Jackson and her collaborating choreographers (read more about Rhythm Nation in the Iconic Moments feature). Professor of Screen Industries at the University of West London, Emily Caston, notes in her expansive book *British Music Videos 1966–2016: Genre, Authenticity and Art* (2020) that along with Michael's 'Thriller' video:

> Janet Jackson's 'Rhythm Nation' was also hugely influential in the UK: directed by Dominic Sena and choreographed by Anthony Thomas, the sheer scale of the choreography, costume, photography and editing of the synchronised dance of the video set a standard that has rarely been achieved since. Together, these two videos established a style that was opulent, dramatic and very slick and that would be inherited and consolidated in the 1990s RnB and Rap videos of Hype Williams, characterised by fisheye lens work and glitzy wardrobes.

Post Rhythm Nation and on a similar professional trajectory to that of Michael, Janet's music video catalogue continued to include music videos featuring the highest quality choreography. Highlights include 'If' and 'Together Again' (1993 & 1997, both choreographed by Tina Landon), 'All For You' (2001, choreographed by Marty Kudelka, Shawnette Heard and Roger Lee) and 'Feedback' (2008, choreographed by Gil Duldulao). Michael and Janet Jackson are responsible for lighting a fire in many young dancers that pushed them to pursue their passion and realise their potential as professional performers.

New Employment Opportunities for Dancers

As the demand for dance in music video increased in the early to mid-1980s, a welcomed by-product was that a new avenue of employment possibilities were created for professional dancers in London, LA and New York. Previously, mid to long term contracted company or theatre work was what would pay the bills for most dancers. Shaun Earl, a dancer who worked on many commercial projects in Los Angeles in the 1980s and could be regarded as one of the first true Commercial Dancers, notes that dancers could make a sustainable freelance living from the early 1980s by dancing with artists in music videos and working on short-term television and film projects. It was a time when dancers working in these industries realised the opportunity which versatility could offer. Rather than being trained rigorously in one technique, in one studio or school, dancers were learning multiple styles 'on the job.' Earl recalls being booked on the 'Fame!' television show (1982–1987), in music videos for Paula Abdul and Vanessa Williams and being challenged to learn different styles and movement dynamics instantly:

> I did all these different things that made me versatile. I didn't come from a studio, which actually was an advantage for me. I was learning and performing things on jobs which were for the occasion or for the 'vibe' of what the choreographer wanted.

Toni Basil, an influential choreographer and dancer, also commented in an interview in 1984 that before music videos "*dancers couldn't get enough work to keep us eating…. as a result of videos, the good dancers are eating now.*" The increase in demand for dancers in music videos led to more auditions for paid jobs, further cultivating a community and an industry which could support freelance dancers. The mix of dance styles and infusion of contemporary and modern dance principles (such as in and Kate Bush's 'Running Up That Hill,' 1985, choreographed by Diane Grey and New Order's 'True Faith,' 1987, choreographed by Philippe Decouflé), meant company-based dancers who had previously specialised in Contemporary, Musical Theatre or Jazz dance, now had a new performance outlet and further employment opportunities in the commercial areas of music video and live performance with a music artist. Being a 'backing or back-up dancer' became a welcome and financially viable alternative to longer contract company work for dancers.

The newer 'street' styles that were emerging were gaining traction as an exciting range of additions to traditional dance styles such as Jazz and Modern dance but they were still only seen as recreational fringe styles and did not yet have a developed, teachable structure or syllabus which allowed them to be studied as legitimate dance forms in their own right. If any Hip-Hop or Funk styles were needed for video and film projects, they were cast from genuine dance crews such as the Rock Steady Crew (Flashdance, 1983) or The Electric Boogaloos (Thriller, 1983). Most dancers did not yet cross over between styles, they were trained in either the 'studio' or the 'street.' This came at a time in the mid-1980s when codified studio Jazz classes were on trend, advances made by Matt Mattox, Luigi and Frank Hatchett, combined with new dance centres such as Pineapple Dance Studios in London, Debbie Reynolds Dance studio in LA and Steps on Broadway in New York gave advanced dancers a secure structure from which to further their dance training, again helping them to sustain a career in a freelance manner, without relying on a company for security and training.

Other 1980s Influences

As with the genesis of any new creative or artistic movement, it is rarely the work of one or two protagonists but rather an organic endeavour involving many different talents, working simultaneously on similar, yet disconnected, parallel projects. In the art world, The Renaissance movement's conception is sometimes economised to have been started in Florence by a small number of world renowned artists such as Michelangelo and Raphael. The reality is that the Renaissance was a wave of simultaneous cultural developments in various different locations across Europe initialised by a number of different philosophers, artists, patrons and social circumstances. Although it may seem grandiose to compare the magnitude of the Renaissance movement with the evolution of Commercial Dance, the point is that in the early development of Commercial Dance within the music video format, there were many contributors creating works in different places, all helping to evolve popular dance on screen and stage at the same time in the 1980s. Dance and popular culture were colliding at a stratospheric rate in London, New York and Los Angeles and nowhere could this collision be observed more vividly than via music videos. In the US, the dance creatives listed earlier (Michael Peters, Vincent Paterson, Jeffrey Hornaday, Paula Abdul and Barry Lather) were major dance contributors and in the UK, choreographer Arlene Phillips plus a host of notable British directors (Steve Barron, Sophie Muller, David Mallet) and British Pop acts such as David Bowie, Sting, Elton John, Queen and Kate Bush were pushing the advancement of movement in music video and developing a notable canon of work:

Jeffrey Hornaday

Hornaday choreographed the successful movies 'Flashdance' (1983) and 'A Chorus Line' (1985), two very significant films for dancers. Both movies offer memorable, 'music video-esque' dance scenes and are set at a time when street dance styles were making their way into mainstream pop culture. 'Flashdance' in particular is remembered as the film which gave international audiences the chance to see Hip-Hop styles directly from the streets of New York on a cinema screen for the first time. In 1986, Hornaday also co-choreographed 'Captain Eo,' a Disneyland 3D song and dance short film featuring Michael Jackson – another inspiring work for early Commercial Dance creatives. In 2003, he earned an MTV VMA nomination for 'Best Choreography' for his work on Jennifer Lopez's music video for 'I'm Glad,' which saw him re-choreographing the iconic chair-dance scene from 'Flashdance.'

Arlene Phillips

Arlene Phillips may be more recognised in the UK for her work in Musical Theatre (Saturday Night Fever, Starlight Express, Fame!) rather than in the realm of Commercial Dance. However, her work in the 1980s in music video and television marked her as one of the early leaders in the formative years of Commercial Dance as an industry, a fact that is sometimes overlooked. Choreographing for her own dance group 'Hot Gossip' lead to regular appearances on UK TV show 'The Kenny Everett Show' and showcased Phillips' choreography which was based on avant-garde Jazz techniques whilst also appearing daring and risqué for the audiences of that time. Post 'Hot Gossip,' Phillips worked with some of the greats of the 1980s on both sides of the Atlantic, helping them refine their presence on camera through their music videos – Donna Summer 'She Works Hard for the Money' (1983), Elton John 'I'm Still Standing' (1983), Tina Turner 'Private Dancer' (1984) and Whitney Houston's 'How Will I Know' (1985) and 'I Wanna Dance With Somebody' (1987), are all clips which benefitted from Phillips's trend setting choreographic direction.

Paula Abdul

In 1989, a few years after helping launch Janet Jackson's career by choreographing many of the music videos from the impressive 'Control' album, Paula Abdul as a solo music artist also featured dance heavily in her music videos. 'Straight Up' (for which she won Best Choreography at the MTV Video Music Awards) and 'Opposites Attract' both present what would become a template for Commercial Dance work – Jazz techniques developed by earlier pioneers like Jack Cole and Matt Mattox intertwined with newer dance elements.

Read more about Paula Abdul in her 'Main Movers' feature.

Barry Lather

Winning the MTV VMA for 'Best Choreography' for Janet Jackson's 'Pleasure Principle' clip in 1988 (also from the 'Control' album Abdul collaborated on) and his work in the same year on Sting's 'We'll Be Together' video, made Barry Lather an influential force in the videos of the late 1980s. He continued to develop choreography on the small screen with a strong acrobatic Jazz style, perhaps more physical than other choreographers of the time. As a dancer, he was well versed in the emerging street styles of the era and this can be seen in his subsequent choreography work, particularly in Prince's extravagant, dance-packed 1989 'Batdance' video featuring an army of Jokers, Batmen and a string of strutting Kim Basingers, all characterised by different particular motifs. He continues to work in Commercial Dance, mainly in live performance direction with established music artists such as Usher, Miguel, Carrie Underwood and Mariah Carey.

Learn more about Lather's career in his 'Professional Insight' feature where he talks about what it is like to work as a choreographer with the world's most established recording artists.

Vincent Paterson

During the late 1980s and early 1990s, Paterson played an important role in shaping the on-screen dance moments for some of the most notable performing artists of the time in Lionel Richie, Madonna and Michael Jackson. Read in more depth about Paterson in his 'Main Movers' feature.

1990–2000: Big Investment and Slick Dance Clips

The prototypal videos of the 1980s had proven that the choreography in a track's promotional music video could be as influential as the melody of the record. In the 1990s, Commercial Dance as a dance genre continued to take shape and become a recognisable, substantive creation. This owed much to consistent exposure of dance and choreography in music video. Although still a young art form, by 1990, music videos were respected by film makers as instruments which provided a free and creative outlet.

Martin Scorsese's direction of Michael Jackson's long form 'Bad' video and David Fincher's influence on the glossy videos of the late 1980s, such as Madonna's 'Express Yourself,' was furthered in the early 1990s by future feature film directors such as Spike Jonze, Michael Bay and Michel Gondry, who created era defining clips for Fatboy Slim, Meatloaf and Bjork respectively. These auteurs contributed heavily to the appearance of music videos of the 1990s as did artists such as Mariah Carey, Will Smith, Madonna and Missy Elliot, who all continued to use choreography prominently in their videos. The clips themselves were increasingly referred to as 'short films' and given the budget to match this moniker – 13 of the top 20 most expensive music videos ever made are from the 1990s (the list features videos from future blockbuster movie directors such as Brett Ratner, John Singleton and Mark Romanek). Complex direction, cinematography and cutting-edge CGI lead to many videos being of feature film quality, giving a perfect platform for choreography to continue variegating at a fast pace. Arguably, the music video director Hype Williams influenced music videos and the choreography in them more than any other director.

The Realisations

Hype Williams

No other music video director has created a signature style as easily recognisable as Hype Williams has. His work in the second half of the 1990s was slick, quirky, fun and extravagant, creating the blueprint for the Hip-Hop video of this era. The 'fish-eye lens' effect he often used in his work became a trait replicated by other directors in the same way that Timbaland's musical beats were imitated. The two went hand in hand from 1994 until the end of the decade. From a choreographic perspective, Hype's work with Aaliyah, Missy Elliot and Busta Rhymes was particularly ground-breaking, using choreographers including Nadine 'Hi Hat' Ruffin and Fatima Robinson to create the steps. The styling, the trippy set-ups and the eccentric, Hip-Hop-based choreography became trademarks of his work and a blueprint, which other creatives would use to replicate his style internationally. Dance often featured predominately in Hype's videos and provided a platform for dance to develop further in the commercial arena –from Blackstreet's 'No Diggity' in 1996 to Missy Elliot's 'The Rain' and Busta Rhyme's 'Put Your Eyes Where My Hands Can See' videos in 1997.

Following the Music

Beginning in the mid-1990s, a big influence over the future trajectory of Commercial Dance was the route which mainstream Pop music took throughout this decade. Previously during the 1980s, choreography was featured regularly in videos that could be generally defined as promos for Pop music, a musical style that has many varied inflections of disco, funk and European centric electro synthesisers (ABBA, David Bowie, Madonna, Kate Bush, George Michael, The Eurythmics). As discussed in the previous chapter, the vocabulary of dance developed accordingly, using genres that were already established, such as Jazz, and combining them with fashionable steps from what was termed at the time as 'Street Dance.'

By the 1990s, radio-played mainstream Pop music was increasingly influenced by R&B and Hip-Hop music which had garnered mainstream acceptance. US R&B artists such as Luther Vandross, Alexander O'Neal and Mary J Blige, Hip-Hop groups like NWA, The Wu-Tang Clan and Cypress Hill had found global audiences in the 1990s, helped by MTV and VH-1's ability to reach younger generations internationally. Family friendly collaborations like Aerosmith & Run DMC's 'Walk This Way' (1986) and Mariah Carey's 'Fantasy' Remix featuring O.D.B. (1995) influenced youngsters heavily, blending the boundaries of what was considered previously to be music that was either black or white. Programmes including 'Yo MTV Raps' and 'The Headbangers Ball' helped to forge the 'MTV generation' (also known as Generation X) – perhaps the first generation raised on musical tastes originating from many different cultures and ethnicities. A 2013 article in Complex Magazine asserts that this genre crossover was the consequence of a generation raised on music of multiple cultural origins:

> The massive, unprecedented crossover of hip-hop and R&B into the mainstream during the late '80s and '90s had produced a generation of white children reared on music by black artists. Corny teen pop artists grew up, and looked to contemporary R&B as a way to express themselves as adults.

R&B, Neo-Soul, Rock, Rap and Electronica were accordingly big influences on the mainstream pop music of the late 1990s and 2000s and the melding of musical styles resulted in musical acts becoming harder to define in terms of musical genre. The Beastie Boys are a fine example of this, their 1994 'Sabotage' track is part Rap/part Rock, with a fun, Spike Jonze directed spoof video to accompany it. Other big sellers of this era such as Mariah Carey, Missy Elliot, Brandy, The Backstreet Boys, Boyz II Men, N'Sync, The Spice Girls, Britney Spears and Christina Aguilera also produced music that often genre hopped from track to track, making use of Hip-Hop, Pop, House and R&B tones to create albums with a large cross-over appeal to consumers. This mix of musical influences also altered the fabric of the choreography in music videos.

Commercial Dance choreography shadowed the rapid evolution of popular commercial music in the 1990s, creating a collage of movement from a pool of dance denominations to suit whichever musical flavour was being exhibited in the video. The dance style became more nuanced, changing according to the sonics of the song – House, Hip-Hop, Salsa, Dancehall, Disco, all trended and built upon the established Jazz/Hip-Hop dance hybrid of the late 1980s and early 1990s.

2000–2010: An Established Genre

The Demise of the 24-Hour Music Video Channel

By the early 2000s, Commercial Dance had become a recognisable dance genre, establishing itself as a fusion of multiple styles. Pursing a career as a Commercial Dancer became an increasingly realistic and viable career choice thanks largely to the efficacy of MTV and the music videos which it had showcased for 20 years. In the mid-1990s, MTV began to change its focus and move away from a channel which promenaded videos on a 24-hour loop. Billboard magazine reported that despite MTV reaching an estimated 77 million households the US in 2001, most of its proposed new programs "had little or nothing to do with music videos" and that it had abdicated itself from its "former role as a 24-hour-a-day music channel." In 1995, MTV in the US played 47,118 music videos. By the year 2000, this number had shrunk to 29,920 as TV shows like 'Jackass' and 'The Osbournes' received the prime time scheduling spots and benefited from the beginnings of a cultural fascination with reality television. By 2001, MTV, VH-1 and BET had all been acquired by Viacom Inc ensuring that this move away from music video programming was also reflected in the scheduling of the two other stations showcasing choreography in pop-based music videos – BET and VH-1.

However, as the 2000s progressed, digital television in Europe and the UK offered free-to-air music videos channels such as 'The Box,' 'VIVA' and 'The Music Factory' which filled the space vacated by MTV. The advent of internet-based platforms such as Myspace and YouTube also began to offer alternative, on-demand ways to view music videos, ensuring that producing music videos continued to be a relevant promotional and artistic tool for record companies worldwide, helping to ensure that the Commercial Dance industry was able to support a swelling number of professional dancers making their money from work associated with the music industry.

Commercial Dance Becomes a Sustainable Career Choice for Many

The 2000s were an era in which many pop artists were producing music videos which centred around a choreographed routine and were using dancers instead of live musicians in their live performances. As well as including choreography and dancers in their music video, an artist would often promote a new release with a team of dancers via a promotional tour of television and award shows such as Top of the Pops (UK), CD:UK (UK), MTV's TRL Live (USA), The BET Awards (USA), The NRJ Awards (France) and Wetten Das? (Germany). With music videos, live television appearances and promo tours, there was finally enough work generated for a dancer to work sustainably as a Commercial Dancer. As the artistic quality and production budgets continued to ascend in the 2000s, so did the level of the accompanying choreography. Individual choreographers began to put their own recognisable stamp on the choreography that was featured in music videos, in much the same way music producers began to become more prominent in Pop and R&B music (Timbaland, Pharell Williams, Rodney Jerkins).

In the early to mid-2000s, a multitude of US-based choreographers offered a style of movement that was unique to them. Each choreographer brought their own flavour to the mixing pot. Marty Kudelka brought a new kind of Hip-Hop with rhythmic precision, Tina Landon offered a variation on House flavours, Brian Friedman worked with a challenging technical Jazz style and Rich + Tone Talauega seasoned everything with their own unique groove. As the content of the choreography in music videos became more distended, so did the necessary versatility required of a Commercial Dancer. Reflecting this distention of influences, Commercial Dance's development in the 2000s can be observed in a number of iconic music videos from this era: *Christina Aguilera's 'Come On Over' (choreographed by Tina Landon, 2000), Justin Timberlake's 'Like I Love You' (choreographed by Marty Kudelka, 2002), Beyonce's 'Crazy in Love' (choreography by LaVelle Smith Jr and Frank Gatson, 2003), Britney Spear's 'Toxic' (choreography by Brian Friedman, 2003), Usher's 'Yeah!' (choreography by Devyne Stephens & Usher, 2004), Jennifer Lopez's 'Get Right' (choreographed by Rich + Tone, 2005), Rihanna's 'Umbrella' (choreographed by Tina Landon, 2007) and Lady Gaga's 'Bad Romance' (choreographed by Laurieann Gibson and Richy Jackson, 2009)*, are all examples of how Commercial Dance was elevating its artistic validity as well as accelerating its growth as an viable industry for dancers to work in. Slick, exciting choreography led by the artist had become a must for many Pop and R&B acts meaning that these prominent US choreographers worked regularly and became sort-after creatives on a global circuit, choreographing and influencing dance work internationally.

UK Talent

In the UK, a rich vein of choreographers were also making moves which ran parallel to their American counterparts, catering for a golden decade in British pop music and Commercial choreography. Priscilla Samuels, Paul Domaine, Gary Lloyd, Paul Roberts, Kim Gavin, Elizabeth Honan, Ryan Chappell and Paulette Minott are some of the leading UK-based choreographers whose innovative work in the late 1990s and 2000s ran laterally with that from across the Atlantic, inspired by the music video visuals created by US directors like Hype Williams, Paul Hunter and Joseph Khan as well as the steps performed by their US creative counterparts such as Wade Robson, Cris Judd and Michael Rooney. This group of British choreographers and creatives made an enduring contribution to UK popular culture by providing relatable steps for artists and bands who were selling an enormous number of units, spurred on by the arrival of television shows such as Pop Stars (2000), Pop Idol (2002) and X-Factor (2005). Many stadium filling musical acts featured choreography in their music videos and live promotional events. Steps, The Spice Girls, Westlife, All Saints, Sugababes, Robbie Williams, Billie Piper, Atomic Kitten, Take That and Blue were joined by musical talent stemming from these hugely popular reality television shows of the late 2000s – Girls Aloud, Leona Lewis, JLS, Little Mix, Cheryl Cole, One Direction and Alexander Burke. This provided even more sustainable employment opportunities for many British-based dancers and choreographers as the radio friendly Pop and R&B crossover gave UK choreographers a comfortable canvas to create work from and increased demand for their work.

The Realisations

Image 5.2 Cheryl Cole's 'Fight For This Love' music video (2009), choreographed by Beth Honan. A rich vein of UK choreographers such as Honan choreographed for many successful UK pop artists throughout the 2000s and 2010s. (FYI: in this still from the video, I am dancing to the right of Cheryl.)

2010s Onwards

The 2010s saw the passing of the baton from the originators of dance in the music video to a new generation of creative artists navigating an industry increasingly entangled in multi-platform media consumption. Artists like Britney Spears, Michael Jackson and Madonna, although still remaining relevant, saw their influence wane on the choreographic offerings in music videos. As the decade progressed, commercial choreography drifted away from the bubble-gum pop dances seen in music videos from bands like N'Sync, The Backstreet Boys or Britney Spears in the 2000s and towards a more serious and creatively artistic path. Fresh choreographer's including Parris Goebel, Keone & Mari Madrid, JaQuel Knight and Charm La'Donna, who had grown up watching videos choreographed by trend setters like Tina Landon, Hi-Hat, Rich + Tone and Michael Rooney, were raising the artistic expectation of dance in music video. The Commercial Dance industry and its associated movement style was now already established, the task for these choreographers was to take this fused genre of popular and social dances and reaffirm its authenticity by studying and adhering to the core principles of the dance techniques from which it is made. Their understanding of numerous specialist dance techniques became more accomplished due to more universally available and internationally based training. Understanding of previously seldom seen Hip-Hop and Club styles had no doubt improved as channels such as YouTube and Instagram made movement research easier, allowing dancers to learn the foundations of these styles in a credible manner.

Traditional dance sectors also continued to blur. Contemporary dance choreographers incorporated more marginalised styles such as Popping and Breakin' into their work and Commercial Dance makers looked to the creative powers exhibited so freely by Contemporary dance choreographers such as Akram Khan, Hofesch Schecter, Anne Teresa De Keersmaeker and Yoann Bourgeois for inspiration. Projects like the Parris Goebel curated series of music videos for Justin Bieber's Purpose album (2015) are a great illustration of the creative freedoms, ambitions and aspirations of the Commercial industry in the 2010s. Featuring a variety of dancers well versed in many different styles, the videos give screen time to a multitude of different genres, utilising the talents of Goebel's own ReQuest dance crew in the iconic 'Sorry,' Keone and Mari Madrid for 'Love Yourself' and Emma Portner in 'Life is

Worth Living.' JaQuel Knight continued to keep dance at the forefront of Beyonce's videos with additions such as 'Formation' (2016) as well as cultivating emerging, choreography focused artists Victoria Monet and Megan Thee Stallion, notably choreographing Stallion's viral 'Body' video in 2020. Other choreographic creatives like Jamal Sims (Jennifer Lopez, Ciara) and Sean Bankhead (who choreographed notable Missy Elliot's 'I'm Better' video) all contributed to Commercial Dance in the late 2020s.

K-Pop's influence expanded in the 2010s, as bands including BLACKPINK and BTS outgrew the South Korean market, gaining in popularity in Europe and the US and subsequently creating an enormous platform for dance in music videos. The quality *and* quantity of choreography in music videos from K-Pop artists has enabled many dancers and choreographic creatives to flourish in this industry as their works are featured extensively on social media and video streaming platforms. K-Pop's fan networks are immense and videos from choreographers like Keil Tutin (BLACKPINK), Bada Lee (EXO) and Sienna Lalau (BTS) have garnered 100s of millions of views (see the Professional Insight feature on Keil Tutin for a deeper look at his career).

The Music Video Legacy

Beginning in 1983 with Michael Jackson's seminal 'Beat It' music video choreographed by Michael Peters, Commercial Dance has continued to secure itself as an essential artistic feature in music video, constantly crossing over into and enriching popular culture, initially with the help of MTV. For four decades, music videos have provided choreographers and dancers with a way to exhibit their skills whilst also providing consistent employment. Thriller, Rhythm Nation, Umbrella, Single Ladies and Sorry reached all four corners of the globe, not just because of the popularity of the song but also because of the enjoyment the choreographies from the associated music videos bought to the millions of people who watched and imitated them on the dance floor.

5b. Musical Theatre and Dance Theatre

Musical Theatre has increasingly become a place of incubation and growth for Commercial Dance. As Musical Theatre scores and soundtracks have become more influenced by Pop and Hip-Hop music styles over the last 20 years, the choreography on stage has followed suit. Mid-20th-century stage classics such as West Side Story, Guys & Dolls and CATS, all have a choreographic base steeped in technical Jazz and classical dance techniques. These cornerstone Musical Theatre shows currently play in theatres on New York's Broadway, the West End in London, in Berlin, Madrid, Paris and Sydney as well as on national tours worldwide, comfortably nestled in theatres next to modern works like In the Heights, Hamilton: An American Musical, Legally Blonde, The Bodyguard, Six: The Musical, & Juliet and MJ: the Musical.

Modern musicals dating from the mid-2000s onwards have incorporated Commercial Dance choreographic inflections into the body of their work, which has seen more dancers with a versatile Commercial Dance training being cast in musicals. The chorus line of many shows now consists of Commercial dancers led by a choreographer also using Commercial Dance styles to help narrate and set the emotional tone of the musical's movement. Adam 'Bo' Boland, a director of the prominent Musical Theatre and talent agency, Collective Agents in London, notes:

The Realisations

The diversification of working choreographers in Musical Theatre has brought a new level of understanding to popular culture into the arts. As agents we need our finger on the pulse. You can create anything in Commercial Dance, its a choreographer's dream, there is no limit to the characterisation – anyone can become anyone through Commercial Dance and because of this I am able to represent a far more exciting range of performers – we need dancers that have the raw skills that are required to execute all areas of Commercial Dance effectively. Previously these skills were a novelty, they are now essential. No two Lockers, Poppers, B-boys or B-Girls are the same, which makes my job exciting, we're no longer looking for a ability to clone, but an ability to interpret and make it one's own.

Choreographers such as Andy Blankenbuehler are utilising Commercial Dance to break from the occasionally limited and rigid structure of Jazz dance in order to compliment the narrative by marrying lyricism, emotion and metaphor to physical movement. Choreographers who predominately work in the Commercial world like Marty Kudelka, with his break from repetition and 'shape orientated' movement, have been an inspiration. Commercial Dance's inclusion into Musical Theatre is pivotal in ensuring a future audience for Musical Theatre.

Choreography in Musical Theatre is frequently used to express a character's emotion or heighten the meaning of a song and it is created for artistic reasons – not in order to necessarily monetise a product. However, the content of movement in more recent shows on the Broadway and West End stage can still be considered Commercial choreography due to the mix of styles which form the body of many choreographers work – creatives such as Andy Blankenbuehler (Hamilton), Gary Lloyd (Heathers), Ellen Kane (Legally Blonde), Sonya Tayeh (Moulin Rouge) and Carrie-Ann Ingrouille (Six: The Musical) are just a few who have found success with this hybrid form of dance.

Image 5.3 Andy Blankenbuehler's choreography for Hamilton: An American Musical moved away from traditional theatre Jazz and incorporated influences from other dance styles such Hip-Hop and Contemporary

The Realisations

Classic to Commercial

Thriller Live! was one of the first musicals on London's West End to use predominately Commercial Dance styles as choreographic influences as it celebrated the song book of Michael Jackson, The Jacksons and The Jackson 5 and went on to run for over a decade. Breakin', Funk styles, Jazz and Disco are all influences on the show's choreography, which in 2006 was re-launched by director and choreographer Gary Lloyd. Lloyd has worked in both the Musical Theatre and the Commercial world, choreographing the critically acclaimed musical 'Heathers' (2022) in London's West End as well as working with artists such as Robbie Williams and Kelly Clarkson in the Commercial world. He believes that the future of dance on the Musical Theatre stage will be enhanced by the increased use of Commercial Dance:

> Shows like CATS and West Side Story are like ballets and could almost exist as stand alone dance pieces, telling the whole story through the choreography. Guys and Dolls, 42nd Street, The Producers and the like are classic musicals that rely on big production numbers to lift the audience and allow the script to travel through darker or more narrative moments. The songs and their choreography become a big part of the arc and the journey of the piece and due to the writing, rely on movement within the style or era in which that piece has been written. Creating this work can be very complex, as in one musical you may need to focus on lavish costumes and a specific grand style whereas another show may require the choreography to be earthy and totally character based.
>
> Commercial choreography in the 21st Century musical is just as energetic and impactful but can also show feeling and emotion within the movement in a much more intricate way, often taking inspiration from Contemporary dance choreography, another style which is fast becoming part of today's fusion. I think the main difference (from traditional Musical Theatre choreography) is that Commercial choreography is still used to represent the younger generation and although in many cases, incredibly creative and powerful, these styles still have years to go before this new fusion becomes considered classic.
>
> I imagine that now Commercial choreographers have broken into Musical Theatre and both mediums borrow from one another, the future of choreography in musicals will be a beautiful blend of styles, attracting the most talented and versatile choreographers to achieve this.

New Choreography for a New Audience

Musical Theatre has been assisted by Commercial Dance in finding a culturally relevant voice again in socially progressive times. The osmosis of popular cultural canons such as pop music and Commercial styles of dance into Musical Theatre has helped with this renewal. Many prominent musicals which debuted in the early to mid-twentieth century are steeped in societal virtues, which now seem stale and outdated. As Boland noted, Musical Theatre has been seeking to secure its future audience. Musical Theatres' commentary and outdated assumptions around race, sexuality and family values needed reconsidering and reframing in order to keep these classic musical masterpieces relevant to a new generation of young theatre goers. For the generations born after 1990, the cultural landscapes of musicals such as Carousel, Oklahoma! and Seven Brides for Seven Brothers can feel like alien terrain. A new generation of musical enthusiasts now see their own socio-political concerns being met head on by accomplished contemporary works such as 'Dear Evan Hansen,' '& Juliet,' 'For colored girls who have considered suicide…' and 'Come From Away.' Social media anxiety, loneliness, social segregation and the consistent threat of global terrorism are typical concerns incorporated into these musicals, mirroring the daily omnipresent news-media minefield navigated by 'Generation Z.' Revivals and re-boots of shows like Oklahoma! (Broadway revival, 2019, dir. Daniel Fish) and Legally Blonde (Regents Park UK, 2022, dir. Lucy Moss) have made attempts to transport popular works into a modern world, incorporating themes of inclusivity and using a cast from multiple ethnicities and backgrounds whilst also using notable commercial twists in the choreographic glossary. Steven Spielberg's onscreen re-imagining of 'West Side Story' gloriously reintroduced the music of Stephen Sondheim and Leonard Bernstein to a younger audience, whilst carefully correcting the original movie's racially questionable approach to casting. The new choreography, although created in a similar classical vein to Jerome Robbins' iconic original work, gave choreographer Justin Peck elbow room to bring an added athleticism to the movement, highlighting the supreme physicality and conditioning of the dancers of today whilst also incorporating intricate rhythms into the movement which complement the music in a way that was not seen in some of the work of the 1960s and 1970s.

Comparably, Christopher Scott's work as choreographer on John M Chu's movie 'In the Heights' is also a benchmark piece of filmic work for modernising the canon of Musical Theatre works. Scott complemented Lin Manuel Miranda's patchwork Puerto Rican Hip-Hop score with choreography as equally diverse and authentic, incorporating a number of Commercial styles. Andy Señor Jr is a musical theatre actor and director from Miami with Cuban heritage, he played the character of Angel in 'Rent' on Broadway and on London's West End and has directed Broadway shows such as 'On Your Feet: The Story of Emilio and Gloria Estefan' and 'Holiday Inn.' He shares his views about the development of Musical theatre and its increased interconnectivity with Commercial Dance styles:

> Over the last 10 years there has been a shift and the focus has been on telling the story through the dance – because the choreographers and directors want to work this way. It was something we did in 'On Your Feet: The Story of Emilio and Gloria Estefan'. Sergio Trujillo (the choreographer) came up with a beautiful narrative about family traditions for which he gained a Tony nomination. Andy (Blackenbeuhler)'s work has introduced a whole new vocabulary to dance in musical theatre – every movement means something. His work was the tipping point in that every movement is advancing the story and the quality of the movement was not what we had seen on Broadway before. Genres associated with Commercial Dance, such as Hip-Hop styles, allow characters and actors to express themselves authentically. I never did those traditional Broadway jazz dance movements growing up, they were not from our culture, it was borrowed. Also, shows we are making now – they deal with real truths we are working on in life presented in a musical fashion and with that comes the reality of our movements as well.
>
> There is also a lot of pre-production done now concerning choreography, budgets have been allocated to allow choreographers to work with the characters really spend more time creating movement which relates to the story. I think you can look at a show on Broadway right now and see Commercial Dance and one thing reflects on the other, there isn't such a disparity as there was in the 80's…it helps us reflect what is going in in the world and also helps us with audiences as that is what they want to see.

The Realisations

Jazz Dance and Storytelling

Jazz dance has long been the 'go to' dance style for Musical Theatre choreographers. It forms the base vocabulary for many musicals in the second half of the 20th century, but is not always the most malleable, adaptive form of dance to work with. Jazz dance connoisseur Bob Borross comments that *"…. It takes fortitude and concentration to delve deeply into the motivations for (Jazz) movements…Saying more with your choreography is always the goal of the choreographer."*

Where Jazz dance sometimes struggles is with 'saying more with the choreography' – expressing subtle emotional notes or extended story lines has not traditionally been Jazz dance's forte, potentially problematic in a Musical Theatre industry which, as Señor Jr states, is becoming increasingly focused on 'telling stories through dance.' Having worked in a number of conservatories, it is evident that, aside from Jazz technique classes, Jazz dance choreography is rarely encouraged or taught, with choreography modules focusing on modern or contemporary dance techniques. Dance educator and scholar Melanie George considers the lack of innovative Jazz choreography in professional practice in her 2022 essay 'Where are the emerging Jazz choreographers?,' suggesting that the students' work *"may be perceived as representing stagnation in the development of the choreography aesthetic, but there is no mechanism for deepening the study of jazz choreography."* George suggests one of the reasons for this stagnation is that

> The lack of study devoted to the craft of jazz choreography is grounded in the manner in which Jazz is taught in the academy, for it is in the academy that formal choreography classes largely take place and promulgate what is deemed valuable.

Perhaps this lack of attentiveness offered to Jazz choreography and its potential creatives in many dance colleges is a cause for limited innovative Jazz dance output relative to other genres such as contemporary or Hip-Hop styles.

So, it remains that Jazz dance is predominately used to express the immediate emotions of the dancer in a particular number, heighten the impact of the music or to 'wow' the audience with the acrobatics and the dynamic physicality of Jazz dance. Bob Fosse used his unique, Jazz-based choreographic works in musicals such as Sweet Charity to provide a quirky and engaging background for the protagonists to dip in and out of as they sang through musical numbers which drove the narrative forward. The cast of characters in 'A Chorus Line' use Jazz dance as a medium to amplify the emotive lines they sing and to entertain the audience with their deft dance skills. As Gary Lloyd suggested, despite the remarkable storytelling abilities of Jerome Robbins and Gillian Lynne, musicals such as West Side Story and CATS could *almost* standalone as pieces which communicate a story solely though dance but there would still be some way to go for these musicals to be as effective if all verbal scripting was scratched.

There have been moments of sole Jazz dance-based narrative theatre, such as Susan Stroman's Tony award-winning dance-based Broadway show 'Contact' (2000) which tied storytelling to loose incarnations of Jazz dance but it is not a concept in theatre that has been repeated many times. Why doesn't Jazz dance 'say more' more often? Perhaps it's that much of post 1950 Jazz dance was created to entertain, to make its audiences happy, to celebrate music and bowl over its audience with the dancer's mastery of difficult technical and acrobatic Jazz dance elements. This is not to say that Jazz dancers do not or should not consider themselves actors playing a role, many do, but rarely in theatre are they ever given the opportunity to play this role over the course of a full 2-hour play, most numbers are short and strive to tell a fairly elementary tale. Jazz dance's existence was always driven by the need to create short, entertaining, artistically powerful ephemeral moments – by its own nature, it's not designed to be a long format, narrative tool. In contrast, many classical ballet works tell complex two or three act stories using only dance and mimetic elements from its distinctive classical syllabus. 'The Nutcracker,' 'Swan Lake' and 'Don Quixote' (to name a few) are all complex tales, communicated effectively using only the physical and mimetic language of classical ballet, there are no lyrics or spoken word to aid the story telling. Jazz dance could employ similar mimetic devices to classical ballet, but it is not a feature that has ever seemed like an aesthetically good fit for Jazz.

Perhaps the larger arsenal of movement options in Commercial Dance, such as Hip-Hop and Funk styles, Vogue Fem plus niche techniques such as Tutting and Krump can assist a Musical Theatre choreographer by offering a sizeable vocabulary upgrade to work with, in comparison to Musical Theatre's traditional *lingua de franca* of Jazz dance. However, despite its rich lexicon of movement, Commercial Dance also finds itself struggling to develop beyond an offering of three exhilarating minutes of dance and tell an expansive story with any emotional depth.

Can Commercial Dance Assist with Theatrical Narratives?

As Commercial Dance dancers and dance makers have enveloped marginalised dance styles, often without a true mastery or understanding of the dance style they are embodying, it has stripped some of its narrative potential and original emotional connection to the movement. Whether its the vivacity of Krump, the confrontational style of Breakin' or the original Afro rhythms which moulded Jazz dance, key genetic strands of the movement are recurrently missing when these styles osmose into the kaleidoscope of Commercial Dance. We are left with a Frankenstein imitation – a sanitised, diminished, shell of a dance that was once emotive by nature. Has this loose imitation of dance styles, which Commercial Dance can be in its poorest form, weakened its ability to carry narrative or emotion at any depth?

In their original and purest form, the sub-styles which make up Commercial Dance, such as original Hip-Hop styles, do not suffer this same lack of emotional and storytelling potency. In the UK, Hip-Hop dance theatre has proved this to be so, with collectives such as Kenrick Sandy and Michael Sante's powerful, Olivier award winning, Boy Blue company producing some remarkably engaging and profound dance theatre including 'Blak Whyte Gray' (2017) and 'Redd' (2019). Emotion is enticed with ease by Sandy's choreography as it draws from the original emotional roots of the movement being performed and is arranged in a way which narrates and further creates a spectrum of genuine sentiment which is easy for the audience to connect to.

Another great example of theatrical narrative being furthered by the use of more sophisticated Commercial Dance associated techniques in its choreography, is illustrated by the progressive work in London of ZooNation: The Kate Prince Company. With its base at Sadlers Wells in London (a traditionally contemporary or classical dance orientated institution) and using mainly Hip-Hop and Funk styles, ZooNation has successfully complied a series of dance-based shows which not only employ high-level production values, comparable to those of a West End show, but also strives to tell stories. Since 2005s 'Into the Hoods' subsequent shows such as 'Some Like it Hip-Hop,' 'The Mad Hatters Tea Party' and 'Message in a Bottle' (a collaboration with the musician, Sting) have all found new ways to use choreography comprised of Hip-Hop and Funk styles plus an array of other genres including Contemporary, Waacking, Krump, Vogue/Fem, House, Commercial Jazz and Lyrical Hip-Hop, to communicate complex story lines. Granted, guidance from a narrator or the lyrics of the song they are performing to give clarity to some aspects of the story but largely, over the course of the show, dance is the prime mover in terms of narration.

The Realisations

Image 5.4 A scene from Zoonation's 'Mad Hatters Tea Party' at the Roundhouse, London, 2016. Featuring dancers from left to right – Manny Tsakanika, Teneisha Bonner, Issac 'Turbo' Baptiste, Bradley Charles, Tommy Franzen, Kayla Lomas and Rowen Hawkins. Sadly, Teneisha Bonner passed away in 2019. I had the fortune to train with Teneisha at London Studio Centre, she was a dancer with a tremendous talent and is hugely missed by the London dance community.

Why does ZooNation succeed at telling stories through dance movement? One reason is that their director, choreographers and dancers (which often come through their own extensive ZooNation youth academy and youth performance company, in much the same way a sports team trains budding apprentices) are well educated in the origins and foundations of the styles they are performing. This ensures a clear connection and comprehension of the emotional root of the dance form. Yes, some of the blended movement style could qualify to be 'Commercial' in nature but it's created and performed in a way which is true to its rudimental values and therefore able to carry emotional weight and a more impactful socio-political message. Dance academic Stacy Prickett, PhD concludes in her journal article 'Hip-Hop Dance Theatre in London: Legitimising an Art Form' that Hip-Hop can be a 'transformative force' and provide 'narrative possibilities' for mainstream theatre:

> Echoing the power of the originating form, hip-hop can function as a transformative force but the innovations summarised here reinforce its position as a mainstream theatrical form, potentially reaching across boundaries of class, race and generation. Narrative possibilities enhance the range of performance opportunities for female performers – be it among commercial street style dancers or 'B-girl' breakdances. In gaining cultural capital within established venues, hip-hop dance theatre and, in the case of ZooNation, hip-hop musical theatre, is building new audiences and attracting the scrutiny of mainstream dance critics.

Lessons from Bourne

The catalogue of work created by Matthew Bourne's predominately contemporary dance company, 'New Adventures,' is a great example of how effective mixing choreographic styles can be at advancing a narrative. Bourne's 'The Car Man,' 'Play Without Words,' 'Edward

Scissorhands' and 'Dorian Grey' all use dance to recount revised narratives of theatrical literature. In The Guardian newspaper's review of Bournes's 2022 revival of 'The Car Man' the extent of Bourne's ability to tell stories using dance is reinforced, describing the work as a *'shatteringly good piece of storytelling.'* The Stage newspaper's review followed with: *"Matthew Bourne's talent as a choreographic storyteller is unassailable. Through an astute combination of silent movie gesture, mime and dance, he taken the fundamentals of ballet and brought them kicking, if not screaming, to a mass audience."*

Bourne strays from traditional classical movement and incorporates other dance dialects into his work, including inflections of lyrical Jazz and very occasionally a hint of Commercial Jazz. In an interview from 2001, Bourne reflects on his work in Car Man:

> The sort of work I'm doing is a bit difficult to categorise, a lot of people say 'is it dance?' and it opens up discussion as to what is dance? I think that any movement set to music, with counts, is dance. A lot of people would argue with me with that, they would say that certain forms of gestural movement or natural movement or social dance isn't real, serious dance. But I mix all those things together.

'Mixing all these things together' and making *'astute combinations'* is similarly a key concept in Commercial Dance. The steady development of Commercial Dance, with its melding of Jazz, Club Styles and Hip-Hop foundations has provided a route for theatre choreographers and directors to tell stories with more complexity by using an extended dance vocabulary, just as Bourne has done over the last 25 years by mixing various theatre dance styles.

Lessons from Blankenbuehler

Andy Blankenbuehler's ground-breaking work on the internationally successful 'Hamilton: An American Musical' has done more than most in the last decade to reframe options for choreography in musical theatre. His choreography on Hamilton is a mix of his solid Jack Cole-esque Jazz roots and the Latino and Hip-Hop flavours he studied whilst researching movement options for the original stage version of 'In the Heights.' He is also a choreographer focused on using his choreographic skills to further narrative. A study of the movement in Hamilton reveals an immense amount of importance has been placed on choreography and transitions that further character and plot development. In the number 'Right Hand Man' the dancers practically narrate the rhymes which are being told to the audience using Blankenbuehler's understated choreographic mix. In an interview with author Lyn Cramer about his time preparing for the stage version of 'In the Heights,' Blankenbuehler describes the advantages of using Hip-Hop choreography as a storytelling device:

> The hip-hop that looked like pantomime was really interesting to me. Several teachers out there had work that was so sharp and chiseled, like Lin's (Lin Manuel Miranda) score. When I watched it, I could see storylines. So I decided that's how I wanted to choreograph. I started imitating everyone I loved. I tried to make Hip-Hop dance a bit abstract, deconstructing it, so I could apply it to the way people walk down the street. I would only use Latino dance in a social setting like the club or the carnival number. Latino and salsa dance would never be turned into story language like Hip-Hop.

Kenrick Sandy and Michael Sante's 'Boy Boy' collective show how effectively Hip-Hop, Funk styles and Club styles in their originative state can transmit emotions and propel a narrative expertly. Matthew Bourne's 'New Adventures,' Kate Prince's 'ZooNation' and Andy Blankenbuehler's progressive work on 'In the Heights' and 'Hamilton,' have demonstrated that blending multiple dance styles, when done with care and authenticity emanating from the root of the dance genre, can accelerate the sophistication with which dance can tell a story in theatre.

The Future of Commercial Dance in Theatre and Musical Theatre

Creative teams working in Musical Theatre are increasingly adopting Commercial Dance styles as their predominate choreographic preference, successful productions from the 2020s including 'In the Heights,' '&Juliet,' 'Hamilton' and 'Moulin Rouge' demonstrate this. Musical Theatre agents in the UK more frequently source dancers or choreographers with a Commercial Dance background. Successful Musical Theatre creatives are realising the potential Commercial Dance has to offer in the theatrical sphere, enabling them to update and build on classic dance shows like 'Cats,' 'Legally Blonde,' 'The Wiz' and 'Fame!'. UK-based Dance companies including Mathew Bourne's New Adventures, Boy Blue and ZooNation: The Kate Prince Company have explored the capability that composite Commercial Dance styles have to drive a narrative forward.

The multiple styles which are at a Commercial choreographer's disposal offer a vast movement vocabulary which can aid in providing effective and complex feature length story telling within the contexts of Musical and Dance Theatre, something that Jazz dance, on occasion, can struggle to do. The key for further progress in advancing Commercial Dance as a theatrical dance form capable of captivating audiences and telling emotive stories is for this rich tapestry of styles to be devised and performed with an understanding, and as a true reflection, of its rudimental emotional roots. If this can be addressed, the future is bound to see increased frequency of use and improved efficacy in how Theatre and Musical Theatre directors are able to use Commercial Dance to tell a story effectively.

5c. Live Concerts and Televised Events

The third segment of 'The Realisations' chapter is 'Live Concerts & Televised Events.' Other than in music videos, live concerts and televised events have offered the most significant platform in which Commercial Dance is manifested. Performed in stadiums to 10,000s of people by an army of dancers and broadcast into millions of homes, these events have provided a cornerstone for professional dance employment and a way to visualise dance in its most immediate and tangible form. Since the mid-1980s, there have been thousands of significant live concerts and televised events which have featured excellent choreography. In this chapter, we consider a handful which have influenced Commercial Dance trends over the last 30 years.

Madonna: The Blonde Ambition Tour (1990)

The Blonde Ambition Tour was performed in 11 different countries, at the dawn of an era when pop music was transcending radio airplay and artists like Madonna, George Michael, Queen and Michael Jackson were performing world tours to hundreds of thousands of fans globally. Madonna's third tour is noted for its innovations (the wireless head mic, the Jean Paul Gaultier designed golden 'cone bra' and the huge production budget), its controversies (it was condemned by Pope John Paul II for its perceived blasphemy and the sexual nature of some parts of Madonna's performance resulted in local police nearly stopping the show on at least one occasion), but it is also noteworthy as a multi-faceted theatrical pop concert which placed choreography and dance at the forefront.

Madonna performs energetic choreography continuously throughout the 16 song set, at times sacrificing her live vocal performance so she can defiantly lead her dancers by example. Choreographed and co-directed by Vincent Paterson and including many of the dancers which were also featured in Madonna's iconic 'Vogue' video of the same year (e.g., Jose Gutierez Xtravaganza and Luis Comacho), the movement evident in numbers 'Causing a Commotion' and 'Where's the Party?' is a great example of the blending of genres that began to occur in the early 1990s, that of weaving Jazz dance formulas with on trend Hip-Hop social steps such as the Roger Rabbit and Running Man. The extra ingredient which Madonna added to her choreographic make-up was Voguing, which gave her dance work an avant-garde dimension many other performers lacked and cemented her as one of the most progressive and socially inclusive artists of the decade.

Madonna's openness to channelling her sexuality via the choreography and her open embrace of the LGBTQ+ community throughout the tour, building on the iconography she began earlier in 1990 with the release of the 'Vogue' music video, pushed the envelope in terms of what choreography associated with pop music consisted of. It was risqué, controversial but mesmerising for audiences, in part due to Madonna's total physical commitment to her live shows. The Blonde Ambition tour drew the blueprint for a multitude of pop artist's touring productions for the next 30 years. Kylie Minogue, Lady Gaga, Katy Perry, Beyonce and Michael Jackson have all referenced the Blonde Ambition blueprint to some degree, particularly in how they have replicated Madonna's infallible determination to lead her pack of dancers from the front throughout her performances. Carlton Wilborn, a dancer on the 'Blonde Ambition Tour,' spoke about his experience to The Guardian newspaper:

> Every single night, the blast-off energy from the crowd was crazy – they were so loud we could hardly hear the music. We had done so much training at this point – the rehearsal process was truly like boot camp – and it was great to finally be in the sweat of it all. When I heard her singing to an audience for the first time: it was like: "Oh shit, she's fucking performing now." And it was a lot of fun working with an artist who had started in dance and who could do all these intricate moves with you….
>
> When I was booked, I had nothing to do with voguing: I was classically trained – the underground art world was not my thing. At the time, voguing was very exclusive to that [New York black and Latino LGBT] community. Now you have all kinds of people voguing and I think that's a great thing. She was able to dive into something that had a strong pulse and felt it was important to get the word out to the consciousness of young gay dancers – it was about helping these people thrive and feel good and powerful."

Kylie Minogue: The Showgirl Homecoming Concert (2006)

Kylie Minogue and her creative director, William Baker, produced a series of innovative live concert tours in the 2000s, which altered global audiences perceptions of what Commercial Dance could be and paved the way for artists such as Lady Gaga to follow in the coming decade. The shows blended contemporary dance theatre with the palpable excitement of a pop concert like no other series of concerts has, before or after. Starting with KylieFever2002, Minogue chose the avant-garde Catalan contemporary dance choreographer Rafael

The Realisations

Bonachela to create the movement for the show. This was at a time in the early 2000s when Commercial Dance was emerging as a genre which heavily infused Hip-Hop dance styles into its cadence. Using a purist contemporary dance choreographer to make phrases for classic pop and disco records was a bold choice which swam against the broader Hip-Hop trends followed by most pop artists at the time. Minogue's creative team also played with ideas of traditional gender roles in the dance world, creating works which embraced gender and sexual ambiguity, again a daring choice at time when Hip-Hop music and other dance styles were widely perpetrating traditional masculine and feminine gender tropes. Taking this creative risk constructed an unlikely theatrical juxtaposition of genres which collided beautifully on stage and assembled a formula Minogue would continue to use on her following tour.

The Showgirl: Homecoming Tour in 2006 was an extension and revamp of the Showgirl: Greatest Hits Tour which launched in 2005 but was cancelled due to Minogue undergoing treatment for breast cancer. Award-winning UK-based contemporary choreographer Akram Khan was added as choreographer, who joined Rafael Bonachela and the Commercial Dance impresario, Michael Rooney, on the choreography team, making for a unique mix of styles. Bonachela brought steps which were proven to work exceptionally well on tracks such as 'Can't Get You Out of My Head,' Khan's intricate and innovative movement phrases added a theatrical, dramatic tone to numbers like 'Confide in Me' whilst Rooney's experience in creating dance which can connect with stadium-sized audiences, provided the larger-than-life pop concert moments.

Combined with costume design by Karl Lagerfeld and Dolce & Gabbana, The Showgirl Homecoming concert's brought high fashion and elite contemporary dance theatre to pop concert audiences, raising the creative expectations of dance in live pop environments. Claire and Jamie Karitzis, two dancers who worked on the tour, reflect on their experiences:

> We had previously worked with Michael Rooney and Raphael Bonachela on the 'Showgirl' tour but never with Akram Khan. Straight away we had an understanding of the 'weight' of choreographers we were about to work with. Each one totally different to the next in various ways – their work, the way they held the space in the studio, how they taught, each as special as the next but it was a very diverse rehearsal period.

Image 5.5 Kylie Minogue notably used a number of contrasting choreographers including Michael Rooney, Akram Khan and Rafael Bonachela to create a fused palette of dance styles in her 2006 The Showgirl Homecoming World Tour. This is a still from the Khan choreographed number 'Confide in Me'

I specifically remember feeling the utter calmness of Akram as he created, he worked in such a mathematical way and at times it was hard to keep up, his number 'Confide in Me' was my favourite number in that tour, it felt so deeply rooted and connected, which is down to Akram and his incredible gift. I was honoured to be apart of that.

The diversity of choreography on the Homecoming tour to me at that time was 'my world', so I don't think I really appreciated where it was taking the world of Commercial Dance like I do now. The feathers, the sequins, the wigs, the make up – it was so truly Kylie and of course the wonderful vision of Willian Baker but it all came together and worked so dynamically with the styles of each choreographer. The quirkiness of Raphael's movement in our medley of 'Shocked', 'What Do I Have to Do' & 'Spinning Around' (which was a marathon of a number)! And then there is the great and wonderful Michael Rooney who produced for us some true 'Showgirl' choreography. It was a tour filled with creatives and visionaries and the energy was always electric.

There was a unspoken feeling on that tour of what a gift it was for the tour to be in existence. Jamie and I feel the choreographic side of the creative team played its part and created visual masterpieces that paved a way for the world of commercial dance.

Michael Jackson: This Is It (2009)

At the time of Jackson's untimely death in 2009 at the age of 50, he was intensively rehearsing for a series of concerts which would have taken place at the O2 arena in London. Many of the rehearsals and the behind-the-scenes footage were recorded by documentary filmmakers. After Jackson's death, this footage was cut together into a concert-documentary which received an international cinematic release later in 2009 via Columbia pictures. Although this concert documentary film could not be considered to be a 'live event' as such as no audience was ever officially present, it is a solitary and remarkable insight into how Jackson's vast choreographic catalogue had been updated for an event that, had it gone ahead, could have found itself on this list anyway.

The film effectively documents the journey of commercial choreography over 25 years – from when Jackson had kick-started the commercial industry in 1983 with his trilogy of dance-based videos from the Thriller album, up to his final hours dancing on a soundstage in Los Angeles in 2009. The choreography team of Travis Payne and Tony Testa expertly melded the template of Jackson's original choreography with on trend flavours and textures which were prevalent in 2009 and translated them onto the bodies of the talented group of dancers assembled by the director Kenny Ortega and Jackson himself. The film's opening features testimonials from each dancer (the dancers selected included an international array of movers including Timor Steffens, Nick Bass, Misha Gabriel, Tyne Stecklein and Mekia Cox) about what it meant to be part of the 'This Is It' project – affirming the influence Jackson had had on their own journeys as dancers.

The choreographic updates to phrases which for years had become iconic on Jackson's world tours like Bad (1989), 'Dangerous' (1993) and HIStory (1997) were created with a nuanced eye, carefully modernised by adding subtle and precise musical and rhythmical punctuations in the choreography – heightening complexity without losing the base flavour and magic of the original creations. Travis Payne was a long-term collaborator of Jackson's, working with him on those original tours, and the updated choreography cooked up by Payne and Testa is a stylish blend of 1990s meets late 2000s. The heightened athletic ability of the dancers is also evident in numbers such as 'They Don't Care About Us' as the work ventures into more physical areas whilst also staying true to the original 'Jackson-isms' around which it was originally created.

This documented concert also offered a way for a new generation of young dancers to experience and understand the rich heritage which ran throughout Jackson's live dance and choreographic performances. Those born later than 1990 may not have experienced the immediate cultural impact that original music video renegades like Jackson had on budding dancers of the time. The dance numbers in 'This Is It' composed a new choreographic score for a vast body of exceptional dance work which reigned from 1983 through to 2009. Dancer Timor Steffens makes an eloquent point about his experience on this project in a 'Meet the Dancers,' This Is It, featurette:

> When I started to rehearse with Michael Jackson, if you look closely at what he really is doing – he is an instrument of music. If you were deaf and could not hear the music and you look at him, you will see the music playing through his body and that just changed my whole view of dance.

Beyonce: Homecoming concert film (2019)

In terms of innovators of dance in the commercial sector, Beyonce Knowles-Carter is the luminescent name for the era of the 2010s. Her drive, the fearless way she moves and her willingness to creatively take risks have put her name at the top of the list of inspirational icons for young dancers who aspire to make professional dance their full-time vocation. The Homecoming concert filmed at Coachella music festival in 2018 uses choreography as the structural backbone of the performance. It features a large cast of exceptional dancers and a full marching band. Every minute of the concert is built on top of the choreography provided by JaQuel Knight and Chris Grant. Devised around references to Historically Black Colleges and Universities (HBCU) culture, the choreography not only includes direct associations such as 'Stepping,' 'J-Setting' and majorette dancing but also includes a spectrum of styles such as Krump, bone-breaking and more generic new style Hip-Hop phrases. Punctuating an endless promenade of sublime choreography, Les Twins provide some rhythmically insane dance breaks, King Havoc and Jasmine Harper perform a Contemporary Jazz/Flexing duet (which again pushes the boundaries of what is possible in Commercial Dance) and a dance duet between Beyoncé and her sister Solange includes a 'ticking fight' and some old school Hip-Hop steps. The all-female support band and the marching band are as much involved in the choreography as Beyonce's core set of dancers are, creating an irresistible chorus of movement on the stage. Crediting every single dancer and noting the Dance Captains in the credits of the film is also a welcome acknowledgment for the dance community.

Playing Coachella as the first black woman to headline added to the weight of the event. The documentary concert film from 2019 is a must see for anyone interested in the development of popular and vernacular dance and to witness the power of inclusivity dance styles associated with the Commercial Dance industry can have. As Beyonce comments in the film:

> Everyone that had never seen themselves represented felt like they were on that stage with us.

The Realisations

Image 5.6 Beyonce jamming with Les Twins in the 'Homecoming' concerts at Coachella, LA, choreographed by JaQuel Knight and Chris Grant (2018)

Image 5.7 Link to 'Crazy in Love' from the Homecoming concert

Kendrick Lamar: The Big Steppers Tour, Live from Paris (2022)

As a Hip-Hop artist, Kendrick Lamar has always swerved towards the creatively innovative, both musically and visually. His 2022 Big Steppers live concert is a canvas on which Lamar and choreographer Charm La'Donna paint a brave, minimalist and constrained body of theatrical, choreographic work loosely built around themes of isolation and quarantine. A live recording of the concert was made in Paris in 2022 and streamed on the Amazon prime platform, allowing the creative details of such a subtle production to be magnified as we view the action through the lenses of the multiple cameras filming the action.

The Realisations

Stylistically, the choreography is not what is commonly seen at a live Hip-Hop concert. It displays staging characteristics often associated with European contemporary dance and immersive physical theatre. La'Donna plays with a constant antagonist energy between moments of order, restraint and stillness which sit juxtaposed to explosions of unconfined, powerful movement mirroring the dynamic and emotive contents of Lamar's music. The opening of the concert sets the choreographic tone for the rest of the show. The dancers march out on the catwalk like stage, performing small, gestural movements in unison as they bounce in time to the dramatic classical composition. They stride together, making synchronised geometric shapes as they move down the stage, a Tetris like feature seen in many of the dance numbers. Even freer numbers such as 'Die Hard' which use a language of movement more commonly associated with Hip-Hop and Commercial choreography are put together in a way which pays the utmost attention to the use of the stage space and the stillness of the dancers, creating both delicate and chaotic moments. The use of only two male dancers interpreting the rhymes and lyrics of 'Swimming Pool (Drank)' highlighted the performers expressive abilities, matching the artistry of Lamar's rendition. Similarly, the way dancers imitate Lamar's natural movement flow and swagger creates a feeling of cohesion between the artist and the dancers. In an interview with Complex magazine, La'Donna explained how she made creative decisions about the choreography in the show:

> The feel. It's literally what feels right for the song. I think when you watched it, I'm pretty sure it felt right to have girls on "Die Hard." It felt right during "Bitch, Don't Kill My Vibe" to have one entity on stage with him. It felt right for "m.A.A.d city" for it to be chaotic in movement. This is all trial—you do it, you see how it feels. If it feels right, it is. If it doesn't, you keep adjusting until it feels right.

The choreography in this concert film is used in a way that heightens the creative qualities of the production by using movement phrases which work seamlessly with other design elements to create a theatrical and dramatic piece of performance art. It demonstrates how restrained and thoughtful choreography can enhance live Hip-Hop performances on a grand scale.

PROFESSIONAL INSIGHT – KARLA GARCIA

Location: New York, USA

Karla is a Filipina-American dancer, performer and educator who's choreographic style stands with one foot in the world of Musical Theatre and the other in the world of Commercial Dance. She was a swing for 4 years in 'Hamilton: An American Musical' on Broadway. As a choreographer her projects include the Netflix film 'Tick, Tick, Boom,' directed by Lin Manuel Miranda and choreographing the 2023 Tony Awards. Her classes at venues such as Broadway Dance Centre and Steps on Broadway provide her students with tough technical combos laced with dance styles from many different areas of the Commercial Dance spectrum.

Before I moved to New York, I was told I would be right for shows like King and I or Miss Saigon – your classic 'Asian' musicals.
Ironically, I was never cast in any of those. I always booked a dance part in the ensemble that was ethnically ambiguous. Before 'Hamilton: An American Musical,' it always felt like

I was not Asian enough, sort of Latina looking but not enough, and definitely not classic looking enough. I've had a healthy career, but I admit, it was tricky trying to figure out where I fit. As a Filipina, I am an intersection of different cultures. The Spanish colonised the Philippines for 300 years, so obviously there are cultural similarities. Some call Filipinos the 'Latinos of Asia.'

It wasn't until Hamilton that I felt like I truly belonged in a production based on my talent and the richness of my cultural background. Now, as a choreographer, I am inspired to tell stories that uplift the BIPOC community by creating worlds where everyone just EXISTS… and there is a place for all backgrounds and perspectives.

Performing Hamilton: An American Musical on Broadway the day after Donald Trump was elected was an out-of-body experience.
The words of the show had never resonated so much until then. I felt like I was expressing loudly what my beliefs and values were through my art. I had been in four Broadway shows and two National Tours, and this was the first time I really felt that my artistic body was a vessel… an extension of who I am as a person. It was intense and freeing.

I was inspired by my god-sister Lamae Caparas.
She was on the National Tour of 'King and I' at age 16 and then went on to tour with 'Fosse.' She is also a Filipina, and we grew up dancing at the same studio. Seeing her leave my hometown and perform on that huge a scale completely inspired me to do the same. I knew it was possible seeing someone who looked like me also reach their dream.

My choreography started shaping from my early training at my dance studio Fran's Studio of Dance in MD.
We did classic Jazz technique with an emphasis on Broadway dance and tap – lots of lines and musicality with a ballet foundation. I also took extra ballet classes at the Kirov Academy and Washington School of Ballet. Then, I studied dance at NYU Tisch School of the Arts and my mind was opened to modern and postmodern movement. The real choreographic influences began when I started performing in Broadway shows and Tours. I was shaped by the choreography of Jerome Robbins, Wayne Cilento, Sergio Trujillo, Josh Bergasse, and of course, Andy Blankenbuehler.

While I performed in Theatre, I was also immersed in the Hip Hop scene in Washington DC and NY. I was fascinated by the underground battle community where people danced foundational styles of Hip-Hop like Popping, Locking and Waacking; and I appreciated the collegiate Hip-Hop competition circle as well. I know all these experiences have informed my choreographic voice and continued to help me evolve as an artist.

Singing was definitely a big learning curve when entering theatre.
I come from a very musical family. My Dad was a musician, my brother plays the sax and piano, my sister sings, and I also play the piano. However, those dancer nerves used to creep in a lot in those first few years living in NY. I continued to take lessons and found songs that I really enjoyed singing for auditions. Then, I got over the 'fear hump,' and started to enjoy it more.

My advice would be to find music you really enjoy and work on the pieces with a voice teacher you love. It's all about confidence, emoting and being able to carry your harmonies in an ensemble. I know some dancers who even have become leads in shows because they really found their singing voices.

The Realisations

Image 5.8 Karla teaches at BDC and Steps on Broadway in New York as well as choreographing for film and performing in 'Hamilton: An American Musical' on Broadway. Photo by Jenna Maslechko

PROFESSIONAL INSIGHT – KIEL TUTIN

Location: New Zealand/Los Angeles, US

Kiel Tutin is one of the most prominent K-Pop choreographers, creating iconic choreography for BLACKPINK, Twice, Somi and Sunmi, amongst many others. Born in the UK, he later lived and trained in New Zealand under Parris Goebel's tuition at The Palace Dance Studio, performing with The Royal Family. Kiel works internationally creating work for artists such as Todrick Hall and Jennifer Lopez, working with her as supervising choreographer on the 'It's My Party' tour and the 2022 movie 'Marry Me.' In 2023, he choreographed BLACK-PINK's headline set at Coachella.

I've found that even K-Pop band members that aren't as experienced or as skilled still have a very strong foundation in learning and performing choreography.
The amount of training that K-pop idols go through when they are trainees basically prepares them for anything, so the more I work with an artist, the more I can see their capabilities. It can be hard not being there physically to teach the artist and help them execute to the best of their ability, but the standard and quality that is synonymous with the K-pop industry ensures that whatever is put out will be polished and drilled, it's not very often that I have to 'dumb down' anything for a member of a K-pop group, they're all incredibly multi-talented.

For me, it always starts with the music.
Instrumentation, rhythm and lyrics usually give me what I need to create, and I feel like I create from quite an intellectual perspective, there's no divine inspiration for me! A lot of my

work is known for pictures/visuals that I create with groups, and for that I try to be inspired by things separate from dance, like shapes, memories and movies. I've always been somewhat of a mimic, with movement, accents, voices, so if I watch too many choreographers or other dancers, I find it coming out in my movements, so I try and avoid that to stay original!

In the Asian music industry, more often than not, it is a requirement to include 'memorable choreography' in the chorus or hook. It's the easier part that the companies want everyone to be able to see and copy. For me it is not necessarily all about the dance move, it is about creating a synergy between the move, the lyrics and the sound of the song, creating something that is unique yet identifiable by a non-dancer/musician, helping and guiding the public to understand a harmonious moment of movement and music.

My time in The Royal Family was really the first time I had any sort of intensive training.
From the beginning we put time and effort into learning many different dance styles, and since it was at a time where there were not yet communities for certain styles in New Zealand, we would learn off of YouTube, watching tutorials and battles and learning what we could. What we learned was for the purpose of a competition, but regardless, those techniques and skills helped create chameleons of dance, being able to learn the basics of different genres of dance without fear. It definitely shaped me and gave me a solid foundation in 'dance.' It created an interesting approach for me, trying to connect with the communities of the styles after having already created a connection with the style is sort of backwards, and not how those styles should necessarily be learned, but some of my biggest influences came from that time and learning in that way. Waacking, Vogue, House, Dancehall are some of my favourite styles that I have always felt connected to and that naturally come out in the way that I move after 'training' in those styles the most, and I try and further my training wherever possible.

I think credit and recognition are never a bad thing.
Honouring the team of people that assist in the success of a project can provide a platform like no other. Crediting on YouTube, Instagram, in physical album booklets should be the bare minimum, in the future I hope to see residuals for media that include choreography, music videos, live performances and tours. The intellectual property and copyright of choreography is a newer territory that more are becoming aware of, and there's a long way to go, but awareness is a good start!

My passion for choreography, dance and music is probably second only to my passion for travel.
Working with artists and performers in different countries can be a completely different process in relation to the culture, customs and normalcy of their respective industries. The K-Pop industry and how it utilises dance is quite unique. Artists that I work with like JLo and Jolin Tsai, have been in the industry for 20+ years, so the process of working with them is a lot more collaborative, they've had longer to figure out what they like, how they want to be represented, what they don't want to do and where they want to push boundaries. Newer artists may be under a more strict direction of a company or record label, as they're still trying to find their fanbase, or individual creativity or pocket as a performer. I can create for JLo while focusing on a feeling or a vibe, but I have to create for a group like BLACKPINK knowing that it has to appeal to millions of K-pop fans around the world, so mentally it can be hard switching between the two, but it's all different, each job is unique and that's partly why I love it!

Image 5.9 Kiel trained in New Zealand with Parris Goebel and has become one of the most sort after K-Pop choreographers. Image is from a dance performance video with Lisa from BLACKPINK

References

5a. Music Video and MTV

Arnold, G., D. Cookney, K. Fairclough, and M. Goddard (2017). *Music/Video: Histories, Aesthetics*. New York: Bloomsbury.

Caston, E. (2020). Movement and Dance. In *British Music Videos 1966–2016: Genre, Authenticity and Art* (pp. 55–71). Edinburgh: Edinburgh University Press. http://www.jstor.org/stable/10.3366/j.ctv177th88.7

Hay, C. (2001). *Billboard Magazine*, February 17, 2001, p. 70.

Mundy, J. (1994). Postmodernism and Music Video. *Critical Survey*, 6(2), 259–266.

Ovalle, P. (2008). Urban Sensualidad: Jennifer Lopez, Flashdance and the MTV Hip-Hop Re-generation. *Women & Performance: A Journal of Feminist Theory*, 18(3), 253–268.

St Petersburg Times, September 2, 1983. https://news.google.com/newspapers?nid=feST4K8J0scC&dat=19830902&printsec=frontpage&hl=en

https://www.britannica.com/art/television-in-the-United-States/CNN#ref1057634

www.complex.com/music/2013/08/best-r-and-b-songs-by-white-singers-in-the-2000s [accessed: 06/10/2022].

www.djrobblog.com/archives/6340 [accessed: 28/08/2022].

https://www.redbull.com/int-en/5-things-you-should-know-about-new-jack-swing

www.yahoo.com/entertainment/steve-barron-recalls-directing-michael-jacksons-billie-jeanthought-people-see-world-will-change-164717351.html

https://youtu.be/tbnxe5p8oSI [accessed: 09/08/2022].

5b. Musical Theatre and Dance Theatre

www.thestage.co.uk/reviews/the-car-man-royal-albert-hall-london-matthew-bourne-will-bozier-zizi-strallen-alan-vincent-review [accessed: 06/2022].

Cramer, L. (2013). Creating Musical Theatre. *Bloomsbury*, 1, 40–43.

Griffin, G. (2006). Theatres of Difference: The Politics of "Redistribution" and "Recognition" in the Plays of Contemporary Black and Asian Women Playwrights in Britain. *Feminist Review*, 84, 10–28.

Matthew Bourne: www.youtube.com/watch?v=G4PnQADUN6M [accessed: 04/2022].

Pithers, E. (2019). Ri Just Gets It: Parris Goebel on moving the dial with Rihanna, Vogue UK, 2nd October. https://www.vogue.co.uk/fashion/article/parris-goebel-savage-fenty [accessed: 02/11/2022].

Prickett, S. (2013). Hip-Hop Dance Theatre in London: Legitimising an Art Form. *Dance Research: The Journal of the Society for Dance Research*, 31(2), 174–190. http://www.jstor.org/stable/43281334

5c. Live Concerts and Televised Events

Big Steppers Tour: www.complex.com/music/charm-ladonna-choreographer-interview

The Blonde Ambition Tour: www.theguardian.com/music/2018/jul/15/dancer-carlton-wilborn-on-madonna-rehearsal-boot-camp-tour

Chapter 6

Iconic Moments

Michael Jackson's 'Thriller'

Choreographer: Michael Peters & Michael Jackson
Form: Long Form Music Video/Short Film
Release date: December 1983

> What I love is the capability of a body to be free in the sense of street or social dancing and, at the same time, do something that is technically hard and tremendously disciplined.
>
> Michael Peters

Michael Peters and Michael Jackson collaborated to create one of the most recognisable pieces of choreography committed to the screen. Arguably the most famous music video ever produced, Thriller is an iconic moment in Music Video history for many reasons – the song, the revolutionary artistry of Michael Jackson, the long 14-minute run-time, Rick Baker's special effects make-up and the sky-high overall production budget (which was previously unheard of in music videos). It is also an iconic moment for dance on screen, building on foundations laid in the previous few years of MTV's existence and elevating dance in music video to a new level whilst also going a long way to establishing Commercial Dance as both a genre of dance and an industry in its own right.

Thriller was marketed as a 'short film' and was distributed that way too, with premieres on MTV and Showtime, accompanied by a behind-the-scenes documentary 'The Making of Thriller.' A deal was also struck to sell Thriller and 'The Making of Thriller' internationally on Beta-Max and VHS cassettes. Although a trend was developing to release 'long form' music videos onto home video (British band Duran Duran had done so earlier in March 1983, with their successful Video-Album collection), this deal is significant in the arc of Commercial Dance's development. For the first time, dancers could study the choreography of a music video in their own home – it was an exciting development, allowing people to watch steps 'on demand' and on repeat. At this time MTV was in its infancy, many homes in the US did not yet have access to cable TV and the home video market was still expanding. Before YouTube and Google provided enthusiastic dancers and young choreographers with instant access to an enormous database of recorded choreography, having a VHS copy of 'Thriller' was an essential study tool for all budding dance artists of the mid-1980s.

The Steps

Choreographically, Thriller was a front runner in the rapid development of dance on screen in the 1980s. The video continued to mix different dance styles (such as Popping and Jazz), crossing over what were niche genres into an enormous commercial market, as Peters and Jackson had encouraged in the 'Beat It' video earlier in the same year of 1983. The movement itself consists of strong Jazz work integrated with staccato, rigor mortis inspired Zombie-like quirks. The choreography references common horror character tropes as well as Jackson's own unique dance affectations such as sharp hip isolations and jumping onto his toes. The opening 4 × 8's of the instrumental dance break are mesmerising – the half-time foot shunts forward from an army of 20 Zombies followed by a shoulder and head snap are ingrained in the imaginations of dancers worldwide. Peter's clear and precise choreography gave Jackson the perfect platform to elevate his own personal performance.

Michael Peters

Michael Peter's was an early leader of dance on screen and certainly a hugely influential figure in the forging of a dance synthesis that would later become known as Commercial Dance. A successful figure in Musical Theatre, he won a Tony Award for choreographing the original 'Dream Girls' on Broadway in 1981 (after watching the premiere of 'Dreamgirls' Michael Jackson proclaimed that it was 'the best play he ever saw and everyone should go and see it!'). He was also a celebrated choreographer in film (working on the Tina Turner biopic 'What's Love Got To Do With It?') and in the music video genre where he worked with many of the greats including Billy Joel and Diana Ross.

Michael Peters could be considered to be one of the first true Commercial Dance choreographers. Upon his death in 1994, the New York Times reported:

> Mr. Peters was also among the first to establish a name for the choreography of music videos, in the process helping to raise their production values and claims to being serious works of popular culture.
>
> His work with Michael Jackson on the "Beat It" and "Thriller" videos, in which Mr. Peters also danced, was a sophisticated blend of musical theatre and pop values. Mr. Peters was also vocal in pressing publicly for more acknowledgement of choreographers in film and began a campaign last year to push for an Oscar for choreography.

Iconic Moments

Image 6.1 Choreographed as a collaboration between Michael Peters and Michael Jackson, 'Thriller' (1983) changed the global perception and expectation about choreography in music videos. In its originality, the short film set a multitude of standards in terms of production quality which have rarely been surpassed since

Image 6.2 A link to the full 'Thriller' short film

Janet Jackson's 'Rhythm Nation'

Choreographer: Janet Jackson and Anthony Thomas.
  With additional choreography by Terry Bixler (chair sequence) and Lavelle Smith Jnr.
Form: Short film/Music video
Release date: 1989

In 1989, Janet Jackson released her Rhythm Nation 1814 album and the choreography focused, long form video to accompany it. It's a video which set the benchmark for dance in

105

music video for the next 30 years. Choreographed by Janet Jackson and Anthony Thomas, with additional choreography by Terry Bixler and Lavelle Smith Jnr, the 30-minute Short Film is directed by Dominic Sena. The film is essentially three music videos for the singles 'Miss You Much,' 'The Knowledge' and 'Rhythm Nation,' tied together by a loose narrative which follows the fate of two street 'shoe-shine' boys. The video is shot in black and white and filmed in a mix of locations including an inner city nightclub, a rooftop and a loft apartment. Despite its film noir shooting style, the sentiment of the video is one which advocates hope, positivity and social betterment, echoing the lyrics of the title track and most of the Rhythm Nation album:

> With music by our side, to break the color lines
> Let's work together to improve our way of life
> Join voices in protest to social injustice
> A generation full of courage
> Come forth with me

It is the final notorious section of this short film which qualifies as perhaps the most significant of all the Iconic Moments mentioned in this book – the video for the title track – 'Rhythm Nation.' Set in a disused, industrial factory with a large group of dancers accompanying Jackson, the video is not just iconic in terms of its choreography but also for its striking visuals – dressed in military-esque black costumes and caps and danced in a hazy, atmospheric warehouse, this final segment is a distinguished piece of music video making.

The Steps

Choreographically, the video was a game changer for dancers and choreographers. What is significant is that perhaps for the first time in a mainstream music video, the multiple dance flavours which are used do not appear as segregated cliques but as one, blended, seamless piece of choreographed movement.

Nearly the entirety of the song is filled with choreography, culminating with infamous synchronised group dance sections towards the end of the track. The choreography is sharp and precise consisting of Jazz isolations, Locking wrist rolls, New Jack Swing's Running Man and technical Jazz solos (including one by Lavelle Smith Jnr, a frequent collaborator with the Jackson siblings and future MTV Award Winner with En Vogue). Thomas and Jackson created choreography that was none of these styles and yet all of them at once. *It was pioneering*. The carefree nature and rough edges of the street elements had been polished to create precise dance lines which are hit on exact counts, elevating the en masse aesthetic efficacy of these 'street'-based styles. Equivalently, the cutting Jazz lines were relaxed to incorporate the groove and heaviness of the Hip-Hop-based steps. Care was taken not to lose the cleanliness of the shapes and maintain the overall powerful image of a large assembly of meticulously precise dancers, an attribute which started in this video and is particularly prevalent now in large dance crews competing in Hip-Hop and 'Dance Crew' competitions.

Legacy

In 1990, the video won a Grammy Award for Best Long Form Video at the 32nd Grammy Awards and also the MTV Video Music Award for Best Choreography. However, the video's influence is significantly longer term. Just as the socially conscious lyrics of 'Rhythm Nation' are as relevant in the 2020s as they were in 1989, so is the choreography. It became archetypal for modern artists in terms of music video performance and choreography. The visual style and nature of the choreography in Rhythm Nation have inspired numerous dance-based projects which all took their cue from this video (see Jennifer Lopez's 'Love Don't Cost a Thing' video, 2001, Cheryl Cole's 'Fight for this Love' video, 2009 and Usher's 'OMG' Grammy performance, 2011). Rhythm Nation 1814's indelible impact on Commercial Dance and the Commercial Dance industry cannot be underestimated, in 2011, Rolling Stone magazine pronounced that:

> She (Jackson) is a brilliant dancer in her own right, and has arguably had a greater long term impact on the choreography of contemporary music videos (than her brother Michael). Her 1989 video for 'Rhythm Nation', in which she and a quasi-militaristic ensemble dance in some sort of urban dystopia set the template for hundreds of videos to come in the 90's and the 00's

Image 6.3 A very influential video in terms of creating a Commercial Dance vocabulary, the choreography by Anthony Thomas and Janet Jackson in Rhythm Nation (1989) incorporated and entwined many new and emerging styles of Hip-Hop dance

Image 6.4 A link to the 'Rhythm Nation' music video

Iconic Moments

Beyonce's 'Single Ladies'

Choreographer: JaQuel Knight & Frank Gatson Jr
Form: Music Video
Release date: 2008

Beyonce's 'Single Ladies' music video features some of the most recognised and imitated Commercial Dance choreography on record. Billboard magazine has dubbed it a 'pop culture phenomenon.' As is often the case with such an iconic moment, it is not just the dance steps that have elevated the video to cult status. As with Michael Jackson's 'Thriller,' it is a combination of the video's direction, song hook, costume and the tremendous performance skills of Beyonce that all fuse together to make an infamous piece of onscreen song and dance. The video is shot in black and white under the creative watch of Frank Gatson and directed by Jake Nava. It features Beyonce forming a dynamic trio with two other female dancers – Ashley Everett and Ebony Williams. Taking inspiration from a Bob Fosse choreographed piece called 'Mexican Breakfast' which appeared on The Ed Sullivan Show in 1969, 'Single Ladies' is a mesmerising video in that the long steady-cam shot appears seamless. The video has static moments which are disrupted in a flash as the camera accelerates to follow the three performers as they sashay across the stark white set, their simple black leotards contrasting against the luminescence of the setting.

The choreography encompasses a range of steps, from trademark grounded Beyonce hip and neck cracks to references to another Bob Fosse Jazz dance scene from the movie 'Sweet Charity.' The three dancers step-gallop and kick ball-change in arcs across the ramped floor with aplomb as Beyonce holds the lens' attention with her performance skills. Knight's expert merging of styles from different eras leads to Jazz fusing with elements of J-Setting, creating a truly memorable piece of movement art which also incorporates some iconic and much imitated steps – specifically the close up 'ring-on-it' hand flick and the jutting walk which Justin Timberlake imitated on Saturday Night Live. Dancer Ebony Williams commented to Billboard magazine about the creative process and researching Bob Fosse's movement qualities in 2018:

Image 6.5 Beyonce's iconic video for Single Ladies (2009) drew from varied dance influences and has become a recognisable moment in 21st-century popular culture. Choreographed by JaQuel Knight and creatively directed by Frank Gatson

Iconic Moments

Image 6.6 A link to the 'Single Ladies' music video

Understanding the tradition of the movement and trying to find similarities in the lines was going to bring it to life and possibly elevate it even more. That is what I think was really cool about how [Gatson and Knight] mixed in the movement with Fosse. Fosse is super musical and is super shape-oriented, and so is J-setting. It's shape-oriented in the fact that one person is copying the other person's shape and the next person's pocket of music, because musicality is so important.

In July 2020, the 'Single Ladies' choreography was officially registered and protected in the US under the 1976 Copyright Act, making Knight a pioneer in facilitating legal protection and licensing for Commercial choreographers and dance artists (read more about this in the *Copyright in Commercial Dance* chapter).

SIA 'Chandelier'

Choreographer: Ryan Heffington
Form: Music Video
Release date: 2014

Although listed as a singular Iconic Moment, it is difficult to include the 'Chandelier' video without mentioning the series of music videos that followed from the artist SIA, all of which feature the dancer and actress Maddie Ziegler and were choreographed by Ryan Heffington. This video and its collective works are of particular artistic note, not just for Ziegler's profound performances and Heffington's powerful and eclectic choreography but also for Ziegler's appearance as the physical representation of the enigmatic singer, SIA. In 2014, Heffington won Best Choreography at the MTV Video Music Awards for his work on 'Chandelier' and it is included here as it was the first in a very original series of works.

Dance is the language and Ziegler is the narrator who reads from a script written by Heffington in these videos which meld so many different forms of dance and physical theatre. Ziegler's immense physical attributes as a dancer are always at the front, highlighting her classical technical prowess and acting capacities. The motif's carried throughout the series include the mimetic use of hand gesture to induce absurd and goofy facial gestures, occasionally representing translations from SIA's lyrics but more often as seemingly non-sensical sensibilities. The 'Big Girls Cry' video choreography is entirely dedicated to Heffington's trademark 'facial physical theatre,' it's form reminiscent of European modern dance leaders such as DV8 Physical Theatre company or Akram Khan. It is not until 2016s 'The Greatest' that Heffington's work shows a slight inflection towards the more so-called conventional music video choreographic forms, with Ziegler leading an ensemble of young dancers and hints of a more grounded, Hip-Hop influence appearing.

Ryan Heffington

What is interesting about Heffington's movement in these videos is that he uses a basis of classical and contemporary forms not often associated with Commercial Dance and yet the platform in which they have been created for (a music video for a Pop artist) inherently distinguishes the form as Commercial Dance but with new transformative parameters, which are laid out in this series of videos. Heffington bravely disregards these pre-conceived ideas of what 'Music Video dance' should be and creates something unique. As a creative force, he has continued to progress the occasionally formulaic patterns of Commercial Dance, creating interesting movement, blending elements of Hip-Hop styles with physical theatre and paving the way for choreographers of the same ilk. This collection of SIA videos helped to encourage a diverse pool of Commercial Dance choreographers, regardless of whether their background is in Contemporary or Hip-Hop dance, to push on with making genre-bending works. In 2016, The New York Times wrote:

> Over the past few years, SIA, with her choreographer, Ryan Heffington, has done more to raise the standards of dance in pop music than nearly any current artist integrating the forms. For SIA, dance is more than a way to give a music video a splash of pizazz; instead, it's "an expression that crosses all language barriers," she said. "If people can't understand the words, they will understand the content.".... Mr. Heffington doesn't believe that dance is underused in pop music—more that it is abused much of the time by adhering to an easy formula. "We established the artist and backup dancers, I believe, in the early '80s," he said. "There has to be evolution, and there is. We're doing it."

Giving the choreographer the freedom to create a dance film which is viewed as artistically valid in its own right was a shrewd move by SIA and her creative team and proved the commercial pulling power of innovative choreography in music video. It spurred other artists to follow suit, such as Justin Bieber's diverse Purpose Dance Video Collection (curated by Parris Goebel in 2015) which featured only dancers, without Bieber making an appearance. By 2020, 'Chandelier' had been viewed 2.5 billion times on YouTube and Justin Bieber's 'Sorry' 3.6 billion times. The audience's appetite for dance in music video is clear, neither SIA nor Bieber appear in these videos, meaning every viewer has effectively streamed a dance film on the strength of the visuals offered by the choreography and dancers, not due to the appearance of the singers themselves.

Iconic Moments

Image 6.7 Maddie Zielgler showing her technical virtuosity in Sia's 'Chandelier' video (2014). Choreographed by Ryan Heffington

Image 6.8 A link to the 'Chandelier' music video

Pink: What About Us

Choreographer: Nick Florez and RJ Durell of the GoldenBoyz
Form: Music video and live performance
Release date: 2017

In 2017, Pink released 'What About Us,' a politically charged song with a dance focused video which continued her collaboration with choreographers Nick Florez and RJ Durell. The video highlights the importance Pink places in using choreography as a tool for both narration and emotional deliverance. What makes the video an iconic moment in the context of Commercial Dance is that the impassioned nature of the dance sequences, combined with the hybrid forms of Contemporary dance utilised, prove how much Commercial Dance can deliver emotionally and how an introspective creative approach to the movement can move an audience.

What About Us

The 'What About Us' video is set in various desolate urban city locations such as a car park, a diner and culminates in a choreography block performed by Pink and her large group of dancers in the aridity of the desert. The clip begins with a choreography section including Pink and her dancers intertwined in an organic group – they catch and support her as her weight shifts from one dancer to the next, creating interesting tableaux's in the process. The lyrics of this first verse include a repeated use of the word 'we' ("we are searchlights, we can see in the dark") and the group's choreography reinforces a collectiveness between Pink and her dancers, suggesting she is singing on behalf of them and as well as the viewer. The video continues on with an emotive same sex duet using movement vocabulary and an intensity associated more-so with contemporary dance. The charged duet uses the fluidity of contemporary dance lines juxtaposed with virile chest isolations and acrobatic physicality, performed with exceptional dexterity by both dancers.

The middle eight instrumental section of the song offers a united dance break from Pink and her dancers in an American diner. Dancers are scattered across the diner on tables and chairs as they execute stirring choreography which heightens the poignancy of the lyrics. The content of the movement uses a grounded, Contemporary Dance base and infuses it with tonal qualities from Dancehall, Hip-Hop and lyrical Jazz. The finale of the video takes place in a desert setting and continues with Pink and her dancers performing fiery and impulsive choreography with a levelling physicality which finally takes them to the sandy floor.

The live performances of this song followed a similar trajectory to the video, using choreography as a structural, emotional and cathartic tool to further the impact of the song's sentiments. In an interview, Pink described the ethos behind the video and live performances at events such as The Brit Awards and The MTV Video Music Awards: *"Each dancer has their own journey within that piece. The story is told through movement, as it is in the video."*

Nick Florez and RJ Durell

Known as the 'Golden Boyz,' Nick Florez and RJ Durell are renowned contributors to popular dance on screen and stage. Established as choreographers, directors and producers, they have created works for the industry's most omnipresent artists including – Madonna (various world tours), Katy Perry (Super Bowl XLIX 2015 performance plus 'Dark Horse' video) and Mariah Carey (VH-1 Divas Special) whilst also choreographing theatrical spectacles like Disney's 'The Little Mermaid Live' and Cirque du Soleils 'Immortal Tour.' Their work on the 'What About Us' video and the song's live promotional events utilises a contemporary dance foundation with subtle input from different styles, requiring their dancers to demonstrate highly tuned, style blending skills underpinned by a strong technical prowess. In this emotive collaboration with Pink, the GoldenBoyz created not just an iconic moment for Commercial Dance but they also reinforced the high level of skill required of dancers who wish to work regularly, and with longevity, in the Commercial Dance industry. The choreography in the video is not easy and requires dancers with multi genre abilities to execute it with emotional freedom.

Iconic Moments

Giving more insight into the creative and choreographic process, Pink continued:

> So I work with Nick and RJ, and they have been with me for a long time. They're incredible. And they get me, they get my sort of emotional need to connect. And also, I'm not a technical dancer. I'm not the best dancer. I fake it 'til I make it. So it has to be more about the intention and the energy, than about… what move you're hitting. So, yeah…it's almost like an interpretive dance of your feelings, of how you're feeling when you're singing that song. I think that "What About Us" is a call to be seen, and also a call to let go of all the trauma that we walk around with. It feels like therapy for all of us…"

Image 6.9 Pink's video for 'What About Us' showcases Commercial Dance's emotive power. Choreographed by the 'GoldenBoyz' Nick Florez and RJ Durell

Image 6.10 A link to the 'What About Us' music video\

Iconic Moments

'The Greatest Showman'

Choreographer: Ashley Wallen
Form: Feature film, 20th Century Studios
Release date: 2017

'The Greatest Showman' feature film is a musical retelling of the life story of P.T. Barnum starring Hugh Jackman and directed by Micheal Gracey. The film is accompanied by an impressive Pop/Rock soundtrack penned by Musical Theatre maestro's Benj Pasek and Justin Paul. It is an iconic moment in Commercial Dance as it set the choreographic standard for a batch of musical movies made in the late 2010s and early 2020s, all of which used Commercial Dance inflections in their choreography sections and marked a fresh approach to dance on the cinema screen. Movies that followed 'The Greatest Showman,' such as 'Mary Poppins Returns' (2018, choreographed by Rob Marshall), 'Rocket Man' (2019, choreographed by Adam Murray) and 'In the Heights' (2021, choreographed by Christopher Scott) were no doubt influenced by the tone and texture of the dance sequences created by Ashley Wallen and his associate, Jenny Griffin.

Dance movies of the 2000s had polarised their choreography to one side or the other of the popular and vernacular dance spectrum – either prioritising a harder Hip-Hop base ('Stomp the Yard,' the 'Step-Up' series) or homing in on the sexuality within the movement ('Burlesque,' 2010, 'Magic Mike,' 2012). The storylines of successful dance movies like 'Save the Last Dance' (2001) and the 'Step-Up' film franchise (2006 onwards) continually restricted dance to belonging to either 'the school or the streets' (Chung & Ofri-Mensa 2016) and the choreography was required to reflect the divergence of these two worlds. The choreography created for 'The Greatest Showman' united many styles, striking a line down the middle, evoking the feel and ambiance of both a Hollywood musical from the 1950s and of a music video from the 2010s. The dance sequences brought a fresh mix of palatable, family friendly dance styles to the screen.

'Come Alive' and 'The Greatest Show' are the notable numbers in the movie which display a choreographic style synonymous with Commercial Dance – blending the sharpness of steps from Jazz technique with steps from House and Hip-Hop styles. Steps within phrases are contrasted: relaxed grooves sit juxtaposed to dramatic acrobatic elements, demonstrating the elite physicality and skill of the cast of dancers. Wallen also brings a particular musicality to the choreography, building phrases on both lyrical and rhythmic patterns in the music – a nuance seen frequently in music video (e.g., Justin Timerlake's 'My Love,' choreographed by Marty Kudelka) and but not as prevalent in large, feature film dance sequences.

Ashley Wallen

Wallen has been a notable presence on the UK Commercial Dance scene since the mid-2000s. Originally from Australia, Wallen made his name in London as a dancer before moving into choreography and working regularly on many applauded international projects. Choreographing tours and music videos for Kylie Minogue, Robbie Williams, Pink and FKA Twigs, Wallen followed his success on 'The Greatest Showman' by choreographing the Netflix feature 'Jingle Jangle: A Christmas Journey' (2020) and the Amazon produced 'Cinderella' (2021). Using the same successful choreographic formula seen in 'The Greatest Showman' made Wallen's dance sequences in both subsequent movies stand-out moments.

Iconic Moments

Image 6.11 The 2017 movie 'The Greatest Showman' set a new trend for the manifestation of Commercial Dance on the big screen. Choreographed by Ashley Wallen

Image 6.12 A link to the number 'The Greatest Show' from The Greatest Showman

Mary J Blige Live Performance

Choreographer & Creative Director: Nadine 'Hi-Hat' Ruffin
Form: BET TV award show, 'Lifetime Achievement' medley performance
Date: 23rd June 2019

In reviewing this performance, Billboard magazine described Blige as "*a transcendent figure in R&B music who should be credited as one of the trailblazers in blending elements of hip-hop and soul, which cracked down the doors for many of the women artists that came after her.*" She has also been a trailblazer in terms of the choreography she has commissioned and performed in her music videos and live performances, courtesy of some of the big hitters in

Iconic Moments

the Commercial Dance industry such as Fatima Robinson and Nadine 'Hi-Hat' Ruffin. It's an iconic moment because it demonstrates the ageless manner of many styles in the portfolio of Commercial Dance. It shows what a timeless quality many of the original social dance styles of the 1980s and 1990s have and how choreographers, such as Hi-Hat in this instance, are able to refresh these dances effectively by integrating trends and nuances which are prevalent in dance today. Created to celebrate Mary J Blige's BET Lifetime Achievement Award, this 20-minute performance took in 11 songs in total, including choreographic highlights 'Real Love' and 'You Remind Me.' Rehearsed over 3 days, Blige is joined by 30 female dancers who rotate on and off stage, giving time for costume and track changes.

Re-seasoning the Flavour

Hi-Hat's choreography, with Troy Kirby as assistant, is a sophisticated update of the foundational Hip-Hop and New Jack Swing flavour prevalent in much of Blige's early work. The choreography marries playful early 1990s Hip-Hop groove steps with a sharper, more nuanced snap of movement, interjecting 'and' counts to refine and accelerate the infectious bounce of the gait as well as providing a seamless flow to the movement. The choreography is also performed by the large group of dancers in close-to-perfect unison, something that was not always accomplished in R&B and Hip-Hop videos of the early 1990s. The costumes and aura of the choreography reference Blige's iconic, and often imitated, videos of the 1990s and 2000s (e.g., Real Love/Family Affair/Love at First Sight).

It's a performance that reminds us of the free and easy spirit which original Hip-Hop choreography could transcribe for both the dancer and the audience. Social steps created for a collective, feel-good environment – Hi-Hat created 20 minutes of dance nostalgia tinged with current Commercial choreographic trends. When talking about the rehearsal process with her dancers, Hi-Hat remarked that rehearsal is "*...not about the dance steps, it's to get it in your soul.*" Every dancer onstage in this Iconic Moment appears to genuinely perform from within themselves – counts and technique are secondary to the communal celebration of Mary J Blige's music, through choreography that is danced from the inside out and because of that, it connects directly with the audience. I challenge you to watch this performance and not want to join in.

Image 6.13 Nadine 'Hi-Hat' Ruffin's choreography for the 2019 BET Awards saw Mary J Blige and her dancers perform old school Hip-Hop grooves with a fresh, updated feel

Iconic Moments

Image 6.14 A link to Mary J Blige's live 2019 BET performance

Rihanna's Savage X Fenty Fashion Show Vol II

Choreographer: Parris Goebel
Form: TV Special/Fashion Show for the Savage X Fenty fashion brand
Release date: October 2020

Directed by Director Alex Rudzinski and Sandrine Orabona, creatively overseen by Rihanna and choreographed by Paris Goebel, the 2020 TV Special for Vol II of the Savage Fenty leisurewear range was produced for the camera due to Covid-19 limitations. This change of focus, from prioritising the live audience as in Vol I, led to an already dance-heavy concept being able to take flight and use the camera lens to guide the audience's eye precisely to Goebel's intricate choreography performed by a chorus of world-class dancers, representing a spectrum of different body types, sexualities, genders and ethnicities. The show is so bare in terms of set and shooting style that there is nowhere for any of the dancers to hide (quite literally, as many sections are performed in lingerie).

The TV special is integrated with insightful documentary footage and talking heads from many of the shows' creatives (including a who's who of the fashion and music world – Miguel, Cara Delevingne, Irena Shayak and Rihanna herself). It became a show underpinned and led by electrically eccentric movement sequences combining so many elements of Commercial Dance.

A Celebration of Differences

Savage Fenty Vol II is an iconic moment in dance not just because of its choreographic aplomb – it also actively expanded the parameters for inclusivity in dance and fashion. The band of dancers performing are part of the show because of their dance ability and natural persona, regardless of disability, skin tone, gender, sexuality or dress size. For a lingerie and home-wear brand to cast their show in this way, it was a timely example

117

to other brands, such as Victoria's Secret, that society's pre-disposed ideas regarding the physical 'template' a dancer or model should be cut from, was stale and no longer relevant in 2020, the year of a society levelling pandemic and the 'Black Lives Matter' movement. Rihanna and Parris Goebel knew they were writing a new chapter in onscreen dance and turned the page for their audience with conviction. Rihanna explained her thinking to Vogue magazine:

> When I imagine something, I imagine everyone I know and love being a part of it. I want to make stuff I can see on the people I know, and they come in all different shapes, sizes, races, and religions, I didn't think it would be such a talking point after the fact; the only thing I could think about was including everyone.

Parris Goebel's Choreography

Parris Goebel is a choreographer who has made an indelible mark on Commercial Dance over the last 10 years. Her choreographic resumé boasts many other iconic moments, such as two superbly executed Superbowl performances, with JLo in 2020 and with Rihanna in 2023. The sociological importance of her work on the Savage Fenty fashion series meant that her work is covered here in Iconic Moments, rather than in the Main Movers profiles but there is no doubt she has been one of the biggest influences on dance of the 2010s and 2020s.

There are few, if any, choreographers who could have created work which binds their dancers as one creative collective and at the same time highlights and celebrates each dancer's own uniqueness. Her choreography is ferocious yet intricate. So much of the effectiveness of Goebel´s work is in the execution of her work from the dancers she has trained so effectively. From her 'Royal Family' dance crew originals in New Zealand to the dancers she uses when choreographing for JLo or Justin Bieber in LA, each of her dancers is required to completely commit and embody the movement.

The Steps

Goebel's group sequences in Savage Fenty Vol II move seamlessly into solos, lyrical gymnastic sections merge into Contemporary dance work, which is also interspersed with Dancehall, Bone Breaking and Krump. The opening sequence is particularly eye-catching, starting with a solo from Goebel herself (displaying an intuitive musicality that is second to none) and featuring a male popping trio which swipes across into an army of dancers criss-crossing in front of the camera. A hint of Bob Fosse's 'The Rich Man's Frug' combined with her teasing staccato-jilted dancehall and sensualised Hip-Hop flow engrains itself on the lens with help from Kendrick Lamar's seductive jam 'Poetic Justice.' Music artists Lizzo and Rosalia are also featured in segments performing Goebel's rich choreography.

The combination of extreme physicality and musicality in Goebel's work is forged and then performed with such ferocity and pride that any young dancers watching Vol II of the Savage Fenty fashion series should see this level of execution in dance as the benchmark they must aspire to achieve.

Iconic Moments

Image 6.15 The Savage Fenty Vol II fashion show saw Parris Goebel and Rihanna challenge the traditional notion of what a fashion show was, incorporating a broad spectrum of dancers from various backgrounds and ethnicities. The choreography combined styles from many different genres of dance

Image 6.16 A link to 'Drenas', a number from the Savage Fenty Vol 2 Fashion Show

'Us Again' Walt Disney Animation Studios

Choreographer: Keone and Mari Madrid
Form: Short film
Release date: 2021

> The finest gesture can say so much, you don't have to be a super physical athlete to move your body and move people.
>
> Keone Madrid – co-choreographer 'Us Again'

'Us Again' tells the story of an elderly couple looking for a spark to reignite the verve in their relationship. It's a short film created by Disney, covering themes of love, companionship and the sadness felt as youth fades as quickly as the photos in which it was captured. The idea of youth being an outlook or philosophy, not a physical state, is what drives the seven enchanting minutes of this short clip. As the director Zach Parrish notes, "Youth is not this thing you have and then lose – it's a state of mind." With no spoken dialogue at all, the story is told purely through movement and dance conceived by choreographers Keone and Mari Madrid.

A Family Affair

There are two elements which make this short film an iconic moment in terms of Commercial Dance. The first is its seamless melding of genres translated by the two lead characters. Snippets of Lindy Hop, Lockin', Uprock, Broadway inspired Jazz and Boogaloo are all apparent throughout the Madrid's mimetic, subtle style. Rhythms are played with, adding a complexity and freshness which updates some sedentary elements of older Broadway style dance genres.

The second element is the film's cross generational appeal. The character's movement vocabulary takes them from Gene Kelly-esque sequences through to phrases reflecting flavours seen in today's new style Hip-Hop combos. The full spectrum of its audience's potential age range is catered for, from the toddler to the Grandparent, there is movement performed which speaks to them. Just as the themes in most Walt Disney films resonate with the whole family, so does the choreography in 'Us Again.' It's a perfect example of how effective Commercial Dance can be as a family orientated dance medium, away from the gratuitous sexualisation that is sometimes seen in many commercial projects.

Keone and Mari Madrid

This husband and wife choreographic duo came to international prominence in Justin Bieber's 2015 'Love Yourself' video as part of Purpose: The Movement short film, co-directed by Parris Goebel. The couple choreographed and danced in Bieber's video, which observes them in a number of settings in their apartment as the emotional state of their relationship is revealed via their dynamic choreography. The Madrids bring an intelligent, subtle and emotional expressiveness to their movement phrases which is not often seen within the canon of projects which could be considered to be Commercial Dance. Their movement demonstrates a physical theatricality married with a precision of gestural hand placement that makes it unique and particularly distinctive – they have designed a way of moving which has been imitated by creators of dance globally.

Iconic Moments

In some ways 'Us Again' feels like an update of 'Love Yourself.' Aged avatars of similar characters which the Madrids embodied in 'Love Yourself,' have been immortalised by Disney animators in 'Us Again.' In both clips, their astute musicality and intimate connection as performers is clear to see. They have created a dance film rich in multi-genre dance acknowledgement, which also speaks to a multi-generational demographic, adding gravitas and respectability to Commercial Dance on screen.

Dance isn't something that you do, but it's how you do everything.

Zach Parrish – Director 'Us Again'

Image 6.17 Disney's short film 'Us Again' (2021) uses the astute choreography of Keone and Mari Madrid to create dance with a cross generational, family appeal

Image 6.18 A link to the official trailer from the Disney short film 'Us Again'

References

'Thriller' – Michael Jackson

Michael Peters – www.latimes.com/archives
Michael Peters – www.nyti.ms/298ef0D

'Rhythm Nation' – Janet Jackson

www.rollingstone.com/music/music-lists/rolling-stone-readers-pick-their-10-favorite-dancing-musicians-18885/8-janet-jackson-178333/

'Chandelier' – SIA

Kourlas, G. (2016). "For Sia, Dance Is Where the Human and the Weird Intersect," *The New York Times*, 19th July [accessed 31 October 2016].

'What About Us' – Pink

Women Health channel: www.youtube.com/watch?v=lP6qLShcSoI

'The Greatest Showman'

BET Awards – Mary J. Blige. www.billboard.com/music/rb-hip-hop/best-moments-2019-bet-awards-8517174/ [accessed: 03/02/2022].
Chung, B. and A. Ofori-Mensa (2016). The School and "the Streets": Race, Class, Sound and Space in Step Up and Step Up 2. In M. Evans & M. Fogarty (Eds.), *Movies, Moves and Music* (pp. 78–107). Sheffield: Equinox Publishing.

Savage Fenty Vol II Fashion Show

www.vogue.com/article/rihanna-savage-x-fenty-volume-two-overview

'Us Again' – Disney short film

www.youtube.com/watch?v=LacJX-1Zjz0

Chapter 7

Main Movers

Brian Friedman

Location: USA
Credits include:
Television and Live performance:
America's Got Talent *Seasons 4, 5 and 6*
American Idol *Creative Director*
Dancing with the Stars *Creative Director and Choreographer*
The Voice US *Creative Director*
Britney Spears *"Slave 4 U" Billboard Music Awards 2001*
X-Factor UK various seasons *Choreographer, Judge & Creative Director*
Music Videos:
Britney Spears, *"Til the World Ends" (VMA nominated 2011)/"Hold It Against Me"/"Toxic"– Choreographer. "Overprotected" Writer, Director & Choreographer*

Style

The technician of the prominent Commercial choreographers, Friedman has developed a recognisable style of his own which features many technical elements from Jazz and Vogue Fem dance styles. His work is fast and physical – when auditioning for one of his jobs, dancers need to be ready to sweat, go 110% and perform some physically demanding steps! Combining these almost gymnastic elements of dance vocabulary with softer dynamics from Hip-Hop and Dancehall styles has resulted in Friedman creating the perfect style for some of the biggest mainstream entertainment television productions in the UK and the US.

Having had a successful career as a dancer working on projects such as Disney's 'Newsies' (1992) and for artists such as Britney Spears, Rihanna and Mariah Carey, Friedman is a choreographer who can demonstrate and execute his work as well as any of his dancers or students can. His tutorials on dance teaching platforms such as CLI Studios, his masterclasses

Main Movers

at Millennium Dance Complex, LA and various international dance conventions are always led from the front by Friedman as he demonstrates his enthusiasm and commitment to the choreography that he creates. He demands a high level of performance integrity, intensity and respect from the dancers in his studio.

Britney and Creative Direction

Along with Wade Robson, Friedman created steps for one of the most widely imitated Commercial Dance routines in Britney Spears' 'I'm a Slave 4 U' video and he also provided choreography for her iconic 'Toxic' video. He has a long-standing working relationship with Spears' and was nominated for an MTV VMA in 2011 for his choreography on her video *'Til the World Ends.'* Friedman has crossed over into Creative Direction and producing, working on Saturday night cornerstone shows such as American Idol and X-Factor (US and UK). He has delivered interesting creative concepts as well as continued to actively dance, teach and create new choreographic works. A strong and confident persona, he will no doubt continue to help shape the world of Commercial Dance as it progresses. Friedman reflected on his abilities in a feature on DanceTeacher.com:

> I think people see my flamboyant, over-the-top dance persona and sometimes mistake that for arrogance. When I'm on the dance floor, I'm confident. I believe in myself as a dancer more so than I do as a creator. I am a dancer. When I'm on that floor I'm untouchable. Maybe in my 20s there was a level of arrogance to it, but I've gotten to the point where I just know that that's my gift, and I own it. I hope people know that's just the artist me. The human me is as normal as can be.

MUST SEE!
Britney Spears *'I'm a Slave 4 U' Billboard Music Awards 2001*

Image 7.1 Brian Freidman uses a strong jazz technique to underpin much of his choreography

Charm La'Donna

Location: Los Angeles, USA
Dance credits include:
Music Video:
Dua Lipa – *Physical/Break My Heart/Levitating, 2020, Choreographer*
Rosalía – *Malamente/ Con Altura/Di Mi Nombre/Aute Cuture, 2018 & 2019, Choreographer*
Selena Gomez – *Look At Her Now, 2020, Choreographer*
Meghan Trainor – *Let You Be Right, 2018, Choreographer*
Live performance:
Kendrick Lamar, *Big Steppers Tour, 2022*
Dua Lipa, *Future Nostalgia World Tour, 2021/2022*
94th Academy Awards, The Oscars 2022 – *'We Don't Talk About Bruno' opening number with the cast of Disney's Encanto*
The Weeknd – *Super Bowl LV Halftime performance, 2021*

Solo artist, director, songwriter, dancer and choreographer – Charm La'Donna is a multi-faceted creative artist and one of the most important recent additions to the carousel of Commercial choreographers actively shaping the industry. As well as being signed to Epic records as a solo artist, La'Donna is combining putting out her own music with a choreography career which includes making moves for some of the world's biggest artists. Winning the MTV VMA award in 2019 for her choreography on Rosalia's 'Con Altura' video, La'Donna has made notable dance works for Kendrick Lamar, Dua Lipa, Meghan Trainor, Britney Spears, Selena Gomez, The Weeknd and Lizzo.

Having trained in dance disciplines including Horton and Luigi at the Los Angeles County High School for the Arts, La'Donna toured with Madonna at 16 years old and has worked closely with Fatima Robinson as a mentor and assisting her from a young age. La'Donna is a choreographer who is able to physically formulate the movement style she puts on the dancers and artists she works with. Seeing her dance in her solo videos, it's clear that she is a choreographer who is more than capable of executing her work at the same level as any of the dancers she books. Her movement style is mainly based in raw and grounded Hip-Hop-associated styles (see La'Donna's self-choreographed solo track 'Queen') although she demonstrates her versatility in projects such as the opening of the Oscars 2022 and Dua Lipa's 2019 Brit Awards 'Don't Start Now' performance by also incorporating Broadway Jazz and softer, Vogue Fem-inspired elements.

Choreographing both music videos and tours, her work has been particularly noticeable from a dance perspective in terms of creativity – namely the Kendrick Lamar's Big Steppers tour (see the chapter on Live events and Concerts) and Dua Lipa's Future Nostalgia world tour. Consequence Sound observed in an editorial review of the tour that:

> With an artist as big as Dua Lipa, you expect some strong choreography, and the dancers last night absolutely delivered. There were roller skating front flips, jazzercise grooves, chaotic club moshes and moments of infectious personality. It felt like every dance move served a purpose, and each style of dance was specific to the content of the songs.

Image 7.2 Charm La'Donna performing in her video for the track 'Westside' (2020)

In an interview with Forbes, La'Donna preaches the philosophies followed by many creative artists in the 2020s – she practises 100% commitment to her work and recognises that her multiple skills combine to make one business brand:

> I think all of my artists need 100% of me. I have tons of assistance, particularly an executive assistant and attorney who help handle some of the business aspects, but when it comes to creative, I am very hands on with my artists. My whole life has been about hustle and motivation so if I take on a project, I have to give it my all no matter what. I do what I love so I can't complain. I feel in freelance, always being hired by others takes away the freedom to work with your people. Having my own business has allowed me to create my own team and surround myself with likeminded individuals who are helping me build my brand.
>
> I grew up in this industry and was fortunate enough to learn from the best. I've been able to apply my knowledge to my own business and determine what I feel are appropriate (payment) rates. At the end of the day, I feel that rates should always be based on level of experience and expertise…I invest in what I believe in. I think it's important to create a valuable team so I think my most critical expenses would be my management, photographers/videographers and publicist.

MUST SEE!!
Dua Lipa – *Don't Start Now, Live at the MTV EMAs,* 2019
The Weeknd's *Super Bowl LV,* 2021

Christopher Scott

Location: USA
Credits include:
<u>Film:</u>
In the Heights, *2020*
Being the Ricardos, *2022*

Step Up 5: All In, *2014*
Step Up 4: Revolution, *2012*
Television:
So You Think You Can Dance Season 15 (Fox USA) *"Violence Broken"/"Runaway"/"Love on the Brain"*
So You Think You Can Dance Season 14 (Fox USA) *"Say You Won't Let Go" (Emmy nominated)/"Prism" (Emmy nominated)*
Selena Gomez *American Music Awards 2015*
Taylor Swift *American Music Awards 2014*

Compared to some of the other choreographers included in the 'Main Movers' features in this book, Christopher Scott could be considered a relatively new choreographer. Scott is a choreographer guiding and shaping the present and future of dance on screen and in commercial performance. A student of the game, he references a multitude of styles in his work whilst maintaining a consistent awareness of transferring authenticity of the movement from the streets through to the final, production ready, choreography.

Intricate angular hand and arm movements sewn tightly to lyrical musical observations blend with bounce and Breakin' floorwork harmoniously. Suggestions of a contemporary dance approach and flow, mix with house and Latin rhythms. None of Scott's work feels synthetic. Every step in his movement phrases appears researched, understood and genuine – there is no dilution of authenticity in his jigsaw-like connection between dance styles – it's a real skill to consistently create quality Commercial Dance of this depth.

In the Heights

Jon M Chu's and Lin-Manuel Miranda's 2020 cinema adaption of Miranda's Broadway smash 'In the Heights' is a choreographic triumph. Hispanic and Hip-Hop influenced, each of the dance scenes pushes the boundaries further in terms of quantity and the vastness of what styles Commercial Dance as a genre can incorporate. The 10-minute opening sequence culminates in a New York street junction full of dancers reflected in the window of the bodega that Usnavi (the main protagonist) stares out from. It is the spark plug for the rest of the movie – a neighbourhood brought to life by music and dance. Scott's choreography morphs Latin styles into harder Hip-Hop choreography and funk, which reflects perfectly the cultural textures conveyed in the music. The viewer can not only hear the Latin, Hip-Hop and pop rhythms but also see them danced to life by each member of the Washington Heights barrio via Scott's movement. '96,000' is an enormous dance number set at a local open air pool. It features one of the largest cast of dancers ever assembled in a modern era American made movie, with 90 dancers on set. During an interview with Backstage.com, Scott gave an insight to the difficulties in securing so many dancers in a movie and also his feelings toward the omnipresent and outdated collective noun of *'background dancers'*:

> We have 75 dancers in the opening number, which isn't even our largest number. For "96,000," we had 90 dancers. And one of the biggest challenges was holding onto them, because as [the studio is] spending money, they're constantly looking at ways to cut down costs. And one of the biggest ways that they do that is trying to cut dancers. And it's funny because when you were referring to them, too, you were saying the "background dancers." And even just that word, it's become this whole movement for dancers to just be seen and to be heard as artists. So a big thing was making sure that they don't feel unimportant to the moment, especially in a movie musical.

Main Movers

Image 7.3 An overhead shot from '96,000,' a number choreographed by Christopher Scott from the movie 'In the Heights' (2020)

So You Think You Can Dance

Scott's creative abilities can be seen in his work on the US version of 'So You Think You Can Dance,' where he choreographed a number of pieces which were then Emmy nominated. The work is choreographed with an awareness of the dynamism of contrasting movement phrases – switching from the smaller intricate movements mentioned earlier to floor work, which travels explosively. It feels like there is always a motivation for the movement references which are chosen, whether steps from Breakin', Funk or Jazz, there is consideration to the journey of the piece created. Speaking to Dance Magazine in 2018, Scott discusses his Emmy nominations and the importance of understanding the choreographer's role on set:

> In film and TV, we're always fighting for better rates and working conditions, more respect. I've learned that if I go on set with people who haven't worked with a choreographer, there's always this awkward moment where I'm talking to the wardrobe department, the art department, the stunt coordinator and people look at me like, 'Why are you telling me what to do?'. Then they see rehearsals and the level of responsibility we have and that starts to change. Emmy nominations help them understand that what we're doing is real, it pushes the story forward, it has a place in the industry.

MUST SEE!!
In the Heights – *'96,000' scene*, 2020
So You Think You Can Dance (USA), Season 14 – *'Prism'*

Fatima Robinson

Location: USA
Credits include:
Music Videos:
Doja Cat – *Vegas*
Busta Rhymes – *Put Your Hands Where My Eyes Can See*
Aaliyah – *Rock The Boat/Are You that Somebody/We Need A Resolution*

Michael Jackson – *Remember The Time*
Mary J Blige – *Family Affair* – (Winner of 2002 MTV Music Video Award for Best Choreography)
Black Eyed Peas – *My Humps/Hey Mama*
Rhianna – *Pon de Replay/If It's Love*
Pharrell Williams – *Happy*
Meghan Trainor – *All About That Bass (as Director)*
Film:
Save the Last Dance
Dreamgirls
Live Performance:
Super Bowl LVI Halftime Show, 2022 *featuring Kendrick Lamar, 50 Cent, Dr. Dre, Snoop Dogg, Mary J. Blige and Eminem.*
Super Bowl XLV halftime show, 2011 *featuring The Black Eyed Peas*

Fatima Robinson's work portfolio has constantly expanded over the last three decades, cementing her as one of the most dominate creative forces in Commercial Dance. Her two stints choreographing for the Super Bowl halftime show have been notable. The first time for The Black Eyed Peas was in 2011, in which Robinson took on the huge task of working with a cast of 1,000 dancers and also became the first woman of colour to choreograph the iconic sporting moment. The 2022 halftime show saw Robinson praised for the dynamic choreography performed by 130 dancers, which accompanied a selection of Dr Dre produced hits.

Remember the Time

I had the fortune to work with Fatima Robinson twice in London – as a dancer on Sade's 2010 'Soldier of Love' music video and on a 2004 TV Commercial for 'Virgin.' At first hand, it was easy to see her ability to tune into the subtle percussive rhythms of the track and create choreography which closely followed the creative pulse of the song. This ability was perhaps nurtured early on in her career – in 1992, when only 21 years old, Fatima worked with director John Singleton and Michael Jackson on the Egyptian themed short film for 'Remember the Time.' Together with Buddha Stretch, they created one of Jackson's most memorable dance sequences with Fatima and Stretch providing the choreography to an acapella Jackson vocal that grows into a transfixing rhythm-track breakdown dance finale. When reminiscing about the experience of shooting 'Remember the Time' with Jackson to The Huffington Post in 2017, Fatima remarked: *"He never wanted you to count the song, he wanted you to mimic the rhythm of the song… for him it was about the emotion and the beat of the song and that drove the dance."* In the video for 'Remember the Time' Fatima uses understated, succinct Hip-Hop rooted choreography phrases on duos of dancers and injects an Egyptian inflection by integrating elements of 'Tutting' (Tutting is a Funk sub-style that consists of angular arm and hand movements, created by forming interesting geometric shapes, often reminiscent of the angular arm lines seen in ancient Egyptian hieroglyphics – the moniker 'Tutting' is in reference to the Egyptian King, Tutankhamun).

Busta, Aaliyah, Mary and Pharrell

Busta Rhymes 'Put Your Hands Where My Eyes Can See' is one of the game-changing Hip-Hop videos of the 1990s. Collaborating with director Hype Williams to create a unique and

Main Movers

Image 7.4 Fatima Robinson has choreographed two Superbowl performances, the first with The Black Eyed Peas in 2011 and the second with Dr Dre, Snoop Dogg, Mary J Blige and Eminem, pictured here in 2022

satirical take on Busta's grandiose Hip-Hop lifestyle, Fatima's choreography in the luminescent final third of the video is grounded with elements of African dance fused with the popular Hip-Hop styles of the late 1990s. Fatima's work with Aaliyah in a series of emblematic videos including 'More than a Woman,' 'Are You That Somebody,' 'We Need a Resolution' and 'Rock the Boat' confirmed her as one of the go-to choreographers of the era.

Collaborating with another big hitting music video director in Dave Meyers, Fatima won the MTV Video Music award for Best Choreography in 2002 for Mary J Blige's 'Family Affair,' a glossy video with contagious dance sections which are led by Mary J Blige herself, fronting a group of dancers. The iconic video helped the song become one of the biggest selling singles of the 2000s and Fatima's accessible, infectious choreography was imitated on club dance-floors all over the world.

Illustrating her ability to relate to any type of dance or personality, Fatima's work on Pharrell William's memorable 'Happy' video project is uplifting. In behind-the-scenes footage of this shoot, Fatima is beside the lens for every shot, guiding Pharrell and his dancers though their movement choices, making sure that the spirit of the song is expressed though the video's various characters in the most captivating way.

MUST SEE!
Aaliyah – 'Are You That Somebody' music video, 1992
Pharrell Williams – 'Happy' music video, 2013
Dr Dre Super Bowl LVI Halftime Show, 2022

Frank Gatson

Location: Los Angeles, USA
Credits include:
<u>Live Performance/Tours:</u>
Usher, *No Way Out Tour, 1998, Director and Choreographer*

Beyonce, *I Am... World Tour, 2009, Creative Director, Choreographer*
Beyonce, *The Mrs. Carter Show World Tour 2013, Creative Director and Choreographer*
Music Video:
En Vogue, *Free Your Mind (1992)/Runaway Love (1993)/Whatta Man (1994), choreographer*
Usher, *My Way (1997)/You Remind Me (2001)/Love in the Club (2008), Choreographer*
Beyonce, *Crazy in Love, Baby Boy (2003)/Ring the Alarm/Upgrade U/Irreplaceable (2006)/ If I Were a Boy, Single Ladies (Put a Ring On It) (2009)/Run the World (Girls)/Countdown (2011), Choreographer*

A founding father of the Commercial Dance industry and its on-screen and stage manifestation. Frank Gatson has shaped the movement of some of the most prominent and influential commercial music artists of the last 30 years. Trained via Alvin Ailey and Broadway Dance Centre in New York City, Gatson's breakthrough job came shortly after moving to Los Angeles when he booked a spot as a dancer in Michael Jackson's 'Smooth Criminal' video in 1988. Shortly after, he began a successful and career-altering creative partnership with 90's super group En Vogue, co-choreographing a number of their videos. Clips such as 'Free Your Mind' and 'Whatta Man' were era defining clips of the early 1990s.

Gatson's movement work in these clips shows a choreographer drawing from street and club styles, using acrobatic elements from Breakin' as well as studio techniques such as Jazz and Horton technique. It is also a period in which he developed an empowering concept of performance movement for artists, coaching them to move freely and with confidence. Gatson's successful ground work with En Vogue as choreographer and Creative Director laid the path for him to develop Destiny's Child. In turn, this would lead him to help coach on the most culturally titanic artists of a generation in Beyonce Knowles-Carter.

Beyonce

Gatson's work as choreographer and Creative Director on Beyonce's early work as a solo artist facilitated the creation of some seminal moments in modern music video. His work with Beyonce promoted dance from the background to the forefront of her live and recorded performances. His choreography and the prominent involvement of support dancers which Gatson oversaw in the early 2000s elevated Beyonce's work further. Beyonce and Gatson's mutually consistent work ethic and similar movement expression synergised, forging a strong creative partnership. Gatson's background in studio-based technical dance from Ailey and his early interest in Broadway musicals such as 'The Wiz' and 'Dreamgirls' appears to have inspired a simple synchronicity in his choreography and brought a theatricality to Beyonce's stage productions which blended with her own expressive sensuality to create a unique palette of performance hallmarks. In 2003, his work with Beyonce was acknowledged as, along with Lavelle Smith Jr, he won his 4th MTV Music Video Award for Best Choreography for the 'Crazy in Love' video.

Influences

Gatson has helped to bring Beyonce's early canon of work a certain signature style – both in terms of movement and aesthetics. This has not been a one-man job, Gatson has been keen to cultivate creative partnerships over the years with other up-and-coming dance creatives, among them JaQuel Knight, Chris Grant, Danielle Polanco and Ashley Everett. All of these dancers and choreographers have helped Gatson to realise his creative directorial visions on behalf of his artists on various different projects. Gatson's collaboration with Knight as co-choreographer on the 'Single Ladies (Put a Ring On It)' video clip is one highlight of these collaborations. A preacher of 'old school' work ethics and tenets, Gatson's association with Beyonce was one which prospered through hard work in the rehearsal room and open collaboration between many talented creatives. Gatson remarked in an interview in 2010 that:

> Beyonce is the best in the game because she rehearses, plans and is very creative. She is nice, she is beautiful, she gets "it", she is honest. She does not waste your time in rehearsal. When you're in rehearsals you work very hard which is exciting. You might say everyone rehearses, but Beyonce is full-out, working harder than the dancers.

MUST SEE!!
  Beyonce – 'Crazy in Love' Music video, 2003
  Beyonce – 'Baby Boy' Music Video, 2003

Jamie King

Location: Los Angeles, USA
Credits include:
Live Performance/Tours:
Madonna, *'Madam X' Tour, Creative Producer*
Nicki Minaj, *'Made in America' Tour, Creative Director*
Madonna, *'Rebel Heart,' 'MDMA,' 'Sticky & Sweet' Tours, Director*
Britney Spears, *'Femme Fatal,' 'Circus' Tour, Director*
Christina Aguilera, *'Stripped,' 'Back to Basics' Tour, Director*
Madonna, *2012 Super Bowl Halftime Show, Creative Director*
Michael Jackson, *Cirque du Soleil, 'Immortal World Tour' Director/Writer*
Music Video:
Madonna, *'Sorry,' 'Hung Up,' '4 Minutes,' Choreographer*
Ricky Martin, *'She Bangs,' Choreographer/Creative Director*
Britney Spears, *'Stronger,' Choreographer*

Live Concert Creator

Jamie King has travelled the employment spectrum of the Commercial Dance industry, shifting from dancer, to choreographer to creative director. He is largely responsible for tailoring and shaping the format of the modern day pop and music concert. He has creatively conceived and directed international stadium/arena tours and Commercial Dance-based concerts by some of the biggest performers in the world. His concepts are colossal and the practical realisation of his mind's eye is slick and fast. Variety Magazine magazine ran a tribute to King in 2011 in acknowledgement of the total box office sales of concerts and tours he has worked on toppling the $2 Billion mark: *"If you know anything about my pop shows they are always big spectacles,"* says King, who, nearly single-handedly took dance-based pop shows into the same realm as the gigantic concert experiences associated with the Rolling Stones, U2 and Peter Gabriel.

It's about really sustaining that artist's career, and showing the theatricality and the size of the artist. You want the fans to leave feeling they have really seen something special. It's the way the screens move; the way the stage is designed; the way the lighting works; the way the choreography moves. It has to all move in a way that is reflective of the artist.

From Dance to Director

King cut his teeth in the industry as a dancer, notably for Michael Jackson on the 1992 Dangerous World Tour (choreographed by Lavelle Smith Jnr). He moved into creative direction after Prince gave King an early career opportunity he couldn't miss – asking him to create a series of new weekly concerts for him to showcase unreleased Prince material. King explained how this unique opportunity arose:

> He took a chance on me…he saw something in me that I really didn't see myself. The second I started choreographing for Prince and designing performances for Prince, I felt like I was in the right place. I was really understanding what my journey was supposed to be about in terms of activity and staging and so on. Prince showed me more of the details of how music is created and how lyrics can match choreography. When lyrics match choreography with moves, you can create magic and energy that the fans relate to.

After seeing Prince's performance at the 1993 American Music Awards which King directed, Madonna contacted him to work with her on upcoming projects and a 20-year creative partnership was born – beginning with her avantgarde *'Human Nature'* music video in 1994. As a choreographer, King also worked with Britney Spears at the peak of her popularity, choreographing the memorable and often imitated 'chair dance sequence' in the video for the 2000 single *'Stronger.'* His resume as a Creative Director is unmatched and his work on projects such as Madonna's 2012 Super Bowl halftime show cement King as a major influencer on the Commercial Dance industry.

MUST SEE!!
    Britney Spears – 'Stronger' Music Video, 2000
    Madonna – 'Human Nature' Music Video, 1994

JaQuel Knight

Location: USA
Credits include:
Tours & Live Shows:
Beyonce *"Homecoming" at Coachella (with Chris Grant)/"Formation" World Tour/"The Mrs. Carter Show" World Tour/"I Am Yours" Tour/Las Vegas*
Jennifer Lopez *New Year's Eve/Live In Vegas*
American Idol LIVE! *2009 & 2011–2012*
The Wiz, *Broadway Show, 2024*

Main Movers

Music Video:
Beyonce *"Single Ladies (Put A Ring On It)"/"Diva"/"Formation"/"Sorry"*
Brandy *"Wildest Dreams"/"Put It Down"*
Megan Thee Stallion – *"Body"*
Zara Larsson – *"All the Time"/"Love Me Land"/"Wow"/*

Pioneer

As well as being one of the first choreographers to secure copyright protection for the steps he is creating, JaQuel Knight has had a hand in realising some of the most notable recent pieces of Commercial Dance work. Working with Megan Thee Stallion, Little Mix, Ben Platt, Zara Larsson and most notably Beyonce, Knight's work is always energised, TikTok-able, often politically vocal and full of Knight's own infectious vibe. In 2020, Megan Thee Stallion worked with Knight on her 'Body' video and live performances and along with Cardi B's 'WAP' video (also choreographed by Knight) provided two of the most significant viral moments of the year. The 'Body' video features movement inspired by the NOLA Bounce and JaQuel's own influences growing up in Atlanta, a Hip-Hop and dance hotspot. Speaking with Knight, it is clear that he is an impassioned advocate for dancers' rights and a connoisseur of dance of all kinds. He explains how he perceives his choreography:

> What my choreography does is connect the people to the art. Connect everyday people – people who may not be dancers. My goal is to find a way to keep the dance inclusive, regardless of where you are from, for all walks of life. Specifically in terms of movement – its the movement of the people.

Beyonce

Knight's work, particularly with Beyonce, has amplified the quality of Commercial Dance and assisted in elevating her to a modern icon of popular culture. Her performances are frequently centred around outstanding dance routines which channel many influences, from J-Setting in 'Single Ladies' (a style developed by Majourette Dance troupes from Jackson State University, Mississippi, USA) to African influences in the Coachella 'Homecoming' concerts. Whilst discussing the content of the choreography for the Coachella concert series in 2018, Knight explained to The New York Times:

> We have created a language with the choreography that has a street vibe and a great line as well. So the body always looks good. And then it's a level of personality on top and feeling — things you really can't teach. It's a combination of technique, street and personality. And magic.
>
> (Having so many different kinds of movement) keeps everything interesting and it doesn't allow your power to become stale. The audience can stay on its toes. We like to have technical moments — we have a duet with Jasmine Harper and King Havoc, where they combined their worlds. She comes from a beautiful ballet background and he comes from a beautiful street background. Use the flexers here. Come out and boom — let's combine a bit of our African training there.
>
> I think for Beyoncé, adding as many different elements of dance as we can is cool. As a Pop entertainer, people see her as being one dimensional: coming out, shaking her butt and going to the next song. So we really tried to steer away from that.

Main Movers

Image 7.5 JaQuel rehearsing with Zara Larsson

He advocates the simple dogma of hard work and dedication, two principles impressed upon him whilst working with Beyonce. He talks about how this has changed him as a professional artist:

> I've learned so much from working with someone like her (Beyonce) – there is no one person out there that can outwork me and I have to give that to her. She's willing to put in the time. There's not many artists out there who are going to sit beside you as you block lighting, as you go through the lighting changes, as you get the camera shots right, you know? She's going to sit right there through the whole thing…She'll even do the fitting right there – she's gonna do it all at the same time!
>
> The most impressive part of it all, is that when she gets on stage, she knows every camera shot, where every light is supposed to be and she'll call you out about it too. So as an artist, if she's able to do that right in the act and on stage, and she wants the best for us and pushes us to be the best – I have to also be the best artist possible. As I've gone on and started my own company with my own team, I really push us to be the best and to work hard and to know that working hard will pay off. That sort of dedication comes from someone as crazy talented as Ms Beyonce Knowles Carter.

MUST SEE!!
Megan Thee Stallion – 'Body,' American Music Awards, 2020
Beyonce – Coachella Homecoming Concert 2019

Laurieann Gibson

Location: USA
Credits include:
<u>Music Video:</u>
Missy Elliott – *The Rain (Supa Dupa Fly)*
Brandy – *Afrodisiac, 2004*
Lady Gaga – *videos include Just Dance/Poker Face /Paparazzi/Bad Romance/Telephone/Alejandro/Born This Way*

Main Movers

Cassie – *Must Be Love*
Katy Perry – *California Gurls*
Tours & Concerts:
Lady Gaga, *The Monster Ball Tour: At Madison Square Garden, 2011 (Creative Director and Choreographer)*
Bad Boy, *The Reunion Tour, 2016 (Creative Director and Choreographer)*
Film:
Honey, *2003*

Laurieann Gibson is a Canadian choreographer who trained at Alvin Ailey American Dance Theatre before becoming Director of Choreography for Motown and Bad Boy records. The breadth of her choreographic work is extensive and much of her movement style comes from a merging of two worlds – the contemporary dance world, which Gibson experienced at Alvin Ailey, and the Hip-Hop world Gibson experienced working under Rosie Perez as a 'Fly Girl' on the TV show 'In Living Colour' in the mid-1990s. Her credits include dancing and choreographing for artists such as Mary J Blige, Sean 'Puff Daddy' Combs and many other artists on the Bad Boy Records roster.

Gaga

Gibson's remarkable creative body of work is notably showcased in her long-standing partnership with Lady Gaga, forming a juggernaut of a creative team. Gaga combined with Gibson to create some of the most memorable music video dance performances of the last 20 years. The 'Bad Romance' (2009) video is a creative showcase both for Gaga and Gibson. The video went a long way to defining Gaga as an artist, articulating her unique fashion, song writing and movement style. Gibson spoke to Billboard magazine about her creative process for creating the dance sections in the 'Bad Romance' video:

> I was with Gaga for quite some time to prior to "Bad Romance" as her choreographer and creative director. Her movement catalog was already designed — I actually had a diary of movements that we created through our collaboration. Finding how an artist moves is like finding their sound. I think that's why all of our videos were so well done: Her style of performing and her particular language of dance was her own. Her rhythm patterns are so offbeat and aggressive. The little movements, the timing — that was really developed prior to "Bad Romance," so when I heard it, I just elaborated on the style of movement that I had created for her from the beginning.... There is a base of choreography, and then I start to decorate it. I was obsessed with the twist and Chubby Checker, and I was obsessed with the tension that I heard in her voice and the machine aspect of the song, so I took that inspiration. When she takes those tiny steps at the beginning of the chorus and covers her mouth, she's doing a bourrée — that was her ballerina moment.

The choreography for Gaga's 'Born This Way' video and accompanying live performance at the Grammy's in 2011 highlight Gibson's broad and technically-based dance education as well as her Hip-Hop roots – the juxtaposition of both of these styles sit perfectly together in her choreography and deliver quintessential Commercial choreography at its best: *"More than any of my artists, I developed Gaga like a dancer. I don't know how you glissade, jeté and then pop your booty—but we're doing it."* Gibson was nominated for an Emmy for her direction of the HBO special "Lady Gaga Presents the Monster Ball Tour: At Madison Square Garden" (2011).

Main Movers

Honey

One of the most notable modern-era dance-based movies is 2003s 'Honey.' A box office burner that made a star of Jessica Alba and was one of the first (with 'Save the Last Dance') in a line of successful dance movies in the 2000s including the 'Step Up' series, 'Stomp the Yard' and 'You Got Served.' 'Honey' told the story of the struggles and successes of a young Hip-Hop choreographer played by Jessica Alba and was loosely based on the journey of Laurieann Gibson. She choreographed the movie and also plays the role of Honey's rival 'Katrina.' At the heart of the movie is a positive message about community and the importance of being a 'genuine person' in an industry in which it can be difficult to know who you can trust.

'Honey' arrived at a busy time for Commercial Dance. Big budget music videos featuring groups of dancers performing choreography (e.g., Justin Timberlake's, 'Rock Your Body' and Beyonce's 'Crazy in Love'), which included both street and technical dance elements were becoming prominent – the last dance sequence in the movie demonstrates Gibson's ability to unite both of these worlds. She commented to dance-teacher.com:

> Hip hop gave me freedom…(and) my training at Alvin Ailey and a combination of Horton, Dunham and Graham birthed my opinion as a choreographer. The core of everything I do is modern.

Gibson has also found success in a number of TV projects including MTV's 'Making the Band,' being a judge on 'So You Think You Can Dance' (US) and in her own documentary series 'Beyond the Spotlight' on Lifetime which shows the hunger Gibson instils into her dancers as they rehearse – in one episode urging them to be 'gladiatorial' as they enter the stage. Sean 'Puff Daddy' Combs pays tribute to Gibson's gladiatorial work ethic as the creative director on Coombs's 'Bad Boy Reunion Tour':

> When you go on a journey, sometimes you need to be led. In order to be able to accomplish stuff like this you need somebody to keep it in order. You need a general, you need

Image 7.6 Lauriann Gibson's work with Lady Gaga has provided notable on-screen Commercial Dance moments. A still from Gaga's 'Bad Romance' (2009) video

a strategist. When you're doing something like this, it can just turn into chaos. The way Laurieann has stepped up and kept us in order and on time – I don't think she's even slept in 2 weeks. Give it up for our fearless leader, Laurieann!

MUST SEE!!
Lady Gaga, *Born This Way, Live Grammy award performance, 2011*
'Laurie Ann Gibson: Beyond the Spotlight,' *TV series, Lifetime, 2018*

Marty Kudelka

Location: Los Angeles, USA
Credits include:
Music Video:
Justin Timberlake – *Like I Love You/Rock Your Body/Suit and Tie/Filthy*
Justin Timberlake – *My Love – 2007 MTV VMA Award winner for 'Best Choreography'*
Janet Jackson – *All For You*
JLS – *One Shot*
One Direction – *What Makes You Beautiful*
Tours:
Justin Timberlake – *Justified/Future Sex Love Sounds/20/20/Man of the Woods*
Films:
Trolls World Tour, *2020*

If Vincent Paterson was the renaissance dance artist of the 1980s (birthing a new era of on-screen dance) and Tina Landon was the colourful realist (providing choreography for prominent pop artists of the 1990s) then Marty Kudelka's understated style which rose to prominence in the early 2000s makes him the impressionist artist of Commercial Dance. Mainstream yet nuanced, his choreographic style reflects impressionism's simplicity of form and its small, detailed brush strokes are reflected in his choreography. Marty Kudelka has had a profound effect on the direction and fabric of Hip-Hop dance and consequently Commercial Dance from the mid-2000s to the present day. A connoisseur of interpreting musical instrumentation and rhythms into his choreography, Kudelka altered the trend from what had often previously been a cardio intensive technique with emphasis on athleticism, into a subtle form of dance that was closely interwoven with the cadence of the track being choreographed to.

Kudelka's movements are minimal and almost mimetic. Smooth, Fred Astaire-esque transitions and snapped Michael Jackson inspired silhouettes are mixed with the rough, confident swagger of the B-Boys of the early 1980s.

I worked with Marty while he choreographed for the band JLS. His choreography felt like an extension of his laid back and affable manner. His dancers learn his choreography via two main strands. Firstly, there is the movement, the mechanics of the steps, and secondly he guides them as they meld these movements with elements of the music production that they may not have noticed before – perhaps a hidden hi-hat or bass line, creating a line of movement punctuated with subtleties and nuances. It requires the dancer to be sharp and specific with their movement, yet expressive and free in their interpretation of the music, almost paradoxically. If the dancer pushes the physicality of the steps too much, the nuance is lost and if the dancer is too lax in their approach, the phrase can appear too vague. The dancers that Kudelka works with find a way to balance both aspects of his choreography, creating

Main Movers

dynamic, harmonic dance. Discussing his choreographic process in 2017 on the Lab Rats podcast, Kudelka explains:

> Way before I got here (Los Angeles), I created this style that people later saw with Janet and Pink.... I literally started studying and dissecting music...breaking apart songs, then I'll figure out a rhythm in my head of what I want to dance to.... I'll stand up, freestyle and create whatever comes out of my body.

New Style, Lyrical Hip-Hop – there are a number of names which emanated from the style of dance that Kudelka brought to the mainstream via his work with Janet Jackson, Jennifer Lopez and Pink. His most notable work has come from his 20-year creative partnership with Justin Timberlake, choreographing and co-directing the majority of Timberlake's prominent contributions to music video and live performance.

Like I Love You

From Los Angeles to London to Seoul, the ripple effect of Marty Kudelka's choreography, firstly from NSYNC's 2000 'Girlfriend' video, followed closely in 2001 by Justin Timberlake's era defining video for 'Like I Love You,' was extensive in the dance community. Through this video and the live stage performances which accompanied Timberlake's 'Justified' album promotion, a global wave of dancers and choreographers became influenced by this 'New Style' Hip-Hop choreography arriving from the West Coast of the US, many imitating Kudelka's musically inspired flow. Timberlake's ease with which he performs the choreography in this video added to the feeling that something new was happening in the world of Commercial Dance and people were taking notice.

This video appeared at the beginning of my career as a dancer and one of the feelings at the time was that Kudelka and Timberlake had cultivated a new, fun camaraderie in their

Image 7.7 Marty Kudelka choreographed and performed with Justin Timberlake at the Superbowl LII Halftime show (2018). Marty is the dancer furthest right in this photo

choreography which appealed to many up-and-coming dancers, it was confident and suave without appearing too brash or arrogant. In an interview with Time magazine in 2018, as they prepared for the Super Bowl LII Halftime Show, Timberlake succinctly described Kudelka's style: *"He has his own style of movement that complements the way that I like to move onstage. It's crisp without being showboat-y."*

MUST SEE!
   Justin Timberlake – 'My Love' music video, 2006
   Justin Timberlake – Super Bowl LII Halftime Show, 2018

Michael Rooney

Location: USA
Credits include:
Music Videos:
Gnarls Barkley – *Run*: (MTV Award winner for Best Choreography 2008)
Kylie Minogue – *'Can't Get You Outta My Head'*: (MTV Award winner for Best Choreography 2002)
Fatboy Slim – *'Weapon of Choice'*: (MTV Award winner for Best Choreography 2001)/*Praise You*: (MTV Award winner for Best Choreography 1999)/
Bjork – *It's Oh So Quiet:* (MTV Award winner for Best Choreography 1996)
Michael Jackson – *You Rock My World*
Film:
500 Days of Summer (2009)
Disney's The Muppets (2012)
Disney's The Jungle Book (2016)
TV and Tours:
Taylor Swift TV performances 2012
Kylie Minogue World Tours: *'Showgirl'*/*'Homecoming'*/*'X'*

"My style is very life orientated, very vibrant and alive. I like breathing life into steps."
Michael Rooney

Michael Rooney's body of work is vast. Over the last 30 years, he has made a choreographic imprint on every avenue of Commercial work – Music Video, Television, Film, Stage and Advertising. Rooney has won five MTV Video Music Awards for Best Choreography, his first in 1996 and the latest in 2008. He is the archetypal Commercial Dance choreographer, able to precisely realise the vision of the director and creative team, creating movement to fill their photographic aperture. Being the son of film star Mickey Rooney and with his first dance job in the TV series 'Fame!', he was on track from an early age to significantly contribute to the world of performing arts.

Style

Rooney's movement is often playful and comedic, as seen in the iconic Fatboy Slim video 'Weapon of Choice,' starring a mesmeric Christopher Walken. Directed by Spike Jonze and showcasing Walken in an unfamiliar dance-based role, Rooney played upon the star's early training as a Musical Theatre dancer and created a dance sequence with Walken which is perfectly tailored to the actor's dance ability and distinctive character traits. In some of his works, the choreographic style echoes the grand dance sequences of Busby Berkley, combined with an unmistakable current quirkiness. The dance sequence in the movie '500 Days of Summer' and Bjork's 'It's oh so Quiet' video have the whimsical feel of the work of Hollywood movies from the 1940s and 1950s, portraying a high street of ordinary people suddenly united in joyous song and dance, a theme also seen in his work on Disney's 'The Muppets' movie. The fabric of his choreography often consists of strong jazz work – triple pirouettes into long allegro lines require his dancers to be fast and technically sound. Contrasting projects, such as Usher's 'Pop ya Collar' (2000) video, show Rooney to be versatile and able to also communicate Hip-Hop styles effectively.

'Can't Get You Outta My Head'

A chameleon of styles, perhaps Rooney's most important work regarding shaping Commercial Dance's progression is his choreography for Kylie Minogue's 2001 world-wide pop smash 'Can't Get You Outta My Head,' which earned him an MTV Award for Best Choreography in 2002. A futuristic meta-masterpiece of pop which was a vehicle for Kylie Minogue to re-launch herself in the world of Pop music after a few years spent focusing on more indie inspired tracks. Electronic music acts such as Kraftwerk and Daft Punk are evidently inspirational creative references, both visually and musically. The male dancers in the video even wear a homage to Kraftwerk in the minimalist red shirt and black tie (taken from Kraftwerk's album cover for Man Machine).

Rooney created movement for this video which blended the natural allure of Minogue's flow with the robotic afflictions of her dancers. The movement is all at once fluid but jolting, sexual and yet agamic. The cyborg-ish elements of the choreography duplicate the sense of the robot characters from Daft Punk's seminal 'Around the World' video (the work of choreographer Blanca Li and directed by Michel Gondry – an essential watch). The angular Cyborg-ish steps interlaced with a smooth Egyptian style 'head-bop' are the perfect physical parallels for the hypnotic baseline of the song, the epitome of cool. In the closing dance section of the video, the question and answer freestyle play between the male and female dancers is punctuated with statuesque hand flashes, highlighting the battle between indulgence vs restraint that runs throughout the choreography.

Image 7.8 Rooney won the MTV Award for Best Choreography in 2002 for Kylie Minogue's 'Can't Get You Outta My Head' clip

The video elevated a relatively successful pop artist to the revered position of a modernistic disco idol and it wasn't just the music and styling that did that. The power and confidence that Minogue exuded through her command of Rooney's choreographic direction was a large part of its success. The video was a powerful marketing tool for Kylie Minogue and also an artistic dance creation from Rooney of the highest level, encouraging Commercial Dance into an artistic realm not ruled solely by the 'bubblegum-pop' dance steps seen in many videos of the early 2000s.

MUST SEE!
Kylie Minogue, Can't Get You Outta my Head, Music Video, 2001
500 Days of Summer, Film, 2009

Nadine 'Hi-Hat' Ruffin

Location: USA
Credits include:
Music Video:
Missy Elliot *"Gossip Folks"/"One Minute Man"/"Work It"/"We Run This"/"Lose Control"/"Get UR Freak On"*
Coldplay *"Princess of China"*
Willow *"Whip My Hair"*
Rihanna *"Diamonds"/"Where Have You Been" (MTV "Best Choreography" 2012 VMA award nominee)*
Tours:
Mary J. Blige/Nas *"Royalty" Tour (Creative Director & Choreographer)*
Rihanna *"Anti World Tour" (Creative Director & Choreographer)*
Television & Live Shows:
The Voice (USA) – *All Seasons (Producer/Choreographer/Performer)*

Polymath

Nadine 'Hi-Hat' Ruffin is a creative that has worked with the biggest names in the music industry, Hi-Hat has hop-scotched from music video, to film to television seamlessly. A choreographer and creative director who appears to have created her signature style by absorbing and observing cultural textures and reflecting them back in her work, Hi-Hat's body of work is expansive. Her projects diverge from music videos including Shakira's 'Waka Waka (This Time For Africa)' and Rihanna's energised 'Where Have You Been' (an MTV 'Best Choreography' VMA 2012 award nominee) to the movie box office smashes of 'Step Up 2' and Justin Bieber's docu-feature 'Never Say Never.'

Missy Elliot

Hi-Hat's work on the highly influential videos with Missy Elliot in the 2000s has been particularly impactful. Partnering with music video director maestro Dave Meyers, these videos are visually striking, subversive and choreographically raw. Missy's ingenuity, playfulness and authenticity as an artist were perfectly channelled to the screen by the choreographer. An ability to make whichever artist she is working with look comfortable performing the dance steps and the song simultaneously is a consistent theme throughout Hi-Hat's portfolio

Main Movers

Image 7.9 Rihanna's music video for 'Where Have You Been' (2012) was choreographed by Nadine 'Hi-Hat' Ruffin

(see Rihanna's 'Where Have You Been' video). Choreographically, her work is charged with Hip-Hop influences and ranges from groove orientated steps to Breakin' and Lindy-Hop (see Missy Elliot's 'Lose Control' video). Hi-Hat's collaboration with Mary J Blige at the BET awards is covered as an Iconic Moment in this book.

Giving advice to young aspiring dancers for 'Dance Informa' magazine, Hi-Hat's passion and commitment to her craft is obvious:

> You can't hop on the band wagon. You have to be passionate and you have to love what you're doing. You can't just say you want to do this because it's the thing and you'll be in the limelight. You have to have the passion, and once you have the passion for it, you're not going to give up. For me, my passion is dance, choreography and creative directing. If I don't dream about my job, then it's not worth having.

MUST SEE!!
   Missy Elliot – 'Lose Control' music video, 2005
   Rihanna – 'Where Have You Been?' music video, 2012

Paul Roberts

Location: London, UK
Credits include:
Live Performance/Tours:
The Spice Girls – *'Spiceworld' Stadium Tour, 2019, Choreographer and Stage Director*
Sam Smith – *'The Thrill Of It All,' World Tour 2018, Choreographer and Stage Director*
One Direction – *'Up All Night Tour' (2011–2012)/'Take Me Home Tour' (2013)/'Where We Are Tour' (2014)/'On the Road Again Tour' (2015)*
Olly Murs – *'Kiss Me,' Live performance, X-Factor UK, 2015*
Robbie Williams – *'Take the Crown' Stadium Tour, 2012*
Music Video:
Harry Styles – *'Treat People With Kindness' (MTV VMA Winner 'Best Choreography'), 2021*
Katy Perry – *'Unconditionally,' 2013*
Paul McCartney – *'Ever Present Past,' 2007*

Pop-Art

Paul Roberts is a choreographer who has carefully blended high-art and high-street popular culture, creating some of the UK's most aesthetically interesting live performances of the last 20 years. From his early work on music videos for pop artists such as Billie Piper and All Saints, his live performance work with Diana Ross through to being an artistic associate with the award-winning Balletboyz dance company, Roberts' work has always strived to engage the audience through grounded angular lines combined with a powerful group execution from his team of unified dancers. His movement is often physically challenging, involving dynamic multi-levelled work and compact spirals of the torso finished with a suave Gene Kelly-esque varnish.

Finding his dance tonality through studying contemporary and classical dance whilst growing up in Lincolnshire, UK (before training at Urdang Academy in London), Roberts later formulated his style by blending his own distinctive movement with the feel of the steps seen in the inspirational US Hip-Hop music videos directed by Hype Williams and Dave Meyers in the 1990s. The result is a choreographer who can find the appropriate context of movement for the creative brief he is handed. This is evident in the vast variety of music artists Roberts has created dance for and the wide spectrum of dance styles in his portfolio – ranging from evocations of Fred and Ginger (Harry Style's 'Treat People with Kindness') to Twyla Tharp inspired motion (Balletboyz 'Alpha').

It's a Team Sport

A noticeable aspect of Paul Roberts' work is the uniformity and commitment he inspires from his dancers. Although choreographers working at a professional level generally have a group of highly skilled dancers at their fingers tips, in Roberts' performances his company of dancers clearly share the same high-performance values in a similar way to how a team of athletes would. My own experiences working as a dancer for Roberts reflect exactly this – he creates an environment in which dancers push themselves to execute the choreography as best as they could for the sake of the team. This healthy competition creates a band of highly motivated performers working together as a company. He defines the types of dancers he likes to work with:

> Even if you are going from dancer to choreographer to producer to director, whatever it is that you doing, you still have to have that desire to want to lift the cup at the end. So when you bring in your team of players, you want them to have the same desire that you have and if they don't, then you don't use them again. You bring in these people that make your team or your squad the best, the strongest and the most brilliant unit it can be…as a choreographer you're only as good as your as your team of players. Yes, you're looking for ability, facility, style and panache and all of that but you want a burning desire behind the eyes and that fight as well.

Treat People with Kindness

In 2021, Roberts' was acknowledged internationally for his work on Harry Styles' uplifting video clip accompanying his track 'Treat People with Kindness' by being awarded the MTV VMA for Best Choreography (and also became the first British person to win the award). The video showcases Roberts' dance work via a 1960s inspired musical theme, uniting smooth dance steps with a playful nature. Robert's choreography and his dancers suave performance

Image 7.10 A still from Harry Styles' 2021 video for 'Treat People With Kindness' for which Paul Roberts won the award for 'Best Choreography' at the annual MTV Awards

provide the perfect foil for Harry Style's confident charisma as he partners the actor Phoebe Waller-Bridge in a memorable finale.

MUST SEE!!
Harry Styles – 'Treat People With Kindness' music video, 2021
Ballet Boyz – 'Alpha' (part of 'The Talent' programme), 2010
Duffy – 'Rain on my Parade,' The Royal Variety Performance 2008

Paula Abdul

Location: Los Angeles, USA
Credits include:
Music Video:
Janet Jackson – *Nasty/What Have You Done For Me Lately/Control/When I Think of You, 1986, Choreographer*
Paula Abdul – *Straight Up, 1989/Opposites Attract, 1991, Choreographer*
Tours & Live Shows:
The Jacksons – *Victory Tour, Choreographer, 1984*

Choreographer

Paula Abdul was a significant contributor to the development of choreography in music video in the 1980s, making her one of the most influential creatives in the evolution of Commercial Dance. Also known today as a TV presenter and judge on Saturday night television mainstays such as 'American Idol,' 'So You Think You Can Dance' and 'X-Factor,' Abdul's work in the late 1980s and 1990s was choreographically very significant.

Beginning her career as an LA Lakers dancer and choreographer, she was scouted and recruited as Janet Jackson's personal dance coach and choreographer, when Jackson was just embarking on her adult music career. Abdul was rewarded with two nominations for the MTV Music award for 'Best Choreography in a Music Video' in 1987 for her work on Jackson's 'What Have You Done For Me Lately' and 'Nasty,' winning the award for the latter. Janet Jackson has been acknowledged in this book as one of the pioneers of Commercial

Dance and it was Abdul who initially coached Jackson, giving her the dance tools and stage craft to re-launch herself as a reputable female artist and step out of the long shadow cast by her older, famous siblings. Abdul's choreography complemented Jackson's strengths perfectly – strong, technical Jazz foundations interlaced with the singer's natural ability to absorb and perform 'street' styles of the time. Abdul told Rolling Stone magazine in 2014 that:

> I'm very grateful, because this was really the big start to my career. When I was introduced to Janet, I was told by A&M Records that Control was going to be an important album for her, and when I started hearing demos, I was really, really excited to work with her. I felt like I had a chance here to really create something big for her.

Performing Artist

Attracting attention for her progressive choreography with Janet, Abdul pursued her own successful solo career in which she released a number of Billboard Top 100 hits. 'Straight Up' was her first solo success and the video is a dance onslaught introduced by Abdul hoofing through a 20-second tap solo followed by four pirouettes into a knee slam. She wasn't messing around. She was a serious dance creative who was directing, very clearly, the direction in which dance in music video in the 1990s would be headed. Abdul performed this track on 2018 on James Corden's 'The Late Late Show' – this performance highlights what a cornerstone video it was – much of the same choreography and styling from the original video was incorporated and the performance feels as crisp and relevant in 2018 as it did in 1989.

Leading the Pack

In 1990, Abdul opened the 17th Annual American Music Awards, fronting and choreographing a 10-minute dance spectacle which earned her an Emmy nomination for 'Outstanding Choreography.' Leading a pack of 16 male dancers, this piece is an essential watch to see the true technical abilities of the dancers she was working with and the demanding choreography Abdul was asking of them. They demonstrate the technical dexterity of classical ballet dancers (triple pirouettes and a double tour en l'air was not an issue for these guys) combined with the corporal articulation of early Hip-Hop dancers of the time, snapping to the sharp snare of Abduls' pop track 'The Way That You Love Me.' This live performance and the accompanying video raised the bench mark further for other pop music acts over the next 10 years, a bench mark she had previously helped Janet Jackson set a few years earlier with her choreographic work in Jackson's earlier videos.

In 1991s inventive 'Opposites Attract' video, whilst dancing with a cartoon cat (MC Skat Kat), Paula playfully throws down elements of top-rocking and Hip-Hop styles alongside her trademark technical Jazz work – again affirming herself as a main player in cross-referencing street styles with Jazz, which developed Commercial Dance choreography rapidly in the early 1990s. Abdul has maintained close ties to Commercial Dance and has regularly appeared as a judge on American TV show's 'So You Think You Can Dance,' 'Live To Dance' and 'Dancing With the Stars.'

MUST SEE!!
   Straight Up, *Music Video, 1989*
   The 17th Annual American Music Awards opening performance, *1990*

Main Movers

Image 7.11 Paula Abdul's 'Straight Up' video (1988) remains a visually striking music video. Abdul's use of a variety of dance styles was impactful on the direction of Commercial Dance in the late 1980s early 1990s

Rich + Tone Talauega

Location: Los Angeles, USA
Credits include:
Tours & Live Shows:
Michael Jackson the Musical – *MJ movement choreography, Neil Simon Theatre, Broadway New York, 2022*
Madonna – *Reinvention Tour 2004/Confessions World Tour 2006/Madonna Promo Tour 2008/Sticky & Sweet Tour 2009/MDNA Tour 2012*
Cirque du Soleil – *Michael Jackson Immortal World Tour/Michael Jackson ONE*
Chris Brown – *F.A.M.E. US Tour 2011*
The Spice Girls – *Reunion Tour 2007*
Jennifer Lopez – *Brave Tour 2007/Seven Wonders of the World 2007*
Music Video:
Jennifer Lopez – *Get Right/Do It Well*
Chris Brown – *Kiss Kiss/She Ain't You/Yeah 3x*
Michael Jackson – *Rock My World*
Madonna – *Celebration/4 Minutes/Sorry*
Black Eyed Peas – *Pump It*

> We'll call it the groove. The groove is in everybody. It's just as simple as tapping of the feet or bobbing of the head. We'll go to the extent of finding that groove -- and finding what makes the body, in a rhythmic way, feel good.
>
> Tone Talauega

Rich + Tone Talauega hail from Richmond, California, USA. If you've seen any music videos over the past two decades, then you will have seen at least one video that the brothers have either appeared in as dancers, choreographed or directed. They have been (and continue to be) iconic contributors to Commercial Dance both on camera and off. Beginning their career as dancers whilst high school age, they garnered attention on screen with their unique movement style and character. Discovered whilst freestyling at a record release party by long time Michael Jackson collaborators LaVelle Smith Jnr and Travis Payne, Rich + Tone's off-the-wall ability to deliver slick, groove orientated steps fast tracked them into the front line of cutting-edge music videos and live performances. Firstly, with Shanice in 1994, then as dancers on Michael Jackson's 1996 History world tour, through to their memorable appearance in the Dave Meyers directed Missy Elliot video for 'One Minute Man' (choreographed by Hi-Hat in 2001), the brothers have vast performance experience from a young age. Tone Talauega reflects that:

> We were those kids in the early 90s – part of that golden age of hip-hop where it was about the freestyle. My brother and I were born and raised on street-dance and all that stuff – there's a code in street-dance which is about originality and coming up with your own stuff, your own vocabulary and your own style….

Rich adds that: *"Our style is a very specific style and it deals with one foot in the street and one foot in the technical world…"*

The brother's natural progression into movement creation was inevitable. Working with Jennifer Lopez in 2005 on the choreographically iconic music video for 'Get Right' earned them the first of many MTV Video Music Award nominations for Best Choreography. Creating for Chris Brown on a number of videos and live performances, including his 2009 'Wall to Wall' video (in which they can also be seen dancing next to Brown), has been a constant in their career. Inflections of Rich + Tone's influence are interwoven with much of Brown's work – swift, House inspired footwork and movement that glides in tandem with the rhythms of the music are some of Rich + Tone's signatory choreographic motifs.

Working with the Greats

The brothers have choreographed five of Madonna's world tours and her 2012 Super Bowl performance. Completing their choreographic carousel of coaching industry leading artists (which also includes Usher, Mariah Carey and Katy Perry), the brothers provided some of the steps for Michael Jackson's Ghost video (co-choreographers, 1997) and one of his last music video performances in the clip for 'Rock My World' (2001), putting together a combo that referenced Jackson's signature steps combined with some rougher movements from the early 2000s era. In 2022, MJ the Musical opened at the Neil Simon Theatre on Broadway, New York, a project that the brothers had been working on for a while as it was subject to delays due to the COVID-19 pandemic. The stage show highlights the sibling's ability to truly embody Jackson's fundamental movement style. Much of their creative direction abilities have been channelled into projects such as Madonna's MDNA world tour (co-directors), Miley Cyrus's 'Bangerz Tour' and four tours as creative directors for The Backstreet Boys.

Rich explained how their consistent work with established performers has enabled them to adjust to what is required of them according to that artist's particular skill set:

> Working as long as we have in the business, you have an eye and your sixth sense comes into play when you meet people. Automatically you'll know who's a star and who's not. I think some people are great because they practice and they work hard at their craft and other people are just born with it. Chris Brown was born with it.

Main Movers

Image 7.12 Rich + Tone dancing either side of Chris Brown in the video they choreographed for Wall to Wall (2007)

He has natural raw talent – something that you cannot teach, something that the only thing you can do with that is coach. Madonna is amazing because she works harder than everybody else. Having been there for five tours and the Super Bowl show, she is the ultimate when it comes to hard work, dedication and focus. How she puts it all together and delivers it – she stands alone.

MUST SEE!!
Chris Brown – 'I Can Transform Ya'/ 'Wall to Wall' music videos
Jennifer Lopez – 'Get Right' music video
Madonna – MDNA Tour 2012

Tina Landon

Location: USA
Credits include:
<u>Music Video:</u>
Rihanna – *Umbrella /Disturbia/Don't Stop the Music/Rehab*
Janet Jackson – *If/Runaway/Together Again /I Get Lonely/That's The Way Love Goes*
Ricky Martin – *Livin' the Vida Loca*: MTV Award Winner – Best Dance Video
Michael and Janet Jackson – *Scream*: MTV Award Winner – Best Choreography (with LaVelle Smith Jr., Travis Payne and Sean Cheesman)
Christina Aguilera ft Pink, May, Lil Kim – *Lady Marmalade*
Jennifer Lopez – *Waiting For Tonight/If You Had My Love*
Britney Spears – *Opps!...I Did It Again*
<u>Tours:</u>
Rihanna – *Good Girl Gone Bad Live!/Last Girl on Earth Tour*
Janet Jackson – *The Velvet Rope Tour*
Jennifer Lopez – *Jennifer Lopez in Concert*

Main Movers

2000's Dominance

Tina Landon was at the epicentre of Commercial Dance's accelerated development in the mid-1990s–mid-2000s. Many of the ultra-recognisable dance routines performed by Britney Spears, Rhianna, Jennifer Lopez, Christina Aguilera, Janet Jackson, Ricky Martin and Shakira are the works of this celebrated dancer turned choreographer. She was also involved in some of the most notorious on screen moments in dance history – providing the choreography for Ricky Martin's internationally recognisable 'Livin La Vida Loca' video and also co-choreographing the only on-screen collaboration between Janet and Michael Jackson in their 1995 'Scream' video (which gained her an MTV Video Music Award for Best Choreography long with Travis Payne, Sean Cheeseman and Lavelle Smith Jr.). Landon's choreography is characterised by its high energy, aerobic and technical base with a seamless integration of House and Hip-Hop styles.

Iconic dance dominated videos such as Janet Jackson's 'Together Again' (1997), Christina Aguilera's 'Come On Over (All I Want Is You)' (2000) and Britney Spears' 'Opps!...I Did It Again' (2000) beamed Landon's choreography into the living rooms of millions worldwide as music videos benefitted not only from an increasingly accessible MTV channel, but also the gradual emergence of online music video sharing platforms such as YouTube and Myspace in the early 2000s. Landon's dance style complemented the musical trends of this era well. Songs such as 'Together Again,' which were arranged over a prominent house beat, providing a base for Landon's natural style of choreography, which often brought together House and Hip-Hop steps with sharper Jazz lines favoured by Jackson in her earlier work. Landon's style of choreography underpinned much of the movement vocabulary for Commercial Dance in the 2000s. Landon described the style of dance she created in an interview with the music magazine show The Loop:

> I think my style is a culmination of athleticism and sensuality. There's actually a really great part in Jennifer Lopez's first video 'If You Had My Love' where we did three completely different sections – one was House, one was Hip-Hop and one was Latin, so it kind of encompasses everything.

The Velvet Rope Tour

Landon's long standing creative partnership with Janet Jackson was formed in the 1990s. Jackson's Velvet Rope Tour and subsequent 'Live at Madison Garden' TV special was recorded in 1998 and featured Landon as a choreographer and dancer along with a talented set of dancers on the Los Angeles scene at the time such as Shawnette Heard, Kelly Konno and Gil Duldulao. It was a very influential piece of work for dancers and choreographers worldwide in part due to its availability on VHS/DVD and also its high production value, which included many theatrical costume and set changes. Rolling Stone magazine illustrated the size of the production in their review of The Velvet Rope tour in 1998, *"Pacing the big event at breakneck speed, the tireless Jackson crammed twenty-six hits, twenty-plus dance numbers, nine costume changes…into two-and-a-half hours of sheer summer-entertainment bliss."*

Choreographically, the concert was highly intensive with much focus throughout the show on the dancers' own stylistic individualities. Dance-only numbers such as *'Throb'* were featured including a section where each dancer was introduced by name, something that has since become a staple of nearly every music concert featuring dancers. Landon's role as a dancer and choreographer really pushed dancers from being seen as 'back-up' dancers to 'supporting dancers,' allowing them to play an integral role in the production.

Main Movers

> **Image 7.13** A long-term collaborator with Janet Jackson, Landon choreographed and danced in the video for 'Together Again' (1997). Landon can be seen to the left of Janet

Influence

The continued influence of Tina Landon's work can be seen heavily in the 2000s when mainstay Pop and R&B artists of the era, such as Jennifer Lopez and Rihanna, worked with Landon to create their live shows and music videos, each having been influenced by her iconic earlier work on projects such as the Velvet Rope Tour in the mid-1990s. Many of the music videos which Landon helped to create in the 1990s and 2000s are seminal works in terms of Commercial Dance and are still referenced today by some Pop and R&B artists. Whilst presenting Landon with an 'Achievement in Choreography' award at the ALMA Awards in 2000, Jennifer Lopez celebrated the choreographer's achievements in her introductory speech:

> Up until now Tina Landon was one of Hollywoods best kept secrets. In the past 10 years she has choreographed numbers for many top artists… and in the process her tight provocative moves have become the standard for popular dance choreography everywhere.

MUST SEE!
  Rihanna – 'Umbrella' Music Video, 2007
  Janet Jackson – The Velvet Rope Tour, 1998

Toni Basil

Location: Los Angeles, USA
Dance credits include:
Film:
Viva Las Vegas *(1964), featured dancer*
Head *(1968) – Daddy's Song, Dancer & Choreographer*
Once Upon a Time in America *(2019), Choreographer*
Music Video:
Talking Heads – *'Once in a Lifetime' (1980), Choreographer and Co-director*
Tours:
David Bowie – *'Glass Spider Tour' (1987), Choreographer*

Main Movers

Better Midler – *'The Showgirl Must Go On' (2008), Choreographer*
Tina Turner – *Tina! 50th Anniversary (2009), Choreographer*

A multi-faceted performing artist, Toni Basil's dance and choreography CV is exhaustive. She has over six decades of dance experience, from working as a dancer with Elvis Presley in a number of films including 'Viva Las Vegas' to appearing with Frank Sinatra in 'Robin and the Seven Hoods' and more recently as the choreographer for Quentin Tarantino's 2019 movie 'Once Upon a Time In Hollywood.' As a founding member of 'The Lockers' in the 1970s, she affected the journey of Commercial Dance greatly. Basil actively brought Locking (and other 'Street' styles) into the commercial sphere using her platform as a regular on mainstream TV as a dancer and successful recording artist – scoring an international hit with 'Hey Mickey' in 1981. From a choreographic perspective, working with innovatory artists such as Talking Heads, David Bowie and Tina Turner have put Basil front and centre in terms of the iconic movement makers of the last 40 years. The videos available on YouTube of her freestyling House at the age of 74 are remarkable and an inspiration to watch.

From Street to Elite

Toni Basil demonstrated a creative foresight only few possessed at a time in the 1980s when dance genres still stayed very much in their own lane, maintaining exclusivity from each other. As a choreographer, her works for the Smothers Brothers TV Specials on CBS in 1987 illustrates her highly tuned artistic vision, one of the performances is set in a Royal French court, with dancers dressed in clothing associated with the elaborate fashions of the 18th century. With Beethoven's 5th Symphony as the music, Basil and her team of dancers showcase various new 'street styles' of the time. Spotlighting the Boogaloo and Popping prowess of Bruno 'Pop n Taco' Falcon, it was revolutionary to see such a juxtaposition of cultural genres nestled together like this when most dance styles were detached from one another. Another avant-garde interpretation on the same TV show was set to Tchaikovsky's original 'Swan Lake' score, it matched Lockers with classical Ballet dancers, showing a willingness to bring together dance genres considered to be at the opposite ends of the social spectrum – from street to elite. Basil's creative daring was awarded with an Emmy nomination for this particular piece. The fact that these creations were transmitted on CBS, a mainstream television channel in the US, further highlights its impact on the mass American audiences of the 1980s.

The Zeitgeist of Multiple Eras

Through the music videos and performances Basil made during her solo musical career, it's clear how she fearlessly delivers numerous different dance styles which were becoming amalgamated into singular choreographic numbers. In her TV performances of 'Hey Mickey' (1982) 'You Gotta Problem' (1982) and 'Street Life' in (1987), fouetté and chaîné turns often appear next to elements of Locking and New Jack Swing, whilst sharp cheerleader-esque armography compliments the dancers Popping references. Although the genres within the choreography were not yet 'blended' as such (as we see in Commercial Dance today), Basil gave global audiences an early peek at the raw street styles coming from the west coast of America and also showed how seamlessly a professional dancer needs to be able to glide from one style to another. In many ways she could be seen as a prototypical Commercial Dance specialist at a time when the premise of a Commercial Dancer did not really exist. Basil raised expectations regarding the level of versatility working dancers would need over the next few decades. Her authenticity, which is tangible after her decades of working at the top, has kept her on the A-list of Hollywood choreographers. Quentin Tarantino explains why he felt Toni Basil was the only choice for choreographer on his movie 'Once Upon a Time in America':

> She was the goddess of Go-Go, one of the great dancers and choreographers of her time. A terrific zeitgesit-y actress…. In the Monkees movie 'Head', her and Davy Jones do one of the greatest dance numbers in the history of movies. They were magnificent together. She knew this world (the 1960s) perfectly.

MUST SEE!!
Hey Mickey! *Music Video, 1981*
Beethoven's Fifth, *Television performance on the Smothers Brothers Special, CBS, 1987*

Vincent Paterson

Location: USA
Credits include:
Music Videos:
Michael Jackson – *Smooth Criminal/Blood on the Dance Floor/The Way You Make Me Feel/Black or White, Choreographer*
Madonna – *Vogue/Express Yourself/Buenos Aires, Choreographer*
Live Concerts:
Michael Jackson – *Bad Tour, 1987, Director & Choreographer/Super Bowl XXVII Performance 1993, Director & Choreographer*
Madonna – *Blonde Ambition Tour, 1990, Co-Director & Choreographer*
Cirque du Soleil – *Viva! Elvis, 2010, Director & Choreographer*

In the midst of a long and varied career which includes significant work in theatre, opera and music video, Vincent Paterson provided direction and choreography for two supreme pop artists at the height of their popularity during a time in the mid-1980s and early 1990s when creatively, Michael Jackson and Madonna were almost without equals. At this time, they not only dominated the radio airwaves and set fashion trends almost weekly but with Paterson's help, they also changed dance and kickstarted the Commercial Dance industry. This era was such a fertile time for dance on screen (the likes of Paula Abdul, Toni Basil and Prince were also creating significant dance material at this time) that Paterson can be considered as one of the first to organically formulate common ideas about what Commercial Dance is. Paterson's directional eye and choreographic dexterity helped these two artists to change the public's perception of dance in the realm of pop music. He used elements typically seen in dramatic theatre work such as opera or ballet and combined them with the freshness and street styled vitality that both of these artists possessed at that time. Paterson developed choreography which allowed room for street flavours, but also kept a tight, crisp texture using the movement from the Jazz styles he trained in.

Late Starter, Fast Learner

Paterson started his dance training relatively late at 24 years old in his hometown near Philadelphia. Having originally studied as an actor and director, he moved to LA at 27 to pursue dance. He worked closely with Michael Peters, assisting him and workshopping together as Peter's slowly established himself as the 'go-to' choreographer of that time. Paterson played the role of lead gang member in Michael Jackson's 'Beat It' video in 1983 and also danced in the 'Thriller' short film, both choreographed by Michael Peters. In an interview with Kristyn Burtt on her podcast show 'Popcorn Talks,' Paterson talks about what a rich and exciting time the early 1980s were for dancers, particularly male dancers, due to the introduction of MTV and the work of artists like Michael Jackson and Madonna:

> …Once Michael and Madonna started to make these incredible videos, very artist knew they needed to have a music video…. MTV was this phenomenal station where you could turn on and watch your favourite artist all day long, all night long, doing what they did best! As a dancer and choreographer it was exciting because dance was really not that prevalent before MTV came back around…. MTV brought dance back, to the States and to the world.
>
> What Michael Jackson did with his videos is he brought men into the dance world in a whole different way…. Michael brought in street dancers and all kinds of dancers and all physicality of dancers. People realised they could get involved and men realised that they could dance, they didn't have to hide in the shadows, straight or gay. They could dance and have dreams and aspirations about dancing – being in a music video or a film.

Smooth Criminal

Arguably one of the greatest pieces of choreography ever committed to film, Smooth Criminal is a masterstroke on many levels. Choreographically Paterson created a body of work with so many influences – from Fred Astaire's coolness in 'The Band Wagon,' to the Jazz dance vocabulary seen in musicals like Guys and Dolls and the Popping elements introduced to Jackson and Paterson by Jeffrey Daniel and Bruno 'Pop n Taco' Falcon. Every set up in Smooth Criminal is expertly sequenced, giving the piece pace and taking the audience on a journey with Jackson as we follow him around the 1930s night club in which it is set. Paterson's work with the supporting dancers, around the tables and various other set ups, are stylistically notable with angular, almost cartoonish movements giving a surreal 'Who Framed Roger Rabbit' feel to the 10 minute clip. The 'anti-gravity lean' and the epically choreographed finale also helped to make this video a seminal work for both Jackson and Paterson.

Blonde Ambition and Vogue

Madonna's Blonde Ambition tour drew the template from which live music concerts have been built from over the last 30 years. Along with the 'Vogue' music video, it also broke ground for the LGBTQ+ community both inside and outside of the world of dance, providing a voice and clear representation on screen for these groups which at the time were very much sequestered from society. Paterson played a key role in both of these culturally crucial projects. The Blonde Ambition Tour is discussed further in the 'Live & Televised Events' chapter.

This period from the mid-1980s to the mid-1990s was a vastly significant era in the development of dance on screen and on stage. The works that were created and performed at this time are foundational stones in the world of Commercial Dance industry, stones that Paterson helped to lay.

MUST SEE!!
  Michael Jackson – 'Smooth Criminal' music video, 1988
  Madonna – 'Vogue' music video, 1990

References

Brian Friedman

www.dance-teacher.com/5-surprising-things-choreographer-brian-friedman-shares-about-himself/ [accessed: 08/09/2021].

Charm La'Donna

www.consequence.net/2022/03/dua-lipa-tour-2022-nyc-recap/2/ [accessed: 22/08/2022].
www.forbes.com/sites/ashleylyle/2019/05/30/choreographer-to-the-stars-charm-la-donna-talks-about-journey-to-the-top/?sh=6b118de84df9 [accessed: 19/08/2022].

Christopher Scott

https://www.backstage.com/magazine/article/in-the-heights-movie-choreography-73467/
https://www.dancemagazine.com/christopher-scott-2596435273.html

Fatima

https://www.huffpost.com/entry/fatima-robinson-talks-sty_n_1022247

Frank Gatson

https://thatgrapejuice.net/2010/12/grape-juice-interviews-frank-gatson/

Jamie King

www.variety.com/2011/music/news/channeling-mtv-devotion-into-a-career-1118039763/ [accessed: 12/09/2021].

JaQuel Knight

https://www.billboard.com/articles/business/9477613/jaquel-knight-beyonce-megan-thee-stallion-billboard-cover-story-interview-2020/
https://www.billboard.com/articles/columns/pop/8467159/beyonce-single-ladies-put-a-ring-on-it-oral-history/
https://www.nytimes.com/2018/05/02/arts/dance/beyonce-coachella-choreographers-chris-grant-jaquel-knight.html

Laurie Ann Gibson

https://dance-teacher.com/technique-laurieann-gibson/
Speaking about to Nolan Feeney about Gaga's movement – https://www.billboard.com/music/pop/music-videos-choreography-iconic-pop-dance-routines-8467302/ [accessed: 10/08/2022].

Main Movers

Marty Kudelka

https://time.com/5118876/justin-timberlake-halftime-prep/
'Lab Rats Culture' Ep 8 Podcast – Stephen 'twitch' Boss

Michael Rooney

www.theguardian.com/stage/2005/oct/17/theatre [accessed: 20/08/2022].

Hi-Hat

https://www.danceinforma.com/2010/12/01/tip-your-hat-for-hi-hat/

Paula Abdul

www.rollingstone.com/music/music-news/paula-abduls-favorite-choreography-moments-of-her-career-188247/ [accessed: 09/07/2022].
Jet Magazine, Vol 78, No. 4. 07.05.1990.

Rich +Tone

https://www.wnycstudios.org/podcasts/soundcheck/segments/291896-ancient-futuristic-and-timeless-choreographers-rich-tone-talauega

Tina Landon

https://www.rollingstone.com/music/music-news/live-report-janet-jackson-94514/
https://www.youtube.com/watch?v=1HpaISOYlJc

Vincent Paterson

www.youtube.com/watch?v=nVBQPi80w2Q [accessed: 13/07/2022].

Chapter 8

Talking Points

The following pieces explore some of the many conversation points pertaining to social and cultural issues which are prevalent throughout the Commercial Dance industry.

8a. Copyright and Commercial Dance

When does a homage become a rip-off? Are there occasions when the phrase 'inspired by' actually means 'stolen from'? These are complicated questions in the arts. Every artist borrows. We are all intrinsically influenced by a particular artist, style or movement, and inevitably the essence of our artistic idols is evident in our work. It is difficult to know when we cross the line from respectful laudation to outright copying. Copyrighting choreography has been a consistently grey area in the world of dance. Recently in the Commercial Dance industry, there has been a cohesive attempt to make this area of law clearer in the US and the UK with creatives like JaQuel Knight pushing through legislative protections for choreographers. As Knight says: "Just as music has to be cleared and paid before use, it should be the same for choreography, right?"

Copyrighting the 'Feeling'

In 2018, after a five-year legal contest, singer Robin Thicke and producer Pharrell Williams were ordered to pay $5.3 million to Marvin Gaye's estate for copyright infringement after their song 'Blurred Lines' was ruled to sound too similar to Gaye's 1977 'Got to Give it Up.' Interestingly, William's later explained that during the recording process "we try to figure out if we can build a building that doesn't look the same, but makes you *feel* the same way." The music producer Rick Rubin commented after the case that this ruling set a dangerous precedent for artist's everywhere as "the *feeling* (of the song) is not something that you can copyright."

This sentiment of not being able to 'copyright the feeling,' or essence of a piece of artistic work, is transferable to dance and choreography....

DOI: 10.4324/9781003109884-8

Talking Points

Jackson, Fosse and Astaire and Learning from the Masters

It's commonly known that Michael Jackson, one of the pioneers of dance in music video and in the live commercial arena was influenced heavily by many dance greats such as Fred Astaire, James Brown, Jackie Wilson, Sammy Davis Jr, Jerome Robbins and Bob Fosse. Take a moment to compare Bob Fosse's snake solo in the movie The Little Prince (1974) to Jackson's first performance of Billie Jean at the Motown 25 celebration show in 1983. The fedora hat, sleek angular posed lines, hip isolations and finger snaps are all heavy nods to Fosse. The Moonwalk (made famous by Jackson in this same Motown 25 performance) was a street move known as the 'back-slide' for many years before it was taught to Jackson by Jeffrey Daniel and before Daniel it was performed by the exquisite tap dancer Bill Bailey in the 1943 movie 'Cabin in the Sky.' Jackson's 'Smooth Criminal' long-form video (1988) is stylistically influenced by a Michael Kidd choreographed scene in Fred Astaire's 1953 movie 'The Bandwagon.' The cream and blue suit, some of the angular dance lines and the 'feel' of the opening sequence are certainly inspired by this film.

Did Jackson rip-off Fosse's movement style, steal the back slide from Bill Bailey and unfairly assume Astaire's cream and blue suit? Did he breach copyright or plagiarise others' work? No, I think it would be cynical and unjust to suggest that this artistic 'borrowing' by Jackson from Fosse, Bailey and Astaire was anything more than an homage to the movers who inspired him and helped to make him the iconic dancer that he was. What makes 'Smooth Criminal' a gem in the history of dance on film is a meshing of classic virtues from Astaire combined with Vincent Paterson's and Michael Jackson's awareness of what was happening on the 'street scene' in the late 1980s and their consultation of astute dance artists such as The Rock Steady Crew, Jeffrey Daniel and Bruno 'Pop n' Taco' Falcon. It was not a theft of ideas. What Jackson did, as many influential cultural movers do, is take the brilliance of those who have taught and inspired him and remould their material to complement his own, finally sprinkling his personal magical movement on top of theirs. Jackson created in himself a performer who was an amalgamation of many legendary dance contributors who had preceded him. Rod Judkins, lecturer in Creative Thinking at Central St Martins College of Art in London, reinforces this idea of artistic license and defends the act of creative 'copying' in his book "You Are More Creative Than You Think You Are":

> One of the secrets to being creative is to analyse and gain an understanding of the genius of others, then rework it for your own purposes. Rembrandt was an apprentice but he went on to produce entirely original paintings. He learned from the masters, but then his unique vision emerged.

These examples from some of Michael Jackson's dance work and how he 'quoted from' previous masters illustrate how prevalent referencing others' work is in the industry of performing arts and highlight the complexity of where we stand regarding legal creative copyright in choreography.

Reference or Robbery?

Beyonce is one such artist who has come under scrutiny a few times for her references to others' dance work in her music videos. The 2011 'Countdown' video courted controversy with its choreographic and styling similarities to Anne Teresa De Keersmaeker's modern dance films 'Rosas danst Rosas' (1983) and 'Achterland' (1990).

De Keersmaeker said in a radio interview with Studio Brussel that *"I'm not mad but this is plagiarism, it's stealing"* – suggesting both a charge of plagiarism (in that no credit to Keersmaeker was given) and copyright infringement (choreography was 'stolen').

Interestingly, one of De Keersmaeker's responses to this episode highlights how two communities, or industries, view the purpose and function of dance repertoire differently. She launched a project in 2013 entitled RE: Rosas! The *f*ABULEUS Rosas Remix Project, which invited dancers to send video clips of themselves reimagining a section of the original 1983 choreography. De Keersmaeker provided a step-by-step video tutorial of the work to aid learning the movement and encourages participants to interpret the scene in their own creative way. Ramsey Burt gives insight to the Beyonce/De Keersmaeker dispute in his book, 'Ungoverning Dance: Contemporary European Theatre Dance and the Commons':

> Artist's value originality for it's own sake, while industries, including larger media corporations, often recycle what has proved successful…Petty (the director), Beyonce and her creative team had set out to capture De Keersmaeker's choreography as part of Sony's marketing strategy on the internet and MTV. They were trying to exploit aspects of the two pieces they had plagiarised in order to maximise their investment in Beyonce…
>
> De Keersmaker and *f*ABULEUS subsequently responded to Sony's plagiarism by making the piece available and giving anyone permission to make their own versions of it. This response is, in effect, an acknowledgement that contemporary dance knowledge is a shared resource – a commons – rather than a commodity from which to generate financial profit.

This idea of repertoire existing as a shared common resource amongst the dance community, is regarded to be what stops people ripping off others' work in order to make a commercial gain. Respecting others' work and the immediate value of originality is the deterrent. Sharing resources is done with the understanding that they are used for creative and artistic fulfilment rather than the more cynical approach taken by Sony, which appeared to be to recycle the original and ground-breaking work and watch the YouTube clicks and video downloads mount up. All part of a reasonable marketing plan – if you respect and credit the work prominently and clearly, which it was not.

Beyonce responded by releasing a statement acknowledging that – "*(Rosas danst Rosas) was one of the inspirations used to bring the feel and look of the song to life.*" That word '*feel*' comes into play again. The claimed intention is not solely to replicate steps or camera set-ups but to recreate the 'feeling' of the other artists' work.

Watch the video for yourself and consider if Beyonce's video is channelling the 'feeling' of De Keersmaeker's work or if it is 'stealing,' as she claims. De Keersmaeker was never officially credited on the 'Countdown' video (according to the director Adria Petty, this was a genuine oversight due to an earlier than anticipated video release date). As Rosas dans Rosas work was not registered under any Copyright law, no further legal action concerning the apparent plagiarism nor copyright infringement was made public.

'Single Ladies' and Its Copyright Significance

JaQuel Knight is one of the first Commercial Dance choreographers to seek and gain copyright protection for the steps he is creating (see the Main Mover case study on JaQuel Knight for more). Knight is a choreographer who has demanded that choreography and dance is defended legally in the same way other forms of performing arts are. With an astute eye for business and also the protection of dance artists, Knight has secured copyright protection for the sequence of steps he created for Beyonce's 'Single Ladies' video and consequently the work became one of very few non-ballet pieces of choreography to be protected under US federal law. He is actively seeking to copyright all of his work and is also facilitating other dance creators of TikTok viral dances to do the same.

The irony with the 'Single Ladies' video is that upon its release, it was also spotlighted from a copyright stance due to the likeness of movement between the final cut and Bob Fosse's 1969 piece 'Mexican Breakfast.' Both Frank Gatson (the creative director of Single Ladies) and JaQuel Knight have addressed this openly. They acknowledge the inspiration taken from Fosse's work and how seriously they treated the R&D phase of creating the steps with Fosse in mind. Knight remembers the thorough rehearsal process:

> I think it's really important for artists to know the history, Fosse being one of the most influential artists – choreographer, director, writer. Besides "Mexican Breakfast," we studied everything 'Fosse' throughout the process. We even had [dancer and Broadway performer] Desmond Richardson come in and teach us some Fosse movements, signature Fosse pieces, and we just continued to study what we can from the tapes.

Legal Talk

So how does a choreographer protect their work in the US or the UK? A choreographer must traditionally satisfy a number of legal requirements in order for their work to be recognised as legally copyrightable. Their work must be:

(a) *original*

The work that is being copyrighted must be original. The law does not protect most social dances or simple sequences of steps as it is impossible to prove the originality of the step. So seeking copyright protection for steps such as 'the Harlem Shake,' 'the Dougie,' 'the Moonwalk' or 'the Floss' would be very difficult to secure.

(b) *a dramatic work*

Problems in the past that choreographers have encountered when trying to obtain copyright citizenship of their work include having to show that their work has a narrative or 'tells a story.' This is due to dance being included in the area of 'Dramatic works' under US copyright law. Earlier choreographers were sometimes refused copyright protection of their work due to not fulfilling the requirement to 'tell a story.' Louie Fuller was unsuccessful in protecting her 'Serpentine Dance' (c.1897) as the presiding judge in the case ruled that although the constructs of the choreography "maybe pleasing... but it can hardly be called dramatic." This was a legal precedent that stood until a change in US Copyright Law in 1976.

Revisions to the Copyright Act in the US and a broadening of the definition of the term 'dramatic work' in the UK has made fulfilling this criteria easier, the law now advocates a more inclusive application of the phrase 'dramatic work' in which it is common to include dance work.

(c) *a fixed work*

A choreographer must also satisfy the legal term known as the 'prerequisite for fixation.' According to the US Copyright Act 1909 (1911 in the UK), the choreography must be 'fixed' (recorded or stored) 'in writing or otherwise.' Accurate documentation of the literal, physical form of the steps is necessary to identify any copying or infringement of the work.

In the pre-digital age, this requirement caused problems for choreographers. Unlike in music composition or screenplays where the composer's notes would be scored or the writer's work printed in a script, most choreography is transferred over time from dancer to dancer, via verbal cues and physical demonstration. However, recording dance work is becoming easier due to the access most of us have to video camera equipment – once a work is recorded on camera it would satisfy the legal requirement of being 'fixed' – although having pieces video recorded does not always solve all problems relating to 'fixation of work.'

Traditionally, with some classical and modern dance works, the movement would be recorded by a notation system such as Benesh Movement Notation or Labanotation. Notating or 'scoring' a piece of dance (in a similar you are able to 'score' music) ensures that a precise record of the dance movements, as created by the choreographer, are logged and not subjected to the dancer's interpretation of the work (something that can happen with a video recording). In securing copyright protection for his work on Beyonce's 'Single Ladies' music video in 2020, Knight had the movement scored using Labanotation by Lynne Weber, director of the Dance Notation Bureau – a very unique occurrence for a piece of non-classical, commercial work.

Copyright law, which can legally secure choreography created in the sphere of Commercial Dance, is slowly becoming a viable way to ensure that dance work is respected and protected adequately. There are even stories of artists voluntarily paying copyright fees to choreographers to use their work. One such case is the South Korean star PSY voluntarily paying K-Pop choreographer Bae Yoon Jung for permission to recycle choreography she had made previously for the band Brown Eyed Girls in his video for 'Gentleman' (2013).

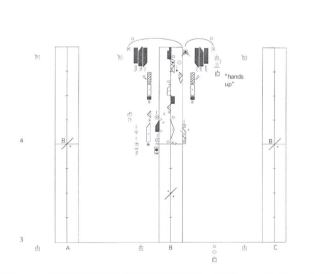

Image 8.1 A section from the official Labanotation of the choreography in Beyonce's 'Single Ladies' music video which JaQuel Knight has copyrighted

However, pursuit of litigation by choreographers is still limited due to a lack of previous case studies which create meaningful recent precedents and the limited financial funds most choreographers have. To avoid more ambiguous cases like De Keersmaeker/Beyonce, dance artists must be encouraged to take note of JaQuel Knight's progressive push to notate and protect his work legitimately. Choreographers creating work of note should consider registering their work and making sure they satisfy the legal measures required. Francis Yeoh, Ph.D., is a dance scholar who's research has centred around copyright in dance. He concludes his paper "Square Peg in a Round Hole: Dance Meets Copyright" by stating:

> The argument for a better accommodation of dance through a greater understanding of the nature and practices of the artform has some validity. In the past judges have in many ways failed to accord dance parity with the other disciplines through the adoption of the idea that dance must tell a story and that it is mere frivolity that is not worthy of recognition. Dance copyright is in a state of flux due to this lack of clarity in the interpretation of the law and the paucity of case law. It is argued that the artform of dance should be given 'equality' of treatment so that it enjoys the same status enjoyed by other authors.

8b. Commercial Class Culture

Dance Class in the Age of Digital Media

Beginning in the late 2000s, dance class structure and expectations changed as digital media became a predominate factor in everyday life. Performing artists were presented with an increasing number of innovative ways to market themselves. As the internet, social media platforms and metaverse development continues to evolve, so will the possibilities for a dancer to get themselves 'seen' by the industry – Instagram, Vimeo, YouTube, TikTok and Facebook have all become visually effective mediums which allow dancers to showcase their abilities and promote their 'brand' directly to 10,000s of potential clients. This has catalysed a change in what students want and expect from a dance class.

Traditionally, a dance class has been a way to improve or hone technique, increase fitness levels, deepen understanding and enhance a student's ability to embody the principles of the style in which they are studying. A new purpose has segued into dance classes – that of providing visual digital media material for the student (and sometimes the teacher or choreographer) to use to promote themselves online. Many classes now devote much of their studio time to digitally recording performances of the combo at the end of class. A 1.5-hour class can devote as much as 60 minutes of the class just setting up and running the choreography in small groups. The groups are often chosen according to the teacher's opinion about which students are performing the material to the highest level – the last (or sometimes the first) group of students picked to perform can be used as a 'demo group,' demonstrating how the choreography should be executed. Stage lights, LED strip lighting, gimbals and specialist videographers have become integral parts of many Commercial Dance classes. Some students are increasingly only willing to paying $20 + for a class which they know is going to be documented on camera and shared online. They want that video package which they can use to accrue 'likes,' followers and reposts online and who knows, if they're lucky, potentially get seen by a choreographer who will book them for a job.

Symptoms of a Video-Centric Class Environment

As classes increasingly evolve into fine-tuned and 'Instagram-ready' performance opportunities, particularly in drop-in dance centres, care must be taken not to lose the very essence of what a dance class' objective is and what it aims to provide for the student. There are, no doubt, benefits to providing performance opportunities within class, but what concerns some dance teachers, choreographers, dance lecturers and students is that the base goals of the dance class are being sidelined. An effective class, in any dance technique, is one that fosters an environment which allows the student to fail freely, securely and without shame or judgement. An effective class is one that presents to the student the core tenets of the dance genre being studied – referencing the key principles and foundations of the movement as well as more advanced notes. A ballet class for instance, uses a sequence of exercises – plies, tendus, port de bras, grand allegro, to first refine and build the dancers vocabulary so that when they do perform the choreography combination at the end of the class, they are putting to use the elements they have been focusing on in class whilst also bringing their own performance spark to the work. Providing bitesize exercises or choreographies which culminate in a short performance opportunities at the end of class is a successful template used in many techniques (Jazz, Modern). Commercial Dance classes, as a genre, have yet to establish a class structure which caters for some of these baseline pre-requisites of a dance class – a freedom to fail and imparting fundamental movement knowledge.

One reason potential reason for this short fall in class learning is that placing so much importance on recording the 'end of class combo,' with the intention of uploading the clip onto social media to promote the class or the students in it, already denies the student an environment in which they can mess up, go wrong or simply have a bad day without having to worry about the judgement of others both in the class and online. Their bad day will be captured on video and potentially posted to 100,000s of people. This may inhibit a student's willingness to challenge themselves and can stop them bringing an element of risk into their class work. To progress at any skill, we have to be willing to push ourselves out of our comfort zone and dare ourselves to meet challenges, which may feel strange or awkward for us. That is more difficult to do knowing that a camera will be on hand to catch any mistakes. Secondly, spending the majority of a class learning only one piece of choreography to perform as a finale to the session can be a limited and ineffective way for dancers (especially those of a lower experience level) to improve their overarching technical skill. There is often no breakdown of the steps or little explanation from the teacher of 'how' to do that glide, wrist roll or double turn in a practical, biomechanical sense. Teaching the choreography intricately is sometimes neglected through to ensure a sufficient, sizeable chunk of material is taught which can then be recorded.

Thoughts from Students

In conversations with dance students, they have commented on a 'cut throat' atmosphere developing in some classes. Student's desperation to be featured in one of the main recording groups (therefore being the first to be featured in the Instagram post and consequently getting more views) means that the classes become environments more similar to a high pressured audition than a class. Students also noted the change in motivations from some going to class – many students were going to classes in which they already know they can perform that teacher's or choreographers material to a high level – they are attending to get the video for the 'gram.' Again, this makes a student more reluctant to pull themselves out of their comfort zone and attend a class where they may be recorded performing a style they are not so confident in, enforcing the idea that these classes diminish room for failure and therefore can decelerate progress. Students did comment on positives of the many camera centric classes that they had attended. Enhancing pick-up skills so that they were 'camera ready' by the end of class was quoted as a positive and a challenge, which they often relished. They also noted that these videos were helpful to use in their portfolio but wished that they didn't come with the downside of promoting a limited learning environment.

A Developing Curriculum

No doubt, learning fast and innovative choreography is an invaluable way to improve pick-up speed and for advanced dancers to further their already high-end mastery of the style – class performance videos require all of these skills to be highly tuned. Furthermore, the environment cultivated in a Commercial Dance class is usually a very positive one, with students adopting the cyphers originally seen in Hip-Hop and Breakin' culture to cheer on others. For highly skilled, professional level dancers, posting videos online can be a very effective tool to promote themselves – dancing next to a well-established, highly regarded dancer or attending a class from a choreographer with a large social media following can highlight a dancer's ability and allow them to be seen by potential agents or choreographers who they previously would not be able to be able to get in the room with.

Kike Granero is the co-founder and co-director 'The Akademics' Hip-Hop dance collective in Barcelona and is also a Hip-Hop lecturer at the Institute of the Arts Barcelona. He has trained in LA as well as in dance studios in London and regularly teaches and choreographs for studios across Europe. He shares his thoughts about the pros and cons of the changing class climate in the Commercial area and the developing industry in Spain:

> I trained in LA for three summers (2011, 2014 & 2022). I look back and realise that I hardly have any videos of those first two summers training in LA. You can hardly find any on Youtube. 8 years later things changed a lot and in my third time training in LA, recording the choreographies – I felt that it had become the main objective of almost every one of the classes I received. I do not feel that this is something necessarily negative, since you learn how to interpret, pick up choreography quickly and to feel secure in front of the camera – I think that is important. But I don't think it's positive either, in the sense that it's over-exploited and that some of the important aspects of going to class and training, have been lost.
>
> The industry is changing, and it is true that, at least in Spain, there is more and more work than before as a dancer and as a creator. I believe that movement generates movement and the need to be seen has turned social networks into a very powerful work tool. It seems that, as dancers or choreographers, we have the "obligation" to create content so as not to "disappear" from the scene. Which, in my opinion, often degrades the quality of what we show, due to the large amount of unfiltered material that is uploaded.

As Granero points out, the dance class industry is changing and videos are an essential tool in a performing artist's self-promotion pack, meaning that more consideration than ever is now needed about how we develop the Commercial Dance classes and masterclasses of the future. There is a push for a more considered approach to class, teachers such as Galen

Hooks (US), teaching platforms like CLI Studios and John Graham (UK) (who teaches out of Base and Pineapple in London) are providing classes in which a succinct, considered pedagogic template for delivering class is put into play. The class avoids a disproportionate focus on recording an 'end-of-class' performance. John Graham shared his thoughts about some aspects of Commercial and Hip-Hop classes:

> I feel like classes could be advertised differently. There could be 'Dance classes' and there could be 'Camera classes'. I think it would be nice to have classes that were labelled more specifically. Maybe in studios when they organise the timetable it maybe more helpful to be more specific (about the focus of the class) rather than say 'Open Class' where teachers can do what they want with that slot.
>
> I'm happy for people to film in my class, if they want to film themselves for progress, even if they want to film it to post, then it's cool…I should invest in a camera though because the other thing is as a teacher, you're actually falling behind if you don't film it! It shocks me sometimes when I see what's getting filmed in some classes, not in terms of the quality (well, sometimes in terms of quality), but also in terms of this being what people want at every level, even at beginner level – they want to be filmed. This has become the culture but I also understand the concept behind us all investing in ourselves. I think there has to be a balance for sure.

Commercial Dance is continually evolving, particularly in the classroom. What a student gets when they walk into a Commercial Dance class largely depends on who their teacher is that day and what part of the world they live in. Perhaps taking cues from how Jazz, Hip-Hop and Ballet tutors structure their classes could help ensure that in the end, the students get solid technical training as well as a well-produced video. Dance students should also be aware that these videos can often highlight their deficiencies as well as strengths to the 10,000s viewers watching on social media.

Shooting videos in classes can no doubt be a useful tool for a student if used as a supplementary performance exercise in a technical dance class but dance educators could take care not to make every class a 'make or break' performance opportunity which inhibits the development of a progressive learning environment. Hopefully, as Commercial Dance develops in an educational sense, classes which place the students' learning trajectory at the centre of their structure will become more commonplace.

8c. Polar Paradigms – Inclusivity and Sexualisation

Despite its relatively progressive outlook, Commercial Dance seems to follow paradoxical paradigms regarding its approach to equitable representation within the industry. The Commercial industry generally takes a relatively progressive stance in terms of diversity and inclusivity. Dancers from different ethnicities, with varying physical attributes, those with disabilities and the LGBTQ+ community are all increasingly represented prominently in many performance projects, particularly over the last 10 years. Fostering diversity and inclusivity within the performing arts industry have become valiant priorities which the Commercial Dance industry can be proud of. On the flip side, the Commercial Dance industry is also frequently called out for using hyper-sexualisation as a prominent marketing device, one which suggests the industry is on a much murkier moral trajectory. Have the sexually gratuitous choreographies in created for some music videos and live performances blurred the lines between engaging dance performances and degradation of the performer and their work?

Talking Points

- **Inclusivity**

    The world of performing arts is frequently cited as a liberal, inclusive and progressive place, but a disconnection to contemporary social attitudes is often evident. Training and working in musical theatre, traditional dramatic arts or classical areas of dance can uncover a paradigm still centred around traditional perspectives regarding gender, race and sexual identity, often embedded in a caucasian, European historical structure. This is not to say there is a reluctance to adapt, but 100s of years of theatre history can be tough to untangle and reframe, hindering efforts to progress and update perspectives. Even before the social movements of the 2010s, such as 'Me Too' and 'Black Lives Matter,' there has been an urgency to make these changes and acknowledgements in all areas of performing arts. In her 2006 article regarding the politics of recognition and redistribution of female British playwrights from black and Asian backgrounds, Professor Gabriele Griffin noted that:

    > the promotion of cultural diversity policies proceeds from an understanding, a recognition, that this diversity has to be recognised and acknowledged. From this spring measures – redistribution of resources – designed to underpin that recognition, and in turn, to integrate or normalise diversity as part of the everyday or contemporary culture.

Griffin adds that she believes that the long march to making redundant the notion of 'cultural diversity' in theatre is well on its way – the make-up of the theatre industry is slowly becoming more reflective of the multicultural nature of US and UK societies. Theatre is actively changing and recognising its historic cultural shortcomings. However, the adolescence of Commercial Dance and the youth of those who are earnestly shaping the industry and the fact it has really only gained traction as an industry in the last 20 years, have enabled it to become a bright beacon for a more progressive and inclusive performing arts industry.

Commercial Dance is increasingly an endorser of inclusivity, regardless of gender, ethnicity, sexuality or physical disabilities. Commercial Dance's channels of performance often present a bouquet of humanity, as clearly indicated by the Parris Goebel choreographed Savage Fenty Vol 2 & 3 Fashion Shows are clear indicators of this (see the Iconic Moment dedicated to Vol 2). Speaking to Vogue magazine in 2020, Goebel states that

> "I hope anyone that gets to experience the Savage show will walk away feeling uplifted and empowered to really love themselves unapologetically" and that "people all over the world, like myself, have been waiting to see themselves represented and celebrated in the fashion world."

Through her choreography, people from all walks of life have seen themselves represented in Goebel's work. Taylor Swift's live performance of 'You Need to Calm Down' at the 2019 MTV VMA's was centred around promoting equality and LGBTQ+ rights. Featuring plus sized model and dancer Dexter Mayfield and representations from all backgrounds and ethnicities, the colourful choreography helped to push Swift's message of social inclusivity. The dancers working with a pop artist are frequently portrayed as part of the artists inner clique – their differences, whether racial, sexual or physical are celebrated, just as they are in Meghan Trainor's 2022 music video and promo performances of 'Made You Look,' which celebrates the disparities between her featured dancers, advancing the idea that they are all part of her 'cool kids club.'

- **Sexualisation**

    Dance in the 20th century and beyond has often characterised male and female roles in a traditional manner – ballet (Sleeping Beauty), musical theatre (Guys and Dolls) and dance on screen (Dirty Dancing) have all enforced long established tropes of gender roles. American art philosopher Noël Carroll maintains that defining a female role in film is too often guided by the dichotomy of 'mother vs whore' (Carroll 1990, 349). A female role can be defined as only one or the other, a trope often carried over into in the dance industry, where a female performer is either a safe, sisterly character or a vixen in stiletto heels – there is no room for an in-between (see Sandy's transformations in the movie and musical franchise 'Grease'). The advertising mantra of 'sex sells' is frequently adhered to in Commercial Dance, where performers of all gender identifications are sometimes overtly sexualised in their appearance and through the content of the choreography. In their paper, "Naughty Girls and Red Blooded Women: Representations of female heterosexuality in music video," academics Railton and Watson note that *"the display of the sexualised body and the potential for that body to be figured as an object of desire or fantasy are crucial to the economies of both pleasure and profit of the pop music video."* Murali Balaji Ph.D., a journalist specialising in diversity and equity, also comments that *"the emphasis on the physical aspects of Black womanhood is amplified in music videos, where sex is often used to sell both the performer (regardless of gender) and the performers image."*

A clear example of 'emphasising the physical aspects of Black womanhood' is in Kanye Wests' 2016 'Fade' video. Featuring the dance talents of Teyana Taylor, directed by Eli Russell Linnetz and choreographed by Jae Blaze, Guapo and Derek 'Bentley' Watkins, the video is a carousel of expertly executed Commercial Dance choreography. The creative team shrewdly utilise the talent and sexuality of the performer, the artistry in the movement and the post-modern cultural references (Flashdance/1980s VHS home work-outs) in order to promote the song. Despite the impressive choreography and dance performance that the video delivers, it could be inferred that Taylor's sexuality is the main promotional tool being wielded in the video – West himself does not feature in the clip. Whether this clip celebrates or diminishes the value of the female form is an argument for its viewers to consider. Regardless of the audience's moral conclusion, there is no denying the strength of the choreography and its dextrous execution by Taylor.

Beyonce's 'Baby Boy' (2003) music video could also be seen as reinforcing the idea of the black female form being used as a commercial vehicle to sell a song. Railton and Watson go on to argue that Beyonce's performance of the choreography in this video and *"its very uncontrollability reinscribes the black female body as available, literally to the look of the spectator and symbolically to the desires and fantasies of both black and white men."* Sexuality in Commercial Dance often reflects the carnal themes of the accompanying music as it strives to hold the audience's gaze – with the aim being to encourage a purchase of the artist's music, the designer's clothing brand or of the perfume that the dance is helping to promote. This marketing tool is perhaps at its most socially innocuous when the performance complements the natural sensuality of the dancer, as opposed to exploiting and objectifying the dancer with hyper sexuality. It is a fine and difficult balance to make – it can make the difference between a project appearing sophisticated and artistically enlightened or gratuitous and empty. Jennifer Lopez's 'I'm Glad' (2003) music video, which also references the movie 'Flashdance' (1983), is another example of a talented and mesmerising artist using their sensual talents to hold the audience's gaze as a promotional tool. Media scholar Priscilla Ovalle offers that the success of Lopez's video was indebted to the combined visual spectacle of racialized sexuality, the female body, and dance performance set in an urban context. Appearing in Flashdance fashion and movement, Lopez's body performed anew the codification and commodification of an ambiguously nonwhite female sensuality within the MTV frame.

The music videos for West's 'Fade,' Beyonce's 'Baby Boy' and Jennifer Lopez's 'I'm Glad' are examples of common instances in music video where the commercial objective of the choreography is to commoditise the performers' sexual allure to generate more views of the video and ultimately sell the song.

Britney Spears' '…Baby One More Time' (1998) and Nikki Minaj's 'Anaconda' (2014) are both notable music videos which have courted controversy in the media due to the choreography's focus on the sexualisation of women of different ages and ethnicities. As of October 2022, these two videos have viewing figures on YouTube of 750 million and 1 billion, respectively. Regardless of whether the viewer believes that the choreographic portrayal of women in the video empowers or devalues, the enormous number of views prove that sex still sells and commercial choreography is sometimes willing to make the most of that mantra in order make a dollar.

8d. A Supporting Dancer

Time's up for the 'Background/Backup' Dancer

A singer doesn't have a 'background' band, they just have a band. Dancers and the choreography they perform are integral parts of many entertainment forums – whether a pop concert, a corporate event, fashion show or a music video. I offer that both of these terms – 'back-up' and 'background dancer,' condescend, subliminally undermine and ultimately diminish the importance and effectiveness of a dancers role.

Justin Timberlake, Taylor Swift, Beyonce and Madonna's live touring productions of the last 20 years illuminate how much of the foreground the 'background' dancers occupy. They are a key part in entertaining the 100,000s of fans who have paid premium ticket prices to see the artist perform in an enormous stadium or arena, something that the artist could not do as effectively without the support of a talented and hard-working cast of dancers. They are as creatively involved as the drummer or lead guitarist. They are as key to the productions success as the lavish lighting and video elements. Dancers offer the artist a secure platform from which they can drop in and out of the choreographed movement when they choose to, feeding off the physical and kinetic energy that pours from the dancers throughout the entirety of the show.

Dua Lipa's 2022 'Future Nostalgia' World Tour (choreographed by Charm La'Donna) uses 12 dancers who are embedded into nearly the entirety of the 19 song set list, providing a foil for Lipa's steadfast choreography to elevate itself further onstage. Journalist Lisa Jo Sagolla acknowledges the impact of 'backup dancers':

> You wouldn't put a Rembrandt in a sleek metallic frame; you'd choose an antique wooden one—something that complements the period and style of the art. Similarly, the right backup dancers can add immeasurably to the performance of a pop star. They bring enormous energy to the stage, and their motion helps focus the audience's attention on the singer. They also frame the star with a particular look and movement style that contribute to his or her image, while their dancing enriches the concert going experience.

As Commercial Dance choreographers continually raise the creative bar, they also redefine and accelerate the artistic expectations of the modern audience. Audiences *expect* the choreography and the dancers to form an intrinsic part of an artist's production, especially with the advent of TikTok and its bitesize snaps of choreography that make the movement associated with the song as important as the song's chorus hook. The fans are as hyped to learn the 4 × 8's of the chorus choreography as they are the lyrics to the song. The enormous success of K-Pop attests to this, the dance and choreography element is a hugely important asset in selling the artists song (check out the 'Professional Insight' feature on Kiel Tutin, a prolific K-Pop choreographer for a more detailed look at this).

A '*Supporting Dancer*' would be a more fitting title for dancers working with music artists. Callum Powell is a British choreographer and dancer who has choreographed The Masked Dancer (ITV, 2021/2022), JLS's Beat Again Tour (2021) and music videos for Take That and Robbie Williams as well as working as a dancer himself on many projects, including the Elton John biopic 'Rocketman' (2019). He discusses the labelling of dancers, particularly in relation to those working in film, stadium and arena tours:

> Using the term 'Supporting Dancer' is way more inclusive and makes a lot of sense… When you work on film now, no-one is an 'extra', everyone is a Supporting Artist.
>
> As soon as you take the dancers away from a live performance you lose a lot of impact, the artist loses support and also confidence in many ways. There aren't many artists who can stand there on a stadium stage on their own, without a dancer, or a group of dancers supporting them, and keep the performance looking as effective. In live events it's easy to see that the dancers also have a big effect on the fans in an interactive and positive way. It feels invalidating and undermining to still apply the term 'background dancer' or 'back-up' dancer.

A *Supporting Dancer* illustrates precisely what dancers hired to perform with artists do – they support them artistically on stage, they increase audience engagement, they help to fuel the artists energy during performances and in the case of tours (which can be long, lonely and gruelling) they often provide support to the artist in terms of community and friendship. Terminology and its social relevance are continually under review, perhaps it's time to reconsider the term 'background dancer.' It is up to working choreographers and dancers to tactfully begin to use more inclusive language so we can take 'background' or 'back-up' dancers out from the shade and create a community of *Supporting Dancers* who can bask in a little more of the light they deserve.

8e. Street Dance versus Urban Dance

Street Dance

As a kid, I was always scouting for anywhere I could find that taught 'Street Dance' classes. In the early 1990s in the UK, they were quite difficult to find but there were few around. They were such fun and exciting classes, introducing us to the steps we saw in music videos on MTV and in the movies. 'Street Dance' classes provided welcome relief from the discipline and sternness of some of our other classes such as Ballet and Jazz. As a classification of dance, 'Street Dance' has become an increasingly less relevant label in the dance community over the last 20 years, but still remains prevalent in the lexicon of popular culture and the general media. As dancer and choreographer Jeffrey Daniel commented in 2013, "I don't call it 'street dance' anymore because it left the streets years ago."

Talking Points

An internet search will throw up suggestions that Street Dance refers to dance forms which have been developed and practised on the streets or in social, non-studio environments sitting juxtaposed to many other modern forms of dance studied at academies and conservatories worldwide including Ballet, Contemporary and modern Jazz – all studio based and cultivated largely in Europe.

Street Dance was/is comprised of dance vocabulary that did not fit comfortably into established, pre-cooked syllabus dance techniques and became the fun, entertaining cousin of these older and 'serious' dance genres. Coined in the 1980s, it was a marketable and media friendly term and quickly became a recognised form of dance that could sit easily alongside other established styles in a local dance school's timetable. Its main components vary widely but largely consist of black and Latino birthed Hip-Hop styles including movement signatures from Breakin', Funk Styles, House and New Style plus many other social or vernacular Hip-Hop hybrids. These original dance styles evolved outdoors, on the streets of New York and LA in the 1970s and 1980s, catalysed by the poor economic circumstances which affected many of the black and Hispanic communities who created these dances. The financial limitations, plus the socially engraved racial segregations of the time, did not grant many in those pauperised communities the opportunity to train in a traditional dance studio setting (see the chapter on Hip-Hop & Funk Styles for more). Just as the characters Turbo and Ozone from the 1984 movie 'Breakin' 2: Electric Boogaloo' teach Street Dance at the local community centre, during the late 1980s and 1990s, Hip-Hop and other popular dance styles were scouted and diffused into dance studio schedules all over America, under the all-inclusive moniker of 'Street Dance.'

Peering through the Safety Glass

'Street Dance' classes have granted safe but redacted access to a family of Hip-Hop and popular dance styles in a conventional and yet removed context. Taking a 'Street Dance' class lets students peer through the safety glass as they peruse original Hip-Hop dance culture in its primal, coarse form without actually needing to engage fully with the culture's original values or history. The advent of Street Dance classes in the 1990s severed many of these dance steps from their original social messages, cultural affiliations and purpose. Has using the term 'Street Dance' subtly removed many of the social and racial associations which are often inherently made with Hip-Hop culture, those associations being to poverty-stricken working class and minority Latin and black neighbourhoods in the inner cities of America? Labelling these forms of dance with a neutral, palatable title like 'Street Dance' all at once sanitised and monetised dance movement emanating from original Hip-Hop culture, giving it a wider demographic appeal.

Television shows like 'Britain/America's Got Talent,' which promote 'Street Dance' crews (Flawless, Diversity), movies (The 'Step Up' and 'Stomp the Yard' franchises) and global 'street dance' competition phenomenon (UDO, 'Red Bull's Dance Your Style') have sold Street Dance to the mass market, bringing pariah Hip-Hop dance styles to suburban dance studios and communities.

Using the term 'Street Styles' is a recent preferred adaption to the term which provides an acknowledgment that this genre is made from subsets of individual dances which were founded in the streets – rather than simply one big dance conglomerate. It may be that identifying these dances as 'Street Styles' revives the relevance of the term 'Street' in relation to dance.

Urban Dance

Factions of the dance community in the US coined an alternate moniker to 'Street Dance' in the 2000s – that being 'Urban Dance.' They felt that some choreography which pulled from a number of different styles (e.g., using Popping, House and Breakin' elements mashed together to create sequences of choreography, rather than freestyled movement) was no longer 'true Hip-Hop' and also viewed the term 'Street Dance' as outdated and tarnished due to its media 'sell-out' association.

'Urban' has a number of definitions, it can relate generally to city life and according to Oxford Languages dictionary, it also 'denotes popular black culture in general.' The original philosophy behind introducing the term 'Urban Dance' is that it would be used to refer to a school of dance techniques cultivated by North American black and Hispanic communities 'in the city', just as the music industry used the term 'urban' to refer to music from the same societies. 'Urban Dance' began to gain momentum in the 2000s as a catch-all term to address this multi-genred and diluted version of Hip-Hop movement. The term could be used to categorise choreography, or the focus of a class, which drew from various different dance forms. International dance competitions helped to spread the phrase globally and it became a widely used title, particularly in Europe (one of the most popular dance studios in Barcelona, Spain is called 'La Urban Dance Factory' and some conservatoires and universities in the UK also refer to 'Urban Dance' classes and programmes).

The End of 'Urban' as an Artistic Category

Language and colloquial terminology changes according to cultural progressions and societal developments. In 2020, after the murder of George Floyd and the rise of the Black Lives Matter movement, American and British society redressed its usage of certain race related vernacular. There has been a conscious push within the music industry to stop using the word 'Urban' as a way of defining a music genre. In 2020, Republic Records, who represent Drake, Arianna Grande, John Legend and Taylor Swift announced that they would no longer use the term 'Urban Music' due to the historically racial undertones associated with the word. 'Urban' was originally applied to black music by radio stations in America in the 1970s in order to market genres such as soul and rhythm & blues music more successfully to a white audience wary of using the word 'black.' Rolling Stone magazine explained in 2020 that disc jockeys began to use "a new word designed to covertly make radio stations that played black music more appealing to narrow-minded white advertisers." 'Urban music' was a term conceived to maximise commercial sales of black music to white audiences and by using it, arguably segregated and devalued black musical genres further. The same year, the Grammy's also moved away from using the term 'Urban' and renamed some categories – the Best Urban Contemporary category was changed to Best Progressive R&B Album. The terms 'Urban Fashion/Music/Dance' have historically separated BIPOC artists from mainstream artists, subliminally detaching, excluding and diminishing the value of the work created. Tyler the Creator, winner of Best Rap album at the 2020 Grammys remarked that *"I don't like that 'urban' word—it's just a politically correct way to say the N-word to me."* The original reason to use the term 'Urban Dance' was to return authenticity to a diluted and mis-represented Hip-Hop dance culture, the expression was no doubt used because it was already palatable in the music industry but its underlying association with 'Urban Music' is one which is increasingly considered to be problematic.

Online dance studios Steezy also dropped the use of the term 'Urban' in 2020 as a category for its classes. A reformulated approach now sees Steezy's classes which were previously called 'Urban,' newly categorised as 'Open Style Choreography,' a term that describes the class content whilst dropping any societal or racial associations. On their blog page, Steezy explain the changes they made:

> "Urban" music. "Urban" fashion. "Urban" cuisine. It's all code for 'from the hood,' and the entire black and brown community has long-since been tired of the label…And as we made BLM donations, moderated panels, and provided resources, it became clear that one of the best things we could do was to quit using the term "Urban Dance" and replace it with a term that promoted a culture of both authenticity and respect.
>
> As a few founding members of STEEZY kicked around ideas, the conversation travelled to the street style battle scene where dancers freestyle using any/multiple styles. These battles are often called "Open Style Battles" as they are literally open to all styles of dance. From there, the term "Open Style Choreography" was born.

Interestingly, neither 'Street Dance' nor 'Urban Dance' classes have typically included any styles with a traditionally 'feminine' or LGBTQ+ origin. Waacking and Vogue Fem phrases seem to rarely been seen in classes termed as 'Street' or 'Urban,' despite both genres being developed on the club scene and outside of a traditional dance studio environment. In terms of their content, the labels 'Street & Urban Dance' appear to largely reflect the early, male-dominated arena of Hip-Hop culture and its related hetero-sexualised dance forms. Perhaps this has further contributed to the dance classification's loss of relevance and validity, further fertilising the growth of alternative monikers such as 'Open Style', 'Street Styles' and 'Commercial Dance.'

Categorising and labelling dance forms can sometimes feel restrictive and counter-intuitive in the genre blending world of the arts. As social and geopolitical divisions become more pronounced, discussions surrounding ingrained colloquial language have occurred in the 2020s on a macro scale across many societies globally, as well as in micro dance communities. The labels 'Street Dance' and 'Urban Dance' have been used for contrasting motivations over the last 40 years: to protect dance, to understand dance and to exploit dance. They have arisen from dancers wanting to defend original Hip-Hop dance foundations and from dance studios seeking to label their classes in a way which reflects recent thoughts around antiquated communal phraseology. These discussions validate the premise that how we define the movements we make can have a societal impact that is felt far from the dance studio.

PROFESSIONAL INSIGHT – RANDALL WATSON

Location: London, UK

Randall Watson is a London based dancer who has achieved what very few do, to work as a Commercial Dancer for top choreographers and artists in both the UK and the US. From touring with Little Mix in the UK to touring with Jennifer Lopez on her 'It's My Party Tour' across the US and dancing in her Superbowl halftime performance, his resumé also takes in work with artists such as Victoria Monet, Katy Perry, Rihanna and Taylor Swift.

Janet Jackson inspired me to dance.
I remember having the 'Rhythm Nation' video on VHS when I was little, I would watch it over and over again. I was obsessed. I knew I wanted to what they were doing from that age.

Tours and live shows require a certain amount of 'out-live' energy.
It's not just about delivering the choreography and keeping it clean with a performance face, like it is in TV work. You have to engage with the audience and make them feel like it's almost a personal experience, no matter where they are in the venue. With TV/Video work you can pull back energy-wise, be smarter about your choices for camera and also be more aware of what your face is doing. Ultimately, you want to look your best. Music Videos live forever!

The most beneficial thing training wise for me was being part of a Commercial Dance group called 'Dance 2XS' in London.
It allowed me to learn from those around me that were currently working as dancers as well as learning to work with others in that capacity. We would have audition-prep style rehearsals, which were a great help when it came to actually auditioning.

Times are different now; there are so many resources and so many avenues to take in the journey to becoming a Commercial Dancer. The advice I would offer is *train, train, train*. Do many different classes, be as versatile as you can to maximise the check. Research, listen to and learn from those already working or have worked.

BE NICE.
No one wants to work with a bitch but also be true to who you are.

I grew up learning choreography from music videos.
Janet, Britney, N'sync, etc. What's crazy is that I knew all the JLO routines. She was always someone I wanted to work for and in 2014, I vowed that it would one day happen. Mad. Fast forward a few years, I'm on tour with her and doing her Superbowl performance.

The biggest difference between working in the UK and the US is the pay.
You make significantly more in the US and collect royalties for jobs too. You are treated more like an individual talent rather than one of many.

In terms of Commercial Dance choreographers, I feel like JaQuel Knight, Parris Goebel and Sean Bankhead are leading the way
They have Commercial Dance choreography and its wide outreach in a chokehold. They've really helped Commercial Dance become even more mainstream. Between the roster of artists within pop culture they have and are leading TikTok challenges with their original choreographies – it's a wrap. They are also delivering steps/styles that are original and very specific to them, which is great.

I believe a good Commercial Dance class has at least one 'end group' to demonstrate the choreography.
It's always good to have a great group who really understand the combination – the final group is a gauge of where your ability is at within that class, or in general. The teacher should be trying to get the best out of you, not just give steps. They should be willing and watchful enough to give feedback to every student to help their growth.

Talking Points

Image 8.2 Randall performing with Victoria Monét on the Jimmy Kimmel show in 2021

PROFESSIONAL INSIGHT – XENA GUSTHART

Location: London, UK

Xena is the choreographer of the West End and Broadway musical hit, Jim Steinman's 'Bat Out of Hell.' She is Scottish and works out of London and New York. Her training was versatile and included studying Locking with Anthony Thomas and becoming an esteemed Breaker as well as mastering studio styles such as Jazz.

Having performed in Musical Theatre (Bodyguard: The Musical), Hip-Hop dance theatre (Boy Blue's 'The High Five and the Prophecy of Prana') and in the Commercial Dance industry (including work for Kylie Minogue, Adidas, Clinique, Sadlers Wells Theatre London and the BBC) Xena has had a unique view of the expansion of Commercial Dance in it's different contexts.

As a Commercial Dancer, you have the ability to work in two industries.
I believe that Commercial Dancers should get some singing lessons and get a recorded singing reel. If you can harness some singing techniques and demonstrate that you can sing and are working on it, you are very likely to be chosen to work in a musical. This is interesting financially and makes you doubly employable. There are roles within Musical Theatre that can mean you progress within the dance department such as Swing, Assistant Dance Captain, Dance Captain, Resident Choreographer, Associate Choreographer, Choreographer, and then as a Creative Director. This experience in Musical Theatre will only heighten your chances within the Commercial world. It's the first time in a long time that I feel Commercial Dancers can have a fantastic and long-lasting career by working in both the Commercial industry and the Musical Theatre industry!

The Musical Theatre scene is changing, rapidly.
More contemporary musicals are including a very commercial take on their approach to music as well as dance and therefore the way they use storytelling. Today you can see many musicals in the West End and on Broadway that are incorporating Commercial Dance,

meaning that the audience demographic is changing and by doing so, it means that going to the theatre has become a much more popular event than ever before. I believe the main inspiration towards this shift in the musical theatre scene is its commercial viability. By making musicals more accessible and interesting to a new demographic means more 'bums on seats' and this has a direct effect on the style of the musical, the music and of course the movement used in the shows.

For me, the process is very clear on how to create movement to music.
I always start with the story, simply because I love to tell stories and I want the audience to go through and make their own mind up. I then listen and re-listen to the music over and over again, getting a feel for the nuances within it. The light, the shade, the energy and I try to feel what energy the music gives me.

I then methodically breakdown these different sections into counts of 8 or in time codes. So I know I may have 8 × 8's of an instrumental with heavy percussion and then 4 × 8's of the melody coming back in etc. Once I have this breakdown of this music, I go back to each section and listen to the different 'lines' in the music, the bass, the drums, the accents, the instruments NOT playing the melody and then the melody. I do this to make sure I know the different layers to each bar of 8. Then as a whole, I map out the story I want to tell to match with the feel of each section I have broken down and see how I can create a beginning, middle and an end. I then begin to choreograph to these sections. I do my best to make every step with the intention to help portray the original story laid out at the beginning.

I like to take inspirations from Gene Kelly, Fred Astaire and Ginger Rogers as well as old school Lockers and Hip Hop dancers like Toni Basil and Tony GoGo. I love blending this with inspiration from the golden era of old school Hollywood Jazz and storytelling. For me, it's important to cover a variety of movement and I do this from drawing on my different backgrounds in dance and my inspirations.

There are significant differences between the UK and the US; they are two different beasts.
In my opinion Commercial Dance is at its absolute highest level in the US, the commitment to the varying styles within that genre is outstanding. The access to the industry's top choreographers, coupled with a high volume of dancers in each studio, breeds this element of

Image 8.3 Xena trained in many different styles, including Breakin'

competition and therefore the standard is constantly being pushed and raised. Their technical ability really does over-shadow many of those training in the UK. I find that the Commercial Dancers in LA also have a very strong foundation in Jazz technique including turns and flexibility – all of this gives each dancer more control over their body and they therefore operate at a higher level than anywhere else I have come across.

With regards to Musical Theatre, I believe the main reason that the level is higher in the US than the UK is down to the fact that the dancers have a strong union. This means they feel protected and valued within the industry and therefore have a higher expectation of them and what they deliver. However, I think the UK does have a real sense of pushing the boundaries in what we see in both the Commercial and the Musical Theatre scene. In both scenes we see new ideas being added to the Commercial Dance style, to commercial shows and to Musical Theatre and I believe this derives from a true sense of innovation that the UK dance scene has.

References

8a. Copyright and Commercial Dance

www.ew.com/music/2019/12/06/blurred-lines-marvin-gaye-pharrell-williams-controversy/
www.washingtonpost.com/lifestyle/style/beyonce-countdown-video-and-the-art-of-stealing/2011/11/15/gIQAj0WbYN_story.html
www.youtube.com/watch?v=uy3LBxKTU8Q
Burt, R. (2016). *Ungoverning Dance: Contemporary European Theatre Dance and the Commons*. Oxford: Oxford University Press.
Judkins, R. (2015). *You Are More Creative Than You Think You Are*. UK, Spectre.
Robert, Y. (2020). JaQuel Knight Is Paving the Way for the Future of Copyrighting Dance. www.forbes.com/sites/yolarobert1/2020/11/23/jaquel-knight-is-paving-the-way-for-the-future-of-copyrighting-dance/
Saucier, A. (2018) Dance and Copyright: Legal "Steps" for Performers. www.itsartlaw.org/2018/10/30/dance-and-copyright-legal-steps-for-performers/
Yeoh, F.S. and C. Waelde (2011). Beyond Text: Music and Dance: Beyond Copyright Text. www.youtube.com/watch?v=uy3LBxKTU8Q

8c. Polar Paradigms – Inclusivity and Sexualisation

Balaji, M. (2010). Vixen Resistin': Redefining Black Womanhood in Hip-Hop Music Videos. *Journal of Black Studies*, 41(1), 5–20.
Carroll, N. (1990). The Image of Women in Film: A Defense of a Paradigm. *The Journal of Aesthetics and Art Criticism*, 48(4), 349–360.
Lhooq, M. (2014). Shocked and outraged by Nicki Minaj's Anaconda video? Perhaps you should butt out. www.theguardian.com/lifeandstyle/womens-blog/2014/aug/22/nicki-minaj-anaconda-video-black-women-sexuality
Railton, D. and P. Watson (2005). Naughty Girls and Red Blooded Women: Representations of Female Heterosexuality in Music Video. *Feminist Media Studies*, 5(1), 51–63.

8d. A Supporting Dancer

www.backstage.com/magazine/article/dancing-behind-stars-57756/ [accessed: 07/2022].

8e. Street Dance versus Urban Dance

www.cosmopolitan.com/entertainment/music/a32827031/grammy-awards-changing-name-urban-categories/ [accessed: 07/2022].

www.rollingstone.com/music/music-features/labels-ditch-urban-1011593/ [accessed: 10/11/2022].

www.steezy.co/posts/the-story-behind-urban-dance-and-why-were-leaving-the-term-behind [accessed: 07/2022].

Chapter 9

Places to Train

Around the time that Commercial Dance was establishing itself as a viable employment sector in the early 1980s, a number of places to train began to emerge in various cities internationally, with New York and London leading the way. These dance centres marked a change from dance training as it had been previously known. Before this period, going to a dance school to take classes usually meant going to one dance tutor or academy – a place where only that style of dance (predominately modern dance or ballet at that time) and their own practised dance syllabi were distributed to its students. Dance critic Elizabeth Kendall wrote an illuminating piece about taking dance classes in New York city in the mid-1970s. She experienced a dance scene bursting with life and reminisces about attending classes in a number of different studios:

> The city's edges belonged more to us. I remember the feel, smell, texture of each New York studio with its own kinetic-aesthetics, which seemed to seep into the surrounding streets. The Merce Cunningham studio on the top of Westbeth in the far West Village, where we practiced his cool, precise motions…The ivy-covered townhouse of the Martha Graham Company way east on 63rd Street, where, in whitewashed studios that almost smelled of blood, we reached up from the floor as if in agony, or got imaginary-gut-punched in several positions….
>
> But SoHo was where I took tap dance with a young female acolyte of the veteran Harlem hoofers. She'd borrowed the key to an empty warehouse on the corner of Prince and Mercer (later a J. Crew store). She would put a boombox on the dusty floor, and we would stomp, shuffle, time-step to its beat.

By the early 1980s, those derelict New York loft spaces and warehouses began to be bought up as new Wall Street money slowly moved into the hip arts haven that is SoHo and the East Village. The dance landscape also began to change, the modern dance boom of the 1970s was being usurped by another dance boom – that of Breakin', Jazz dance and the aerobics classes which saturated international pop culture. By 1983, Jane Fonda's dance inspired work out videos and audio albums were international best sellers and 'Flashdance' was selling out at the cinemas. There was an increased demand for tuition in dance styles other than just the Euro-centric studio techniques of Ballet and Modern Dance – the new and evolving study of Jazz and dance-based aerobic classes were all sought after. The demographic calling for classes were not only professional dancers or serious students of dance, but the classes also provided a way for everyday people to keep fit and enjoy dance as a hobby.

Economic and cultural changes shepherded in the idea of 'drop-in' dance classes. For a small, one-off fee, people could walk in off the street without pre-booking and take a Jazz, Tap, Ballet, Salsa, Street Dance or Modern class taught by different teachers in the same building – a candy store of dance offerings all under one roof. This business model is still the one used today in cities internationally. Developments over the last 20 years have led some dance centres to specialise in the Commercial Dance industry and its associated styles whilst maintaining the drop-in or pay-as-you-go business model.

The following dance centres have had a significant impact within the dance industry and offer specialised classes suitable for a training Commercial Dancer in the 2020s.

9a. BASE Dance Studios

London, UK

A relatively recent addition to the dance studio circuit in London, BASE dance studios was set up in 2018 by Dax O'Callaghan and Aston Merrygold, two entrepreneurs with a depth of performance experience rooted in the Commercial world. BASE is a dance centre created to cater for predominately Commercial dancers, choreographers and students. Naming each studio after influential performers, all of which have made an indelible mark in the world of Commercial Dance reflects its direction – Jackson, Timberlake, Britney, James Brown. Whilst training for upcoming live performances in 2022, Janet Jackson made BASE her resident dance studio whilst training with choreographer Dean Anthony Lee.

Co-Director Dax O'Callaghan describes some of the objectives the founders have for BASE studios and what they hope to offer the dance community:

> We feel it is vital for choreographers to be able to have a home where they can express their choreography and work on their craft whilst teaching the next generations. More importantly, with the commercial dance scene within the UK running under a very unstable structure, it is important that dancers have a place to come together and gain consistency in their training. BASE is also a place for them to share their experiences, socialise, and network.

Contact:
  info@basedancestudios.com
  4 Tinworth Street, Vauxhall, London, SE11 5EJ

9b. Broadway Dance Centre

New York, USA

In 1984, Richard Ellner, business executive and lover of the performing arts, oversaw the transformation from the buildings previous life as Hines-Hatchett Performing Arts Centre to

Broadway Dance Centre. Maurice Hines (older brother of Gregory Hines) and Frank Hatchett had previously developed their school from Jojo's Dance Factory, a dance school founded by prominent Broadway dancer/choreographer Jojo Smith with Sue Samuels. Hatchett and Ellner continued to develop the centre over the next few decades, attracting dancers from all over the world.

Broadway Dance Centre was one of the first dance institutions to disrupt the market and change perceptions of what was previously perceived as a 'dance school.' Expanding on a business model first germinated by Jojo's Dance Factory a decade earlier, BDC offered a schedule made up of classes in a plethora of dance styles, from beginner to professional level and given by different specialists in that particular style. Located west of Times Square in the centre of Manhattan, dancers no longer had to travel to four or five different locations in the city to keep up their dance training. Economically and creatively, it was a win-win situation as dancers saved money and travel time and teachers did not have to worry about administrating their own schools, they could just focus on teaching. It became a place where famous faces from television and film mixed with Broadway chorus dancers whilst offering a central focus for the professional dance community.

BDC now resides at West 45th St in New York, offering multiple different technique classes a week across seven studios, each with an observation area, creating a notable sense of community and support for the dancers attending classes.

Contact:
Info@bwydance.com
322 West 45th Street, New York, USA

9c. Pineapple Dance Studios

London, UK

Pineapple Dance Studios, or simply 'Pineapple,' as it is known locally, is a drop-in dance centre located in Covent Garden, in the heart of London's West End. It was opened in 1979, when Debbie Moore OBE converted a disused former pineapple warehouse to a multi-floor dance establishment hosting high quality dance studios. The centre established itself in the early 1980s, at a time when dance was making a significant imprint on US and European pop culture, heavily influencing music and fashion trends. Realising the new cultural influence dance had at this time, Moore shrewdly created a Pineapple clothing brand, referencing the quintessential dance trademarks of the 1980s – lycra (developed specifically for dance by Moore), track pants, leg warmers and sweatbands, making the Pineapple logo a recognisable part of streetwear in the UK. The power of dance trends and Moore's entrepreneurial talents saw Pineapple floated as public company in 1982 and Moore became the first woman to take her company to the London Stock Exchange. In 2010, a successful, 15 episode reality TV show about Pineapple aired globally, boosting Pineapple as a recognisable international brand.

From a Commercial Dance perspective, Pineapple has been a cornerstone of many professional dancer's development over the last 30 years. Classes in a myriad of dance styles fill the centre 7 days a week and it is also regularly used as a rehearsal and audition venue for some of the biggest Commercial Dance projects in London. During my time as a working dancer in London, a big chunk of all my rehearsals or auditions took place at Pineapple and queues can regularly be seen winding through the streets of Covent Garden as audition hopefuls wait in line to audition for a music video, cruise ship or new West End show. Management companies for artists such as Beyonce and Madonna have booked studios at Pineapple for their projects multiple times over the last few decades.

The television show and the clothing brand have resulted in Pineapple becoming a popular tourist attraction but the high quality of the teachers offering classes remains and the youth performing arts programmes which Pineapple runs has ensured that it maintains its position as a world-class dance centre for both students and professional dancers alike.

Contact:
7 Langley Street
Covent Garden, London
+44 (0)20 7836 4004

9d. Millennium Dance Complex

Los Angeles, USA

Millennium Dance Complex (MDC) has established a home for itself at the epicentre of the west coast Commercial Dance Industry. Previously known as Moro Landis Studios, the project has been overseen and developed since 1992 by Ann Marie Hudson. In 1999, the centre moved premises to Ventura Blvd where it reopened as its current carnation – Millennium Dance Complex. MDC was created with Hip-Hop dance styles at its core. Just as Pineapple and Broadway Dance Centre had been forged in the fire, which was ignited by the popularity of 1980's Jazz dance movement, MDC launched itself when the commercialisation of Hip-Hop culture was influencing global trends – the fashion, the music and the dance styles. Hudson recalls in an interview that:

> When we left New York there was nothing called Hip-Hop dance in any of the professional dance studios, when we arrived in Los Angeles every studio had one on their schedule. I quickly tried to get a read on the L.A. dance scene. The talk was that hip-hop was a passing phase and didn't belong in the 'real dance' world. I remembered that's what they said about Rock and Roll in the fifties and decided to co-mingle the classic dance arts with this new urban movement. It was this fresh expression for the next generation of dance. A raw force that would come to break across all pre-established boundaries and unite cultures around the world.
>
> Our faculty was created from raw talent walking through the door. No resumes required at the beginning, each candidate was tested out in the dance class and hired on pure ability. The momentum of the hip-hop classes was building right along with the Jazz and Ballet. The students were trying everything, embracing the new, the old and each other.

MDC is a place frequented by working professional choreographers, either giving masterclasses, taking auditions or working through rehearsals, it is an important cog in the Commercial Dance industry. The teaching and masterclass rota includes established choreographers such as Yanis Marshall, Brian Friedman, Marty Kudelka, Ian Eastwood and Tina Landon. As dance class videos began to become a prominent part of class culture and studio marketing strategies in the early 2010s, Millennium emerged as an internationally recognisable venue, with masterclasses getting millions of views on social media channels and MDC's 'red wall' becoming a famous performance space in the process.

Contact:
Millennium Dance Complex
11528 Ventura Blvd
Studio City, CA 91604
(818) 753–5081

Places to Train

Image 9.1 Kashika on tour with Finnish artist Evelina (2022)

PROFESSIONAL INSIGHT – KASHIKA ARORA

Location: Finland

Kashika is relatively new to the Commercial Dance industry. She graduated from the Institute of the Arts Barcelona in 2022 and has embarked upon her professional dance career in Finland, touring extensively with the music artist 'Evelina.' She is based in Finland and is also of Indian heritage. She hopes to inspire dancers from both India and Finland to follow in her footsteps.

The dancers and talent in India is incredible; they have their own style of movement and are all so unique.
I was not really aware of the dance industry in India until I went to take some classes there earlier this year. There is an industry in India, especially in Mumbai (I am sure you might have heard of Bollywood). However, a lot of the dancers that are booked for Bollywood (from what I have noticed) are Caucasian, but there are also quite a few who are also Indian. I would love to explore working in India at some point, since I love travelling and working in different countries.

It is a game changer when you are surrounded by people with the same passion and drive as you, that for me is inspirational.
Seeing the way people that have been in the industry longer than you handle situations, their professionalism and the way they work is always rewarding to see, since you can always learn from people around you, even when you are on assignment. It is also interesting to see the different ways in which choreographers teach, since it inspires me to diversify the ways in which I could teach. So far nothing has been scary, I am the kind of person that thrives under pressure and am always up for a challenge.

I never thought that I would have gone to University to study Commercial Dance but I am grateful that I did.
Originally, my dance training mainly included Hip Hop, Heels and Commercial. However, the training on the course included Ballet, Jazz, Tap, Contemporary and Aerial. Learning

different styles consistently not only helped me become more versatile but also helped me with my confidence, with textures, cleanliness and helped me introduce a more versatile movement quality in my dancing.

I believe that a dancer is always learning. You should never get too comfortable about where you are at. The commercial industry is constantly changing and it is important to keep up with it. Because of this, I still keep up my training by going to classes here in Finland, taking online classes and also learning/choreographing with my friends who are also professional dancers. Also, if classes in Finland get too repetitive, I take a couple of weeks to go to places such as Barcelona or London to take classes; it is extremely refreshing.

I absolutely adore Parris Goebel. I believe she IS Commercial Dance.
Not only is her movement and dancing inspirational, but her journey to get to the platform she is at now is extremely inspirational. What makes Goebel stand out is her movement quality because it is a mixture of so many different genres of dance, and the dancers she works with are so diverse and that is empowering. Other than Goebel, Charm La Donna, Kyle Hanagami and Latrice Kabamba are choreographers that inspire me.

I enjoy working in Finland.
I am extremely grateful for the amazing jobs I have been able to do here because I feel like it is a step closer to my hopes of being able to inspire dancers and individuals like myself of a different ethnicity to follow their dreams. The dance industry in Finland is quite small, but diverse. It's all about networking, getting yourself out there, and at the same time staying true to your goals. The industry in Finland is like the industry in any country, but since Finland itself is not the largest place, it makes the industry tight-knit too.

When I was growing up, I never really had someone to look up to who 'looked' like me and was in the industry, and I hope to be that person and be able to inspire at least a few individuals in the future.
A few things I have come to realise and learnt is that number one, you should never take anything for granted and two, you should always celebrate an achievement no matter how small or big it is because at one point in your life, that is where you wanted to be. In terms of my career in the future, there are lots of things I would love to achieve and I am sure they are the type of goals that quite a few dancers have. However, a huge goal I hope to achieve is to be able to inspire individuals of Indian descent to follow their dreams of being in the industry since it is still not that common of a career that is supported and looked at in the same light such as being an engineer, doctor, lawyer etc.

PROFESSIONAL INSIGHT – NATHAN J CLARKE

Location: Madrid, Spain

Nathan J Clarke is a choreographer working out of Madrid. Originally from Australia and after a long career in London working as a Commercial dancer, Nathan has choreographed projects such as The Voice UK for 4 consecutive years, Strictly Come Dancing (UK), Dancing on Ice (UK), The Greatest Dancer (UK), the Olympic closing ceremony 2012 and the X-Factor Italia.

In 2022, he developed and choreographed a residency show in Las Vegas entitled 'Rouge.'

In my career, I've been so lucky to have been in certain situations and to be working on certain projects.
As a Commercial dancer, I really remember the feeling of taking to the stage in front of an audience of over 40,000 fans on the 'Circus' stadium tour for the band Take That. It was a defining moment for me and most of the cast. It's when I knew the move to London was 100% the best thing I ever did and all the blood, sweat and many tears became worth it. The audience were there for the band but we were appreciated and what's more – we were really dancing. Strong, hard and complex choreography. It was a true spectacle and I felt part of something really ground-breaking.

In my choreographic career I feel every job is a 'pinch-me' moment, to be playing out my passion day by day with the pure purpose to create works is incredible. I have worked extremely hard, but unfortunately that isn't all it takes in this industry. I got my chance and held it. From early childhood, I was obsessed with Las Vegas and the dream of one day working in a show there. My career as a dancer passed and though opportunities arose, I never quite got there, but very recently I got my chance. I opened my first Las Vegas show as a Commercial choreographer and had my most satisfying 'this is what you do' moment.

I began training in Australia at the age of 7 after a long process of elimination in every sport imaginable.
I definitely wasn't great at everything I tried, but I couldn't find that satisfaction or challenge that made me want to continue until my Mum finally managed to get me into a Jazz class at a local dance school. I hated it. I cried and cried and couldn't wait for it to be over. The next day I felt that for some reason I had to go back. I obviously did and then Jazz became Tap then Ballet then Musical Theatre then Acro then private lessons. I was hooked. From age 7, I was going to dance classes 6 days a week. From as far back as I can remember, it was tough. Fiercely competitive, strenuous and from what my parents remind me, expensive.

Although London and Los Angeles both appear to be the only two 'places to be' as a Commercial dancer, as we've seen recently – New Zealand, Australia, Paris, Stockholm and Denmark, for example, have and are producing some of the most extraordinarily talented dancers and choreographers to hit the industry in a long time.
That being said, there is a definite gravity towards LA and London due to it being the two epicentres for the music industry, which in my opinion is where Commercial Dance was born. The two go hand in hand. These may be the most exposed cities, but as I've travelled and worked, I've discovered that every major city has its own buzz of Commercial Dance. Milan for example is one of my favourites worldwide and I have choreographed some of my most memorable commercial works there using local talents.

Staying current with trends in the music and fashion industry is a big factor in being a credible Commercial choreographer in my opinion.
This goes hand in hand with taking risks and pushing boundaries within styles. Fusing contemporary dance with Hip Hop, Swing with Popping and Locking, Voguing with Latin. Nothing is off bounds in Commercial Dance and one of the most enticing elements that I've discovered is that there really are no rules. 'Commercial' means to me 'exposed,' 'seen.' It's dance to be witnessed, which in turn invites criticism alongside praise.

Dance is an art form and completely open to interpretation in most forms, whereas Commercial Dance must sit within boundaries of the environment for which it is commissioned. Whether a music video, a tv show, a live tour, the role of the choreographer is to create a piece to fit within the overall creative vision – usually that of the creative director. Managing to fit in these realms while pushing boundaries within the movement and your choreographic vision is what can really make you stand out as a Commercial choreographer.

I really love to work with an assistant when creating new commercial works, the time alone together in the studio bouncing ideas is possibly my most enjoyable moment in the creative process.
Choosing an assistant that's right for you can be difficult, but talent aside, personality plays a huge part. Essentially, your assistant is an extension of you. You want them to grab the choreography in the style that you do it yourself; you want them to sell it to you in those times of self-doubt (there's many). And for me, the assistant role really comes in to play when you have your cast together in the working studio. I personally need a real positive, go getter that will get things going before I've even had the chance to. Often as the choreographer in the commercial world, there are many issues and changes that arise during your rehearsal period and dealing with artists, clients, producers and managers all come into play during these rehearsal days. A great assistant won't let these distractions take time away from the task ahead and will push the cast to where they possibly can without you. An assistant who is versatile in all styles is a must for me as my work covers all aspects of Commercial Dance and mixing this with a great personal bond, respect and a lot of trust can lead to a long term working partnership.

What's next in Commercial Dance? I don't believe any of us know until we are faced with it. The art of digital media is constantly evolving and being fused with dance, creating works that are interactive with digital aspects have long been a thing, but today I believe it is pushing boundaries. Contemporary choreographers spend months and months researching these elements and test driving new technology and for this, I am forever grateful. Once that technology is in its workable stages, it generally finds a way to us in the Commercial world where we can expose it to the public within our medias of television and stage. My hope for

Image 9.2 Nathan on set of The Voice (UK)

the future of Commercial Dance is to maintain its level of exposure. Dance is to be celebrated and enjoyed and within the realms of Commercial Dance, as artists, we are entertaining the world.

References

www.mdclv.com/millennium-story/ [accessed: 06/2022].

Kendall, E. (2020). New York City's Gift of Motion, *The New York Times*, 1st July 2020 [accessed: 06/06/2022].

Chapter 10

Academic Insight

This chapter includes four articles contributed by dance scholars and academics from a variety of backgrounds. The articles connect their various areas of academic and professional expertise with the Commercial Dance industry.

Litza Bixler is a choreographer, dance academic and screenwriter. She choreographed the iconic zombie dance in the cult movie classic 'Shaun of the Dead' as well working on projects such as 'Scott Pilgrim vs the World' and many award-winning TV commercials. In 2022, she was artist-in-residence at the University of Wisconsin–Madison. Litza's insightful contribution, *"Dancing on a Cliff Edge,"* explores the challenges Commercial dancers face as they navigate living from job to job as a cog in the 'gig economy.'

Daria Lavrennikov, Ph.D., is a dancer, performer, choreographer, curator and artist-researcher originating from Moscow, educated in the US and now based in Barcelona. She gained her Ph.D. at the Federal University of Rio de Janeiro. Her essay *"Collaborations between Early 20th century European and American concert and Commercial Dance: Tamiris and Nagrin"* discusses how Modern and Contemporary dance work continues to resonate in the Commercial industries. She highlights how 'uptown dance meets downtown dance' by focusing on the careers of two early contemporary dance pioneers and their body of work: Helen Tamiris and Daniel Nagrin.

Joseph Mercier, Ph.D., is a choreographer and performance maker based at the Northern School of Contemporary Dance in the UK. His Ph.D. at the Royal Central School of Speech and Drama analysed ballet cultures in relation to gender and sexual politics. His work centres around examining queer studies, choreographic practices and performance politics. Focusing on Disco, Waacking and Voguing, Joseph's essay *"Punkin' and Werkin' It: The Queer Roots of Commercial Dance"* looks at these dance sub-genres and their relationship to the Commercial Dance industry.

Armando Rotondi, Ph.D. is an academic, journalist, writer, and theatre practitioner from Italy. He is Full Professor in Performance Theory and Storytelling, and Leader of the MA Creative Performance Practice at the Institute of the Arts Barcelona (validated by Liverpool John Moores University). He achieved his PhD at the University of Strathclyde in 2012, working on translation and adaptation in theatre, film and performance. His essay *"A reflection on*

Hip-Hop, hegemony and appropriation" discusses appropriation vs transculturation within Hip-Hop culture.

10a. Dancing on a Cliff Edge

By Litza Bixler

Dance professionals produce entertaining and creative work for stage and screen and appear to lead glamorous lives untroubled by mundane concerns such as financial uncertainty. Yet behind the curtain, their lives are often characterised by unpredictability and precarity. The aim of this chapter is to offer a glimpse behind that curtain, in order to examine the precarity of freelance work and its impact on commercial dancers and choreographers.

Through interviews and an online survey, freelance dance professionals described a life of insecurity, rejection and constant self-promotion. But they also talked about the freedom, variety, autonomy and flexibility that freelancing affords them. For them, freelancing is like walking a tightrope, where balance and failure are equally possible. And, as one choreographer put it, "the floor underneath is always uncertain."

The Precocity of Freelance Work

Freelance entertainment professionals are independent contractors or specialists who are hired to create a film, show or other creative product. Once a job is complete, the workforce is disbanded. There is a high rate of turnover in the industry, and many talented and experienced people leave (Caves 2000). Freelancers are not considered employees, so there is little government oversight and much of the labour is unregulated. Workers fend for themselves, in an environment where labour is plentiful and jobs are frequently scarce.

Precarity is baked into freelance work via several structural mechanisms: it's inconsistent, unpredictable, short-term, temporary, and there is a lack of institutional support. Entertainment unions and social insurance programs can help to ameliorate some of this precarity, but a 'wild west' environment frequently pervades.

Balancing Risk and Reward

Entertainment work in general is high risk, but even more so for freelance dance professionals. Compared to other entertainment workers, their pay is often lower and their risk of injury is higher.

Dance freelancers must balance a desire for freedom, autonomy and creative expression with a tolerance for risk, insecurity and uncertainty. For many, the trade-off is worth it: with enough skill, flexibility, persistence and confidence, they avoid plunging to their metaphorical deaths. But the abyss is ever-present; and if security is the goal, freelancing rarely achieves it.

Methods

This article presents results from an online survey and 18 one-on-one interviews. Subjects were recruited using a convenience sample drawn from the author's professional network.

The survey was sent to approximately 400 dancers and choreographers, with a response rate of 10% (40 respondents). All participants quoted in this chapter are professional dancers, choreographers and educators aged between 25 and 48. They work as freelancers; in theatre, pop music, television, advertising and film.

Results

Dancing on a Cliff Edge

Perhaps the most salient theme expressed by respondents was that they often felt like they were dancing along a cliff edge. Their work is creatively fulfilling, challenging and exciting partly because it's unpredictable and temporary. But it is also extremely precarious, and requires perfect balance at all times to avoid disaster. Diane, 36, who has been freelance for over 20 years, said: "It's like I'm balancing on a tightrope, and I'm assuming I'll fall off to the right, and then I'll fall off to the left… but I'm hoping for balance."

Mark, 35, specialises in urban dance styles and started freelancing at a young age. He used a similar metaphor.

Sometimes you're on a tightrope and you're just back flipping your way across it, 'cause you've got tons of work and it's amazing. And sometimes you can fall and it can be, like, death.

Tripp, 45, is an experienced choreographer who has been freelance for nearly 20 years. He noted that freelancers are always questioning their abilities and often feel insecure: "You never really think that you're good enough – or even when you think you're good enough, you know that you're gonna get knocked over soon," he said.

Individual Coping Mechanisms

Individual coping strategies for managing precarity fell under three broad categories: mindsets, flexibility, and hustle.

Positive/Optimistic Mindsets

Participants were often future-focused, and believed that their futures would be bright. Jordan, who has been freelance for 28 years, said:

> As a freelancer you have to be very focused on [the future]. I don't know if it's about having faith that you'll work, or being able to pivot, or it's just the practice of knowing that you're not quite sure what your future entails. It's like, am I practicing my faith or am I having faith in my practice?

Previous research has suggested that self-employed people are often overoptimistic and overconfident about their entrepreneurial success (Parker 2009). In this study, 83% of the survey respondents said they were "optimistic" or "extremely optimistic" about the future, and 12.5% said they were "somewhat optimistic." On the other hand, 0% indicated that they were "pessimistic about the future."

About 90% indicated that they were relatively "comfortable with uncertainty" and the majority (69%) were confident that they could "pay their bills" each month. Diane expressed this confidence succinctly: "I know my fixed expenses, and I believe I have the opportunity to create value that is equal to or more than my fixed expenses."

Pedro, 38, is a Spanish choreographer based in the UK. He has been freelance for most of his life and noted that he is "generally quite a positive person," even if he's been without work for a while. "[A job] always ends up coming in," he said.

Freelancers wait patiently for their stocks to rise and for their ships to come in, and believe in the upward trajectory of their careers. Like Carter, 28, who said, "With time, I'm seeing gradual upgrades [in my career], Like every time you go up a level you get a new ability, a new toy, or you know, a power-up."

Such optimism may not be entirely misplaced: 75% of respondents said they were rarely out of paid work, and gaps between their jobs ranged from a couple of weeks to four months.

Growth Mindset and Learning New Things

Most participants exhibited what Decker (2006) has called a growth mindset: a belief in their ability to improve, grow and change through practice. This mindset was underpinned by a general love of learning. As Diane put it:

> I love to be learning even more than I love to be dancing. […] So I often find myself taking a risk in the direction of something I believe in, and being rewarded by a very rich learning experience, and an even richer group of people.

For Tripp, learning and improving his skillset was his way of keeping competition at bay:

> If you're not consistently learning and sharpening your tools, you know, people are just gonna take over. And then I guess you just have to like, eventually wither away.

Several of the participants also noted that they often had to learn new styles or skills, confessing that they would assure clients that they could perform certain skills in order to secure a job, even if they couldn't. They would then quickly "pick up those skills before the job."

In essence, positive and growth mindsets mean that participants feel responsible for their successes, even if luck and external circumstances play a role.

Flexibility and Adaption

To thrive in a competitive and labour-saturated industry, freelancers must create and respond to change. Sometimes this means changing roles, moving from one place to another, or adding strings to their bow. For instance, Steve is an experienced performer and event producer who stays flexible by having his fingers "in as many pies as possible." Diane observed that adaptation is key: "We get paid at varying intervals, varying amounts, from varying sources. But once you know that, and adapt, it's awesome," she said.

Pivots were sometimes motivated by pay. Samantha, 39, a US-based choreographer and director, spoke of how she felt undervalued, leading her to shift from choreographing hit Broadway shows, music tours and films to directing narrative film:

> I started to pivot into narrative directing, because honestly, as a choreographer in films and commercials, I felt a little underpaid and undervalued. […] So why not go where there's like a future, where I'm potentially valued, and where there's a system in place?

Most participants described themselves as nimble and frequently moved from one creative path to another. Sometimes these pivots occurred due to external factors like injuries or lack of work, while others were motivated by boredom, shifting priorities, pay, or a desire for new challenges. Like Diane, who often changed direction in order to push herself. Over the course of her career, she's danced in pop tours, choreographed for film and TV, and now hosts a podcast and runs an experimental dance company.

Others pivoted due to injury, aging, or both; like all performers, they have to face up to the reality that their bodies are vulnerable. Silvio, 48, decided to build a 'portfolio career' out of several creative specialties when he recognised that his performance career had a shelf life:

> You start thinking, how long can I rely on this? Because our job is very much physical. So it was like, I need to focus more on something that I'll be able to rely on in the future. […] I'm not putting all my eggs in one basket.

Managing Injury

Many interviewees experienced an injury at some point in their careers. A serious injury can derail a career or a desired transition, as Matt, 36, a dancer and stunt performer discovered:

> I went to this audition for this live stunt show. And I started thinking, Wow, this is really fun! I think this is the job I want to do. But then I broke my collarbone. And it took me about 9 months to fully get back to work.

Diane and Ada are both choreographers in their mid-thirties who lost their voices due to overuse. Like all choreographers, they use their voices frequently in their work – they shout out counts and directions, they cheer on performers and trainees, they whoop and they holler. After surgery and what Diane called 'weeks of silent recovery,' they returned to work. Ada revealed that the experience 'terrified her,' and both said they had to remain vigilant to prevent reinjury.

As these experiences show, flexibility can be forced upon freelancers by external events. It is possible that many of the long-tenured participants in this study secured their professional longevity by expanding their range and remaining flexible in the face of change.

Hustling All the Time

Participants described 'hustling' as scouting for work, having their fingers in a lot of pies, self-promotion, and/or hard work. Carter, 28, spoke of his experience as a Los Angeles-based dancer and choreographer:

> It's like you're walking down a dark tunnel, and there's a light, but you don't know how far it is or how long it's gonna take to reach it. So you just gotta stay on top of what you're doing. You can't really slack, you gotta hustle. And you're kind of hustling all the time.

Sarah, 37, observed that "being on all the time" was particularly draining. She said, "it's just this never ending hamster wheel of trying to get work, versus wondering when the work's gonna come in, versus negotiating what that work looks like."

Interviewees mentioned that constant hustling helped them to secure and create future work, to manage uncertainty, and to shore up their material and psychological resources. At other times, hustling simply helped them to "feel productive and busy," allowing them to ameliorate anxiety and to maintain a sense of autonomy. For example, Pedro said:

Academic Insight

> I've got these little things that I already do myself, instead of having to wait for someone else to book me on a job. So I think these things probably carry me through. Because if I'm not being asked to do jobs. I've still got my own things to worry about and do admin for, and stuff. So I think it would take me quite a while [to worry about not working] because I still feel like I'm kind of busy.

Side Hustles

Every freelancer in this study had one or more 'side hustles,' non-entertainment jobs that generated supplemental income in order to survive. They sometimes called these 'day jobs' or 'side gigs,' and many participants had two or three. Commonly-mentioned side gigs included service-sector jobs; fitness work and teaching.

Jordan, 40, often works in education: "My family has always done entertainment as a side hustle whereas I did the reverse. Entertainment is my main career and education is my side hustle."

Briony, 40, is an actress and a ballet dancer who taught and took other side gigs in order to pay for technique class: "God, over the years I've worked in bars, in restaurants. Anything, you know, just to earn money, so I could do class," she said.

At one point, Carter had three dance-studio jobs at once, in addition to working at Starbucks and a home-goods store. But he noted that, "just the Starbucks and home-store stuff were side hustles. Anything that isn't to do with dance is a side hustle for me."

Conversely, Jordan aimed to keep all of his work dance-related:

> Sometimes your side hustle can pull you away from your goal, so I always try to make sure that [the side job] funnels back through dance so I'm still building [my career].

Ultimately, side gigs provide a much-needed buffer when there are gaps between jobs, sometimes even blossoming into secondary or portfolio careers when an income stream dries up or falters.

Institutional Structure

Institutional structures such as unions, state benefits and insurance can help dance freelancers manage risk, gain respect and make plans for life events such as retirement. Although institutional support varied between countries, the majority of the participants in this study wanted entertainment unions or other professional associations to step in more often, especially when state support was weak.

Unions and State Support

Several of the US film choreographers were involved in an ongoing unionization drive, and their comments reflected an acute awareness of the precarity of their specialism. For example, Jordan observed that, "if there's an injury to my body, I can't work, or I have to pivot; whereas [people with steady employment] would have some kind of benefits laid out for them." Several of the US-based freelancers complained about the complexities of the American healthcare system and those not already represented by the Screen Actors Guild wanted a union to provide group-based health and unemployment insurance.

UK respondents rarely discussed health or other forms of insurance, presumably because the UK's national insurance program provides these types of support. On the other hand, they often mentioned wanting stricter working hours, written contracts and other benefits associated with traditional employment, such as holiday pay and private pensions. As Pedro noted:

> If I could wave a magic wand, you would get benefits in your payments. You know, like holiday pay. Or you could get a pension included in your fees. Basically, right, just have it function more like other jobs.

Samantha pointed out that dance work in film was treated differently than unionized stage dance work:

> In theatre, like, the [Stage Directors' & Choreographers' Society] protects us pretty well. Our rights are important. And then I tried to carry those expectations over [to film]. But it felt like the Wild West. I was shocked and it's demotivating.

By comparison, Silvio noted his positive experiences in Germany, where performers are supported by insurance policies that are specific to their profession.

In Germany, I felt like as a performer I was treated well. I felt like I was honoured and seen as a proper worker and doing good for the society rather than like, oh, you're just doing your hobby… we had to pay insurance, like from your wages – you didn't even realise that the money was taken. And then when you decide "I'm gonna change career," they give [that fund] back to you.

Respect: from Others, from Ourselves

Many of the participants observed a lack of respect for dance professionals within the entertainment industry, as well as in the broader culture. Sophia, 47, is an Italian dancer who has been living and working in the UK for over 15 years. She observed that "when I say I'm a dancer, people ask whether I do pole dancing!" Audrey expressed a similar sentiment:

> When people think "dancers", they think faffing around in skimpy outfits. There's always going to be that snobbery… even in the West End. They just don't respect it.

Mark often performs physically demanding 'tricks' and 'acro' which are sometimes considered stunts. He noted that "when someone's a stunt performer, there's instant respect. But if you say you're a dancer? There's no respect there."

Some interviewees expressed the opinion that dancers "don't have enough self-respect," or suffer from a 'scarcity mindset,' which led them to accept lower pay and poor working conditions. Steve, who performs less frequently now and is often in a position to hire performers, suggested that dancers are simply unaware of their material worth.

In the UK, dancers are often paid so little, out of ignorance more than anything. Dancers are told "this is your value," and they go "okay, sure." But they don't think about the years of training and the money they've spent on college, travel, training… etc. So it's just not knowing their own material worth.

Steve also sees a clear connection between pay and feeling valued and respected. He said:

> I take a nominal margin from anybody who works for me because I'd much rather they know they're getting paid well, because that engenders loyalty and [they feel] respected. The flip side is if you make people work for nothing, you'll never get the best out of them because there's always that little poison nugget in their mind [...] so this is how much you value me?

Unions: Respect and Collective Voice

Many interviewees agreed that unionization was one remedy for this perceived lack of respect. Several pointed out that when unions fight for better pay, safer working conditions and reasonable hours, they also engender respect for the workers. As one participant noted: "for me, being in a union shows that you respect yourself and your profession. And if you respect and value yourself, then producers will also respect and value you."

For many interviewees, a sense of solidarity and collective voice was important because, as Jordan observed, "when people feel like they are alone on an island, they will not advocate for themselves."

Commercial dancers and choreographers in the UK are not represented by a union. Instead, agents or the freelancers themselves must negotiate hours, pay and working conditions.

Some of the UK dancers mentioned that Equity, the union representing actors and some stage dancers, lacked power or didn't fight hard enough for them. But most, like Tripp, said that the benefits of being in a union outweighed the costs. "Sometimes you have to be very direct to get a direct reply," he said. "So yeah, it's good that there are unions, even if [Equity] doesn't have much power here – it sets the record straight."

About 50% of the survey respondents were already in a union, and 50% were not. All of the non-unionized respondents either 'definitely' (71%) or 'possibly' (29%) wanted to join one. Similarly, most of the interviewees said they would join a union if one targeted towards commercial dancers and choreographers became available.

When asked how essential entertainment unions are to the economic security of freelancers, 61% indicated that they were 'somewhat' or 'very' important.

Retirement and Future Plans

Most respondents said that they would continue freelancing for some time, and several expected to continue 'until the end.' Matt, who viewed being an artist as incompatible with retirement, put it like this:

> I think I would still be freelance to the end, because I feel like people that are in more corporate jobs – there's that burnout point where people need to retire. Whereas I've always wanted to stay in the artistic world. And I don't think there's ever a point in time that you retire from being an artist. So I'm like, why would I want to retire from that?

Diane also envisioned freelancing for most of her life, but talked about how difficult it can be for freelancers to retire, even if they want to:

> You know I look at some of my mentors. I know one super-well-known choreographer who is still working, still having to be working, and she turns 80 this year! And then I look at my dad, who is retired and lounging at his pool. I would love for all of us who've been destroying our knees and hips and voices to get to sit some place quiet

and feel relaxed. I know a lot of our peers don't like taking vacations; they love to be working and that is fine. But wouldn't it be great if there was a choice?

Anthony, 23, is a young dancer new to the Los Angeles dance scene. Nevertheless, he has started thinking about retirement and observed how different it looks for freelancers:

> I come from a family of educators and people in healthcare, so they all have very specific retirement plans set up through their professions. And I've talked to them a little bit about what it would look like for me to set something like that up. But [as a freelance artist] it's just a totally different experience.

Bryony, 40, observed that freelancers are "so in the moment, you never think about what's gonna happen if you can't do this anymore. Because in that moment, you're loving it."

Similarly, 20% of survey respondents indicated that they would "never retire," another 22.5% said they "hoped to retire someday but didn't think they would be able to," and another 37% said they would "retire later than their peers."

Conclusion

Despite these frustrations and challenges, 73% of the survey respondents said they enjoyed being freelance "frequently or always" and the remaining 27% said they enjoyed being freelance "sometimes."

Ultimately, freelancers build resilience by recognising and accepting that there will be feasts and famines and a few dark nights of the soul. As Diane put it:

> Things will be a little bit great, and things will be a little bit shit. No matter what gig I'm on, or agency I'm with, or what city I live in, my life will be a little bit great and a little bit awful but mostly somewhere in between.

When compared to other entertainment workers, dance professionals are especially flexible. They change roles often, they take on multiple side jobs, and they are ready to pivot in response to any challenges that arise. They are also likely to reframe periods of unemployment and rejection through a positive lens and to approach their work with a growth mindset. As Tripp said:

> People would say, you're not working, and I'm like, no I am working. But you're not making any money, they'd say, and I said well I'm investing. I'm becoming valuable in order to earn money. Then sooner or later, I discovered that acceptance. You know, I'm earning as much as someone working in a grocery store. But I'm doing what I love and I'm not working every day, and I'm working out of my own choice.

Anthony described how freelance work creates a tension between flying and feeling grounded:
There's a freedom to [freelancing] which I love. Like a bird, there's freedom in the flight, but at a certain point, you need to rest, to come back down to Earth… and look for worms.

Another dancer was more blunt: "I love dancing, but I also have to pay my rent."

Academic Insight

10b. Collaborations between Early 20th-Century European and American Concert and Commercial Dance: Tamiris and Nagrin

By Daria Lavrennikov

Looking at the relationship between contemporary dance and Commercial Dance, and the contemporary and modern techniques and choreographers that have resonated on the Commercial Dance world, this text will focus on how early American and European modern dance has manifested itself in commercial styles – zooming into the work of two important choreographers from the second generation of modern dance. As a contemporary dance practitioner, teacher, performer and choreographer, in this text, I indirectly dive into my own personal versatile dance history. This includes the dance history of my mentors and teachers, during my studies in the US (at Connecticut College and Concord Academy). This is a dance heritage that interlaces the fields of contemporary and modern dance, physical theatre, ballet, folk dance and aspects of Commercial Dance (the last made up of the diverse genre of dance including Jazz dance, Hip-Hop, Break Dancing, Broadway musical productions, television and film).

Both concert dance (that which includes contemporary, postmodern, modern dance and ballet) and Commercial Dance are rooted in a diversity of evolving dance styles and techniques, as well as other complimentary artistic disciplines. Both have been influenced by and surged within a diversity of cultures and subcultures, and through their exchanges and confrontations, modes of resistance and resilience by way of the movement and live arts. This includes constant interactions, exchanges and syncretism between European, Africanist, Asian and diverse indigenous heritages from the Americas. Both are challenging if not impossible to neatly define, due to their multiple manifestations, family branches and modes of dance studies throughout the world. Yet simultaneously concert and Commercial Dance are constantly changing, evolving and adapting in accordance with the arts industry, socio-political movements and phenomenon, cultural idiosyncrasies, and the artistic movements and individuals that push and question the boundaries of what the disciplines are, could be, and revisiting what they have been to reinvent new branches and directions. What cannot be denied is that each form, style and technique of both contemporary and Commercial Dance is informed by a series of previous ones, and each new artist creates new systems of teaching, creating and performing by digesting, appropriating and redirecting earlier artist's principles, materials and mechanisms. The development and prosperity of these dance forms are also interdependent with reaching, engaging, and expanding the kind of public that could be interested in and attracted by the work, both as students, professionals, practitioners as well as the general public.

I will focus here on two figures, Daniel Nagrin and Helen Tamiris, with their training and artistic work primarily in the US. Their hybrid artistic work is rooted in and manifests itself in both modern and contemporary dance, as well as its inspirations from jazz and vernacular dance styles. In particular, their approaches and aesthetics reiterated the Africanist presence in American dance in dialogue with European dance and theatre forms, such as the polycentric and polyrhythmic ways of working with music and movement improvisation. Both have likewise had an influence on the development of Commercial Dance as well as the greater performing arts industry in the US, with its reverberation throughout the world. I had the honour to take a workshop with Daniel Nagrin, during my studies (Concord Academy Dance Festival) and he was a central mentor and teacher of two of my teachers and mentors,

Richard Colton and David Dorfman, during my high school and undergraduate education. The second artist is Helen Tamiris, who participated in the origins and development of the dance form of modern concert dance in the US from the late 1920s through the 1930s. Then post 1930s, through the 1940s and 1950s, she solidified a place for modern concert dance in the musical theatre of New York's Broadway, becoming an acclaimed Broadway choreographer. Tamiris was initially Nagrin's teacher and mentor and would become his artistic and life partner. Both were key figures in creating and reflecting on the bridge between modern and jazz dance as well as blurring the boundaries between high art and vernacular forms, both their works featured popular culture, symbolism, and social realism.

To offer a contextualisation of the time, for many dancers and choreographers of the time between the 1930s and 1940s, post-war period, employment opportunities were scarce. The major ballet and modern dance companies were still in their beginning phases. Musical comedies and films became important performing platforms offering artists not only experience but also more substantial financial rewards. Although some people criticised and disliked these branches of work for their commercialism and considered them inferior to the pursuit of what they would refer to as "serious or high art," the interaction of the two spheres resulted in developments for both sides. This critique came with the roots of 'modern dance,' termed as such in 1927, and emerging with a belief that dance should reflect contemporary attitudes and issues; the pioneers Martha Graham, Doris Humphrey and Weidman claimed that dance should 'provoke, stimulate and inform' rather than simply entertain. Many dancers and supporters centred their debates on issues of accessibility versus vanguardism. The question they most often argued about was: should dancers try to make their work more accessible to a mass audience or preserve their modernism by creating experimental work for themselves and for their peers? The increased presence of ballet and modern choreographers in musical theatre required a higher level of proficiency for the dancers and resulted in more complex and experimental choreography than the dancing and routines of earlier years based on precision and repetition. Dance gained more importance in musical productions in general. The works of modern choreographers were in turn introduced to a larger and more diverse audience, learning to increase their appeal. Among the choreographers who worked for musical theatre or films were George Balanchine, Katherine Dunham, Agnes de Mille, Mikhail Fokine, Lestor Horton, Hanya Holm, Doris Humphrey, Helen Tamiris, Jerome Robbins and Charles Weidman. Balanchine introduced the word choreography to Broadway with On Your Toes (1936). Unlike most earlier dances in musicals which existed as separate production numbers, his ballets were integrated with the plot shifting the dramaturgical construction. American choreographers Fred Astaire, Gene Kelly, and Jerome Robbins also mixed and experimented with ballet, tap, jazz, ballroom, gymnastics and everyday movements in their productions. The borders between modern dance and the commercial theatre were porous. Dancers had already been complimenting their small earnings by performing in commercial shows and nightclubs, but this kind of commercial work for concert dancers grew noticeably after the war. This occurred mainly because a ballet based dance began to appear as the major form, alongside tap, on Broadway and in films giving modern and ballet dancers new opportunities to work in shows and Hollywood. George Balanchine had been using ballet in the shows he did for Broadway and films in the 1930s and early 1940s, and Agnes Mille was likewise credited with integrating the ballet technique in Broadway musicals in 1943 with Oklahoma. By 1945, ballets and ballet-based dance became solid and consistent parts of many Broadway musicals. The majority of these dances were not done without pointe shoes and could be performed well by modern dancers who were often more available than ballet dancers due to contract obligations.

Another key figure who received less worldwide acclaim, but contributed to both the development of modern and Commercial Dance, is earlier mentioned Daniel Nagrin (1917–2008), a performer, choreographer, teacher, and writer. He was considered a minor pioneer of American modern dance, and dedicated his latter life to teaching and solo performance. He was referred to as the 'great loner of American dance' by Dance Magazine. He had an influence on many American contemporary choreographers including Bill T Jones, Meredith Monk, Richard Colton, and David Dorfman amongst others. In an interview Bill T. Jones describes him as an artist dedicated to humanism and romanticism: "an artist as warrior, who's battle is with sloth, insincerity, indecision, and the artist must win this battle in daily life efforts to commit to clear ideas and procedures." Nagrin lived, exchanged, and collaborated with a rich and challenging community of Jazz musicians. His choreographic work drew on jazz movement and music as well as modern dance and classical music, rooted in gestures and a quality of presence and movement that were uniquely his own. Anna Kisselgoff wrote about Nagrin, in a 1994 review in The New York Times: "The gesture is the movement, and gesture, as acting, is never imposed upon the movement […] no specific technique springs to mind, no school or tradition provides a ready context." He incorporated words and images into his performances, and was interested and engaged in video and sound design early in his career, spanning from the mid-1940s into the 1980s. My contemporary dancer teachers and mentors David Dorfman and Richard Colton referenced and considered Daniel Nagrin a key influence in their artistic development, hybrid interdisciplinary visions and improvisational dance practices. In this sense we could say that Nagrin was way ahead of his time and simultaneously rooted in and in dialogue with popular dance forms and theatrical methods that would allow them to pave another more porous pathway for dance that would branch out into multiple dance forms, both commercial contemporary and those that today are more difficult to distinguish due to collaborations between downtown and uptown circuits.

Created in 1948, his most well-known solo's are 'Strange Hero,' using a raw jazz style that depicts a portrait of a gangster, and 'Spanish Dance,' with reinvented elements of flamenco. Don McDonagh wrote in 1997 in Dance magazine: "For him, jazz was not a finger-popping, torso-twisting genre of self-involvement but a tool to explore character." He began his professional career with Anna Sokolow and continued with Sue Ramos who introduced him to jazz dance. He would then continue on to perform with the modern dance choreographer Helen Tamiris discussed here, who choreographed for Broadway musicals as well as being a pioneer of American modern dance. When Nagrin began to work with Tamiris in 1941, Tamiris' way of working was to allow the dancer to work improvisational and through metaphors under a directed framework to find the movement that she wanted: "Dancing is simply movement with a personal conception of rhythm" she said. She was not interested in imposing her own movement or codified techniques or styles on the dancers, developing movement improvisationally, believing that the body knew how to move. In this way, dancers would create movement out of improvisation for their own bodies, rather than imposing a movement style (Gruen 1988). She would find metaphors based on sense memory to distort and abstract movement allowing dancers to access what is not real and make it real through the imagination, going inside the body with the action.

Likewise as a result her dancers had no recognisable Tamiris style or technique (Schlundt 1972), which contributed to her receiving less visibility amongst the other modern dance pioneers (Franko 1995). Compared to Graham, Humphrey, and de Mille, there was a contrast in recognition and popularity, due to the critics who referred to Tamiris' works as 'mediocre and amateur.' According to Nagrin, Tamiris modes of working improvisation and dedication to social, political and artistic views distanced and alienated the general public. Dealing with social issues and concerns, of the oppressed, of the time including racism, poverty and war;

her work was considered socio-politically responsive and her social realism was comparable to that of Anna Sokolow's and Mary Wigman's in which the purpose of dance was the confrontation of the public (audience) with political and economic issues, especially after WW I. What dance historian Marc Franko terms 'socially relevant,' 'non-formalist' 'proletariat art' was seen as conflicting with the 'bourgeois' art of the Big Four. At this time, Franko claims that the most "hotly contended issues" were the politically intertwining, complex notions of "form versus content and heritage versus innovation." This affected Tamiris' not being given protagonism both during that time as well as part of the understanding of today's dance history.

In 1928, in her concert program, she wrote the following manifesto: "Art is international but the artist is a product of a nationality […] There are no general rules. Each original work of art creates its own code…We must not forget the age we live in." In contrast to other modern dance pioneers, such as Martha Graham, Doris Humphrey, and Hanya Holm, Tamiris' trajectory explored non-formalist methods including blurring the boundaries between what was understood and categorised as high art and the vernacular. She was considered to be one of the first choreographers to use jazz and spiritual music to explore and stage social themes, working with jazz music and dance on Broadway, because this was the dance of America and her understanding of what she should be doing (Nagrin 2001). Her works were set to well-known spirituals, such as "Go Down Moses" and "Swing Low, Sweet Chariot," conveying the theme of oppression with an intense physicality. Nagrin said that "jazz was in the very bones of how Tamiris defined America." However, most dance critics of the time did not treat jazz with seriousness or respect.

Nagrin claimed that,

> Tamiris was one of the founders. She was self-defeating in terms of history and schools, because what she was doing was working from the moment. Each class was different. There was no schema, only that you were constantly thrown into yourself.
> (Nagrin cited in Dunning 1982)

Socially oriented content based work was not in fashion and was openly criticised, stigmatised and labelled as Marxist. Dance critics such as Martin and Horst disregarded the leftist revolutionaries, and Martin omitted them, including Tamiris, in his books during the 1930s. The critics of the time aimed to construct a simplified view of modern dance based on formalism. They favoured the works and ideals of those choreographers who used Horst's or Laban's formalist, traditionalist principles such as Graham who was Horst's personal partner, Humphrey, Weidman, Wigman, and Holm (Kane 2002). Martin recommended the Big Four (that is, Martha Graham, Hanya Holm, Doris Humphrey and Charles Weidman), to initiate and establish both the dance programs at the universities and summer dance workshops from 1934 to 1942, that today continue to be based in structured formalism. Tamiris and Nagrin appropriated non-formalist acting theories to dance instead.

Furthermore, what was of concern to Tamiris and can be considered an influence on commercial and contemporary dance is the interest in certain artistic approaches to eliminating clichés and communicating the inner life, finding diverse metaphors to do this. Both Tamiris and Nagrin's work contains the "non-formalist notion of form following content, or content-then-form." This differentiates Tamiris and Nagrin from most choreographers of this time, in specific the Big Four, as this approach is philosophical and socio-political rather than technical and form-based. According to Tamiris: "Dancing is simply movement with a personal concept of rhythm […] The aim of the dance is not to narrate (anecdotes, stories, fables, legends, etc.) by means of mimic tricks and other established choreographic forms." For her, feeling and emotion come from doing. The foundation of Tamiris's choreographic method

Academic Insight

likewise reflected Stanislavsky's influence through the Group Theatre. They would explore "who you were, where you were, what you were doing, and how you were doing it" (Nagrin 2001). Moreover, an inspiration for Tamiris was that as a young actor, Stanislavski discovered improvisation by working alone to develop his character roles. Tamiris offered neither theories nor codified technique, just that the body was allowed to move in whatever way was natural for each. Having a central influence in Nagrin's works, he claimed "she (Tamiris) always probed and searched for new forms to express her central concern for human dignity" (Nagrin 1988). Unlike the "Big Four" dance pioneers, Tamiris was known to be willing to explore any method to attain her art form, was concerned with human dignity, and blurred the boundaries between high art and the vernacular. The other American modern dancers would not incorporate the vernacular since 'popular' was translated as 'not artistic' at this time.

The major influences on Nagrin's work came from (1) the Russian theatre director Konstantin Stanislavsky, (2) modern dance pioneer and his professional dance partner Helen Tamiris, (3) the technique of Joseph Chaikin's open theatre and (4) Jazz music and jamming. These main inspirations contributed to the development of his system of choreography, called 'the Nagrin method.' In the case of Daniel Nagrin's methods of teaching and creating, he did not focus on design or form but dedicated himself to the necessity of the action and assumed the work would have design, form following function (Nagrin 2001). In part, this is likewise a result of never receiving formal instructions from Tamiris on choreographic design or structure on Broadway or in his solo works, but rather focusing on the need to discover the inner life that fired movements. Although both dancers were known to influence and inspire one another's methods of working.

Nagrin began to work with inner conviction, movement metaphors, content rather than form, and combined virtuosity. This method is likewise based on Stanislavski's teachings to "find truth not in trying to look like something or someone but in doing-acting" (Schlundt 1997). Thus, Nagrin's concept that the entire person is doing whilst dancing is a driving force and major influence in his work and teaching (Nagrin 1997). His method works from a specific image. Nagrin defined the term 'metaphor' as "a transferring from one word the sense of another […] a figure of speech in which one thing is likened to another, different thing by being spoken of as if it were that other" (Nagrin 2001). According to Nagrin, metaphors are so common that they are in every thought and every movement; every action can be seen as a metaphor for something else, and anything can be done in dance through a metaphor. Most dance metaphors cannot be articulated clearly but can be felt and experienced, and he suggests that "this ambivalence is a characteristic of metaphors" (Nagrin 2001). These concepts coming from Chaikin inspired and were implemented into Nagrin's Workgroup. A device that he explored and then borrowed from jazz music was jamming, the improvisational study of an emblem through storytelling using words, movements, sounds, and silence to clarify meaning and attention. In 1957, he created his first solo program and in 1970 formed the Workgroup, a significant improvisational training and performance ensemble. "Its central focus was to explore the possibilities of interactive improvisation and to develop the forms and skills to perform improvisation for the concert-going audience."

Concluding this text, it is important to make mention that today the exchange and influence between contemporary dance and Commercial Dance, or as it is sometimes classified from uptown to downtown dance, continues to be essential to both forms. Today diverse contemporary choreographers, in particular between the US and Europe, yet also spanning the world, are being invited to collaborate with the "uptown dance industry" in large scale Broadway productions, as well as in commercials, films, music videos, large-scale events and concerts as well as Netflix series. Thes exchanges and partnerships bring innovation to both fields and enrich them through other aesthetic values and modes of working. Contemporary dance choreographers continue to enter, influence and collaborate with the Broadway (uptown) dance industry, including Bill T Jones, Mark Morris and Ronald K. Brown who are among the contemporary choreographers who have done this work over the years. Twyla Tharp is likewise a key figure who began her work as part of the postmodern dance movement and then migrated into a hybrid dance form that bridged contemporary and Commercial Dance collaborations. Most recently, as discussed in the article by Sylviane Gold in Dance Magazine, titled "These Downtown Choreographers Are Reshaping Dance on Broadway," written in November 2019, world renowned contemporary choreographers like David Neumann, Camille A. Brown, John Heginbotham, Anne Teresa De Keersmaeker, Sidi Larbi Cherkaoui, and Sonya Tayeh have been collaborating in choreographing productions with acclaimed Broadway directors such as Diane Paulus, Rachel Chavkin and Daniel Fish, Ivo van Hove and Afra Hines opening Broadway to new influences and practices. According to Afra Hines, a Broadway director, Gold Neumann's Hadestown process is:

> refreshingly different from that of some 'old-school' Broadway choreographers: If you're coming from the concert world, obviously you're not looking to make millions of dollars; you're more concerned with the art of it and the creation process of it. David is not restrained by thinking about what the Tony voters are gonna think, or comparing it to his last Broadway show. That is super-cool, and puts the whole room in a different mind-set.

Therefore, the artists are bringing a willingness to experiment, and engage and invite the dancers to take part in the creative process, in a context where artistic decisions and financial decisions are always in a delicate balance on Broadway, where large amounts of investor money and maintaining a status are often at stake. Concert-dance choreographers coming to Broadway encounter a new working environment of multiple producers, multiple collaborators, big budgets, high costs, ingrained traditions and strict union work rules.

This willingness to experiment and engage in the singularity of each performer in the creative process was likewise the case of Daniel Nagrin and Helen Tamiris discussed throughout this article, as both their careers fluctuated between the commercial and contemporary dance circuits and the challenges and success that this brought them in their work. These exchanges, fluctuations, and permeations between dance fields have existed from the beginning of the century for a variety of reasons and with different levels of repercussion and influence on the fields. At the centre of these collaborations, there is dedication to embracing and merging a diversity of movement vocabularies as well as exploring and developing the shifting relationship between music and dance. Likewise, there is an interest in merging vernacular and high art forms, engaging a diverse and wider range of audiences via new technologies, artistic and social platforms, spaces, models of artistic production, and collaborations with the music industry, cinema, fashion, sports and product design.

10c. Punkin' and Werkin' It: The Queer Roots of Commercial Dance

By Joseph Mercier

This chapter traces some of the influences that queer subcultures have made to Commercial Dance, focusing on Disco, Punkin'/Waacking and Voguing. I suggest that these forms have had major influences on many aspects of Commercial Dance practices in wide-ranging ways, but focus here on three key areas: one, the introduction and development of specific gestural and physical vocabularies; two, the development of dance music and club cultures, and the resulting social changes that these brought; and, three, through the introduction of performances modes that draw on camp aesthetics, fem styles, and playfulness with gender and sexuality. In tracing the history of these dance forms, I am also telling part of the history of the music, fashion, culture and social practices to which they are intrinsically linked.

A noticeable trend with each of these historical accounts, is the development of a set of practices within subcultural communities that gets brought into mainstream, commercial focus by a key producer or medium outside these communities: John Travolta (Disco), Soul Train (Waacking) and Madonna (Voguing). This repeated narrative points to the wider issue of the imbalanced relationship between subcultures and the mainstream: mainstream capitalist cultural production is fed by subcultural materials but frequently displaces them from their original context. Halberstam (2005) defines "mainstream culture within postmodernism… as the process by which subcultures are both recognized and absorbed, mostly for the profit of large media conglomerates" and suggests that "most of the interested directed by mainstream media at subcultures is voyeuristic and predatory" (p. 156, original emphasis). Questions of appropriation are abound in many of the examples I draw on. The dance practices I am writing about have emerged, in large part, in response to exclusion from the mainstream, and so when these materials are used without credit or inclusion of the original producers, that exclusion is magnified. While my aim here is to give credit to these queer subcultures for their influence on mainstream practices, I am by no means suggesting the way that mainstream cultural producers have drawn from these subcultures is appropriate, fair or ethical. I acknowledge this in order to contextualise this discourse within the disadvantage and sense of otherness experienced by many of the queer, black and Latino communities that originated these dances. So, even as I am telling the story of the influence of queer cultures on mainstream Commercial Dance, I am also telling the story of mainstream Commercial Dance's appropriation of these queer cultures.

Disco

Perhaps one of the most dominant images of the Disco era is John Travolta in Saturday Night Fever (1977): the white suit with black lapels, sitting into one hip with his famous finger point, "projecting his disco cool and working class hero status" (Hylton 2022, p. 182). But this is an image from the later years of disco when it began to enter mainstream consciousness and as Hylton points out, those "famous arm points… hid the true history of those famous arm moves" (ibid). The roots of this image take us back to the beginning of that decade to New York's underground queer clubs. In 1970, David Mancuso held parties in his apartment in NoHo which came to be known as The Loft, while The Sanctuary was started by a duo known as Seymour and Shelley in a former, floundering straight club (Lawrence 2011b). These spaces intersected with the political consciousness developing from gay liberation, feminism, civil rights movements and anti-war movements (ibid). The new dance floor was a heterogeneous mix of people across a spectrum of gender expressions, sexualities, races and ethnicities, drawn to a new mix of sounds. As Garcia (2014), notes:

Music was an essential part of these gatherings, and the sound of these events would eventually develop into the style called disco. The sound was a mix of soul, funk and Latin music with a driving, four-four kick drum pattern. It took its name from discotheque, the French word given to nightlife venues that featured recorded music instead of live performances (Garcia 2014). This sound gave way to a new way of how club goers related to music and as Lawrence suggests, "contributed to the forging of a relationship between the DJ and the dancing crowd that continues to inform the core practice of contemporary dance culture" (Lawrence 2011b, p. 232).

Not only did disco introduce a new kind of music, it also shifted the way bodies related to one another on the dance floor. As Lawrence argues, disco decentred the heterosexual couple at the heart of pre-disco social dances, including "Waltz, Foxtrot, the Lindy Hop (or Jitterbug), the Texas Tommy and the Twist" (2011b, p. 231). Instead of facing one another, with one partner (the man) leading the other (the woman), club goers started dancing on their own without partners shifting the relational possibilities of social dance forms away from a man and a woman dancing together. Sexuality and gender are significant here, for two reasons. Firstly, the sexism of partner dances – that is, in which the man always leads – was subverted, allowing women the freedom to dance to the music without having to 'follow' the man. Secondly, at the beginning of disco, it was not only taboo, but in many places illegal, for two men to dance together (Lawrence 2011b). Disco dancing emerged as a way for queer people to dance without 'dancing together' as they would be required in other social dances. This had a profound influence on the development of club cultures: by untethering dancing from the imperative to dance in couples, this opened up new possibilities of how bodies moved to music, socialised through movement and expanded the gestural repertoire of club and commercial dancing – as I describe below in the section on Waacking.

Towards the later part of the 1970s, disco began to attract a wider audience, drawn to the infectious, danceable music and a perceived sense of glamorous, disco cool. Disco clubs started popping up around the US and internationally, including famous clubs such as Paradise Garage (1976) and Studio 54 (1977) in New York. As Garcia (2014) notes, "this was also the period when many of disco's best-known artists launched their careers—Donna Summer, Chic, The Bee Gees, KC And The Sunshine Band." And this of course was also the release of the enormously successful Saturday Night Fever, which became the second most popular film of all time (Lawrence 2006) and brought disco firmly into mainstream attention. As Hylton notes, "the film was a feat of misdirection… in the history of disco" (2022, p. 182), displacing it far away from its queer underground roots. This new commercial version of disco "replaced the polymorphous priorities of New York's progressive venues with the flashing floor lights of 2001 Odyssey and the hyper-heterosexual moves of John Travolta" (Lawrence 2006).

Disco's moment in the mainstream cultural spotlight was relatively short-lived and its lustre faded gradually in the early 1980s. Over saturation of the market and too much distance from its original queer, black and Latino contexts, it lost much of the core principles that made it seductive in the first place: bodies creating community, freedom and self-expression through movement and music in permissive, diverse spaces. Lawrence writes, that, "whereas the dance floor had previously functioned as an aural space of communal participation and abandon, it was now reconceived as a visually-driven space of straight seduction and couples dancing, in which participants were focused on their own space and, potentially, the celebrity who might be dancing within their vicinity" (Lawrence 2006).

Disco became superficial and contentless, unable to hold the cultural imagination of a mainstream audience. This was instrumentalised and perpetuated by the 'Disco Sucks' movement, started by a group of rock DJs and producers, jealous of Disco's meteoritic rise in popularity. There was undoubtedly a homophobic and racial dimension to this backlash (Garcia 2014; Lawrence 2006). Even the slogan 'Disco Sucks' was a homophobic double entendre that "evoked the way in which disco drew dancers into its seductive, beguiling rhythms as well as the action favoured by so many of its most dedicated participants" (Lawrence 2006).

Academic Insight

The movement was successful in framing disco as 'superficial' and 'artificial' (Lawrence 2006). The 'Disco Sucks' movement, also used this label for the subcultures from which disco emerged, dismissing the original creators as silly, camp and to be viewed with suspicion.

Disco gradually fell out of popularity into the 1980s, but of course disco never really died. It "dovetailed with 80s dance-pop, new wave and industrial music" (Garcia 2014), especially in Europe and morphed into what we now called dance music. Of course, there are specific examples of contemporary artists explicitly referencing disco, such as Madonna's 'Hung Up' (2005) and Alex Newell/DJ Cassidy's 'Kill the Lights' (2016). However, the legacy of disco on Commercial Dance cultures is even more widespread. Disco revolutionised the way we moved and socialised to music, establishing the foundations of contemporary club cultures out of which a wide arrange of styles and practices emerged, such as waacking, locking and house.

Punkin'/Waacking

The origins of Waacking take us to the other coast of America: Los Angeles in the early 1970s. Here Waacking emerged out of the queer Black and Latinx underground disco scenes. Suraji (2016) contends that it developed as a way for the impoverished youth of the club scenes to 'let loose,' finding physical expression for their sense of stigma and exclusion. They drew physical and performance inspiration from old Hollywood silent film stars, Fred Astaire, Charlie Chaplin, Looney Tunes, Bruce Lee Films. The original Batman TV Series (1966–1968) was an influence and the term Waacking is derived from the onomatopoeic fight scenes: Bang! Thwack! Whack! (Suraji 2016).

The dancers who developed the style, originally called it 'punking,' derived from the term 'punk,' which at the time was a derogatory slur for gay men and sex workers. Suraji suggests that the name punk/punking was coined by DJ Michael Angelo as a playful inside joke among him and the dancers to describe what they were doing on the dance floor: they were punking – that is, queering or 'gaying' up – the music. As Bragin (2014) notes, Punkin' "indicates a stylised movement behaviour that expands set vocabulary, incorporating elements of large locomotion, dramatic gesture and facial expression, and narrative" (pp. 63–64). Whacking – I explain the spelling difference below – referred to one specific part of the dance (Bragin 2014; Suraji 2016): "the fast, rhythmic arm whipping that is the defining characteristic of the style." The dance form started to gain notice, especially after several of the Punks – including Arthur Goff, Tinker Toy, Andrew Frank and Tyrone Proctor – began appearing on Soul Train (1971–2006), the televised variety show originally hosted by Don Cornelius. Because of this attention the name was changed to distance the dance from its overtly queer connotations and make it more palatable for a mainstream audience. It was called variously 'the Cagney' after Hollywood dancer James Cagney, and the 'Shabba-doo' – named after the first straight dancer to learn Waacking form the original Punks, who combined it with locking – and then finally it was called Whacking (Suraji 2016). Shaba-doo, changed the spelling, dropping the 'h' and adding an 'a' to distance the word from possible violent or sexual connotations (ibid). However, "[i]n their own world it was Punkin'… Punkin' was how they lived, how they expressed who they were" (Sanchez in Bragin 2014, p. 64).

One of the original Punks and Soul Train dancers, Tyrone Proctor gained further mainstream attention when he won the dance competition on American Bandstand (1959–1989) with his partner Sharon Hill in 1975 (Easter 2020). Proctor went on to work regularly with funk and pop singer Jody Watley as part of the Outrageous Waack Dancers, and he can be seen in her 'Still a Thrill' (1987) music video. In the 1980s Proctor moved to New York City where he joined the dance group Breed of Motion, with two well-known vogue dancers: Willi Ninja and Archie Burnett. This is a key meeting between the two forms that are often thought of as a set of related styles, even though they have very distinct origins.

The AIDS pandemic in the 1980s and 1990s was a time of crisis for many queer subcultural communities. As members of these communities fell ill and died, focus turned to activism and protest. The Punkin' community was equally affected and many of the original punks died from AIDs related illnesses during this period (Bragin 2014; Suraji 2016). Proctor and Victor Manoel were two of the only original punks to survive and remain active, Proctor would go on to choreograph for Johnny Kemp, The Isley Brothers and New Kids on the Block (Easter 2022); Manoel performed who performed in Saturday Night Fever, also danced on tour with Grace Jones, David Bowie and Toni Basil. Waacking went dormant in the late 1980s and 1990s. In the early 2000s, "street dancers researching early Soul Train styles picked it up again" (Bragin 2014) and Brian 'Footwork' Green started teaching Waacking class at Broadway Dance centres where one of his students was Kumari Suraji (Suraji 2016). The form gained more widespread mainstream attention in 2011 when Suraji choreographed a dance, performed by contestants Sasha Mallory and Ricky James on So You Think You Can Dance (Bragin 2014).

Voguing

To trace the history of vogue dancing, it needs to be contextualised in the wider Ballroom culture of Harlem, New York from which it developed. The Harlem Balls were/are community: a hybrid space, part fashion show, beauty pageant and club night, developed out of the Drag Balls that originated in the 1920s. Tired of the racial biases in the Drag Balls of the time, Crytsal and Labeija held the first Harlem Ball in 1972. It was called "The First Annual House of LaBeija Ball" (LaBeija) and started the ballroom scene as we know it (LaBeija). These primarily, Black and Latinx, trans and queer spaces, are/were a place to celebrate and play out the fabulousness of difference and otherness. Participants of the balls were organised into houses and competed for prizes in various categories, like executive realness, military, face, body, butch queen first time in drag, etc. When vogue dancing became part of the balls, the category of 'vogue fem' was introduced. The balls also developed a distinct vernacular and vocabulary that has seeped into mainstream pop cultures; phrases such as work/werk, reading, fierce, slay, realness and shade – to name but a few – all come from the balls.

The house was, and still is, the centre of Ballroom. Often named after fashion houses, supermodels and glamour: Mugler, Xtravanganza, Balanciaga and St. Laurent. They have a familial structure, led by a parental figure – usually referred to as the house mother, or sometimes father, depending on that person's gender expression – who is responsible for organising and looking after the children of the house. The house mother decides who and in what categories the member of the house will walk in. But the house mother often played a deeper role in house members' lives: these chosen families regularly became a replacement for difficult family lives, often as a result of homophobia or transphobia. Many of the houses developed out of financial and emotional need and became strong support networks for the children of the house (LaBeija n.d.). This is an important point that I'd like to highlight, especially as this conversation moves to vogue's more mainstream exposure. The grass roots community responsiveness and care enabled by the self-organising house family structures is one crucial aspect of ballroom culture that has been ignored or abandoned in the mainstream exposure of the art form. As Jamal Prodigy (Chatzipapatheodoridis 2017), "Now because the scene is becoming so much more commercialised and appreciated in mainstream media, you have some houses that are being developed strictly as production companies" (p. 4).

The origins of vogue dancing are credited to Paris Dupree in a story recounted by vogue DJ David DePino (in Lawrence 2011a):

> It all started in an after hours club called Footsteps on 2nd Avenue and 14th Street... Dupree was there and a bunch of these black queens were throwing shade at each other. Paris had a Vogue magazine in her bag, and while she was dancing she took it out, opened up to a page where a model was posing and then stopped in that pose on the beat... Another queen came up and did another pose in front of Paris and then Paris went in front of her and did another pose. This was all shade – they were trying to make a prettier pose than each other – and it soon caught on at the balls.
>
> (p. 5)

Lawrence notes, an alternative story places the origins of the dance with black gay inmates of Rickers Island prison, who practiced it to attract attention (Lawrence 2011a). This new dance practice was originally called 'posing' and then voguing, referring back to the moment described above (ibid). This posing to music quickly developed, and was combined with movements from Egyptian hieroglyphics and martial arts films. This is now known as 'Old Way.' In later years, some of the voguers began studying dance in more formal settings – such as colleges and universities – and started combining vogue with more virtuosic movements: this became known as New Way. Overtime five key practices were developed and identified, known as the 5 elements of vogue: Catwalk, Duckwalk, Hand performance, Floor Performance, Spins and dips.

Vogue gained widespread attention first with 'Paris is Burning' (1990), Jennie Livingston's documentary of the Ball scene. The form further captured mainstream imagination when Madonna released her song and music video, 'Vogue' (1990), and the subsequent Blond Ambition Tour (1990), drew on ball culture. It was created with and featured vogue dancers from the ball scene like Jose Gutierez and Luis Camacho, both from the house of Xtravaganza. The film Truth or Dare (1991) documents parts of the tour and Madonna's relationship with the dancers. It portrays Madonna as a kind of house mother to the dancers. However, this relationship soured as the dancers began to feel exploited or used. This is chronicled in the documentary Strike a Pose (2016), in which six of the seven dancers reunite 25 years after the tour. Both Livingstone and Madonna have come under criticism for the way they've used vogue as an instrument to further their careers (Harper 1994; Hooks 1992). Madonna especially has been criticised for the way she has drawn on vogue, which mirrors the way she has used many of the practices in her performances. Chatzipapatheodoridis (2017) notes that "[h]er history with urban sub/cultures is constantly under debate wherein appropriation and borrowing are the notions most contested with Madonna's readership" (p. 5).

Voguing's relationship to mainstream Commercial Dance and performance cultures has ebbed and flowed over the decades since Paris is Burning and Madonna's 'Vogue.' But it has maintained a presence in dance cultures and vogue has certainly spread far beyond its beginnings in Harlem. Key figures like Willi Ninja, the legendary founder of the house of Ninja, were instrumental in spreading the practice and he successfully pursued his dream of taking vogue internationally, especially to France and Japan (Chatzipapatheodoridis 2017). Chatzipapatheodoridis suggests that there has often been a tension in Ballroom cultures between community and ambition: he notes for instance in Paris is Burning, how many of the voguers being interviewed speak of the desire for success, glamour and stardom.

Vogues influence on mainstream culture has accelerated in the past two decades. The meteoric success of Ru Paul's Drag Race (2009–present) has introduced aspects of voguing and ball culture to a wider audience, especially through much of the vocabulary of the show, as well as elements like catwalks. Some of the dancing that features in many of the challenges draws on vogue, in both the specific movement vocabulary, but also in its femme presentations. Other TV shows have introduced vogue cultures to mainstream audience such as Pose (2018–2021), a fictional drama series that chronicles the lives of voguers and their houses. HBO's television series Legendary, currently on its third season, is a reality show in which vogue house compete highly produced dance numbers in hopes of winning 'Superior House' and a cash prize. One of the judges off Legendary is Leiomy Maldonado, from the house of Prodigy, who became known to a wider audience through her performance in the music video for Willow Smith's 'Whip my Hair' (2010). In the video Maldanado "schools the children" on her famous hair whip, that many credit her with inventing, before Britney and Beyoncé – Maldanado herself makes a claim to the invention of the move (Davis 2017). Well it is always difficult to know for certain the providence of specific movements; it is very plausible that Maldanado was an influence on the development and use of this 'hairography.' Certainly, this makes sense in the wider narrative of the influence of vogue on pop culture and Commercial Dance, introducing a distinctly femme vocabulary, that has been variously used in music videos and concerts by artists such as Britney Spears, FKA Twigs, Lil Nas X, Rhianna and Beyoncé – to name a few. As Chatzipapatheodoridis, even with mainstream exposure, [v]oguing… has maintained it signifiers of queerness and its ability to be embodied in the praxis of gender and race' perhaps more so than Disco and Punkin'/Waacking and voguing has perhaps stayed more intact as a form and subculture than the other two forms as it entered mainstream attention. Nonetheless, all the influence of all three dance forms is significant in Commercial Dance cultures and reaching beyond the style specific dance moves. Al three forms have shifted fashion, language, music styles, introduced new ways of moving to music, and created new relationships for social bodies to interact with one another through music and movement.

10d. A Reflection on Hip-Hop, Hegemony and Appropriation

By Armando Rotondi

The following contribution is a critical reflection on some specific characteristics and elements related to Hip-Hop culture. It will consider aspects concerning orientalism and cultural hegemony, as well as it will take into account very briefly the concept of subculture.

In fact, we do not want to enunciate a history of Hip-Hop, but by taking this history for granted, the aim is to develop a theoretical reflection that could be useful for the academic debate and the professional world. If a common point among the various scholars on Hip-Hop is the strong, almost intrinsic relationship between Hip-Hop and the economic and social context, it is almost automatic to read Hip-Hop through the lens of cultural hegemony and in relation to a dominant cultural hegemony. Developed by Antonio Gramsci, as well-known, cultural hegemony is the dominance or maintenance of power by one class over another through the use or imposition of a culture. The concept of cultural hegemony clearly falls within the pertinence of soft power – as theorised by Joseph Nye Jr. (2004) – and differs from hard power in having a less physically invasive interference and without the decisive use of brute force. Soft power is rather the use of power and authority in a veiled way, through the imposition with other forms of ideologies and culture. Cultural ideologies of the ruling class become the dominant ideology and culture, but also, many times, considered as the only legitimate and 'right' forms of culture and ideology. In other words, cultural hegemony – as soft power – codifies and canonises the worldview of the ruling class, making the subaltern classes followers and addicts.

A discourse on cultural hegemony – which could be accompanied by a discourse on Orientalism in a broad sense, as knowledge and stereotyping of the other – is necessarily at the basis of our reasoning considering the peculiarity of Hip-Hop that from a condition of subculture and culture belonging to a specific marginalised community has become almost dominant, due to the development of industry and the evolution of a market that has changed possible original forms. In other words, Hip-Hop transformed itself through the process of 'appropriation' and from a marginalised condition into a dominant one not without criticisms, contradictions and controversies.

Framing the Context: Music, Culture, Dance

In the seminal book *Prophet of the Hood* (2004), Imani Perry investigates in detail the main elements of what the author considers the poetics and the politics of Hip-Hop. However, Perry, professor at Princeton University, focuses almost exclusively to the music sphere and to the one that we can define as poetic and literary. Perry selects and analyses hip-hop songs and clarifies connections between musical styles and genres. Specific case studies are, for example, the narrative strategies in songs by artists such as Tupac Shakur, Public Enemy or Ice Cube, in relation to: the imagery that they help to build and that they use; the purpose that these songs may have; the clash with the predominant culture. The contribution also investigates the roots of hip-hop music and culture, as now universally known, identifying the three forms of primary influence coming from Jamaican cultural tradition. Also in this field, Perry's analysis looks at musical aspects and at the ones correlated to the use of language only. Perry calls, indeed, *outlaw language* that language that finds its source reference in Jamaican culture and that has been used in Hip-Hop music in order to demarcate a difference from the *mainstream American vernacular*. Secondly, Jamaican influence appears as clear in the instrumental combination and in the rhythmic speech. Finally, Perry considers, as noted by Cyan D'Anjou, "the innovative styles that fuels the art and entices its creators to cultivate ever-more captivating and catchy tunes to which to dance with any means possible" (D'Anjou 2020, online).

In other words, Perry's book "examines the rhetorical, narrative, and discursive structures and positioning" (Ibidem) of Hip-Hop, "referring to African-American culture; metaphors and exhortations; verbal and visual intertextuality; and American law" (Ibidem).

Despite the recognised relevance of Perry's book, with a theoretical horizon that includes obviously cultural and social studies, the area of investigation is reduced mainly to the music field in relation to songs, as said, overlooking other aspects. In addition, there is the tendency of a complete overlapping of Hip-Hop and rap, not considering, in this way, rap as one of the four pillars of Hip-Hop. In her very articulated review of four books on this topic (including the one by Perry), Juliana Chang states at the beginning, rhetorically asking herself: "What is hip-hop? The most obvious and immediate answer is that hip-hop is rap music: rhymed lyrics that are mainly rapped, rather than sung, over sampled beats" (2006, p. 545). Chang is, however, conscious that it is a very simplistic overlapping, and is also aware that Hip Hop cannot be reduced to music only, even if the music is putted in relation to the wider frame of African-American society, culture and community: "However, the story of hip-hop is not just the story of a musical genre" (p. 546), Chang openly declares. Then, she continues: "An often cited distinction is that rap is the music, while hip-hop is the culture" (Ibidem). On this point, and in relation to the universally understood four Hip-Hop pillars, the author notices: "In the early days, hip-hop comprised 'four elements': DJing, MCing, breakdancing, and graffiti. In this paradigm, hip-hop emphasizes virtuosity of technique and technology? A virtuosity that is understood as style. Hip-hop style is a way of dance, dress, hair, body movement, and speech" (Ibidem). In their literature review, Derrick P. Alridge and James B. Stewart say: "According to many Hip Hop aficionados, Hip Hop culture consists of at least four fundamental elements: Disc jockeying (DJing), break dancing, graffiti art, and rapping (emceeing)" (2005, p. 190). It is a whole and in this way should be investigated, then.

Without entering in the specific analysis of the four pillars on which there is a vast literature, it is possible to focus for a moment on the dance aspects only, noticing that most of the sources related to Hip-Hop culture tend to consider less the dance field compared to the music and the rap elements as well as to the more general social and cultural implication of the Hip-Hop culture. In other words, main references to Hip-Hop are in relation to music and songs. Borrowing a concept from another area of dance studies, we may ask ourselves, as Serge Lifar was asking himself in his famous *The Choreographer's Manifesto* (1935), what is the relation between dance and music and if dance can finally be considered not anymore under the umbrella of music. All this, despite the fact, as noted by Marcyliena Morgan and Dionne Bennett, that: "There is a growing body of scholarship on hip-hop as well. Academic analyses of hip-hop culture began to appear in the 1990s and include the 1994 publication of Tricia Rose's *Black Noise: Rap Music and Black Culture in Contemporary America* and Russell Potter's *Spectacular Vernaculars: Hip-Hop and the Politics of Postmodernism*" (2011, p. 179).

In the case of Hip-Hop, even if we said they should be investigated as a whole of the four different components, it seems in any case that academic studies usually create a possible hierarchy, in which hegemonic relations are not only between a predominant culture and a subculture – as we will see – but also among the four pillars themselves.

From this perspective, our speech is looking at Hip-Hop dance from a cultural studies perspective, putting the idea of hegemony among dominant culture and subculture at its core. For this reason, our perspective is far, for example, from a book such as *Hip Hop Dance: Meanings and Messages* (2007) by Carla Stalling Huntington, a contribution also very criticised, for example, in a review by Takiyah Nur Amin (2010). Specifically, Stalling Huntington analyses hip-hop dance as a text, almost in a semiotics way, and specifically she traces the evolution of this text from the African American dance from the Diaspora to the global scenario.

Hip-Hop between Subculture and Global Phenomenon

Considering the cultural studies perspective with hegemony at its core as the starting point, a reflection on culture and subculture is obliged in order to continue. Although firstly dated 1979, Dick Hebdige's *Subculture. The Meaning of Style* still remains an essential seminal source for a first understanding of what subculture is and, consequently, dominant culture. Even if it is focused exclusively on the British context – the one of punk, for example – and not on the North American environment, it is essential and even more interesting for the historical time when it was written, almost contemporaneously to the development of the movement, genres and subgenres that Hebdige was going to analyse. Additionally, *Subculture. The Meaning of Style* gives strong theoretical elements that consider sociological, historical, semiotical and also philosophical aspects that help in framing what 'subcultures' are. In this case, Hebdige's work is also almost contemporary to the specific case of Hip Hop and, thanks to that, it can be used and applied as a possible lens or filter to read Hip Hop culture as a subculture, at least in its early phase.

Academic Insight

In defining subculture, Hebdige moves from a quote by French playwright Jean Genet – one of the most controversial intellectuals and writers of the 20th century – in order to propose some basic considerations in understanding subculture. Subculture is "submersive implications of style" (Hebdige 2002 [1979], p. 2) and the fundamental themes are gravitating around the "status and meaning of revolt, the idea of style as a form of Refusal, the elevation of crime into art," considering with the expression 'crimes' also the simple possibility of 'broken codes.' Following this initial thoughts, Hebdige proceeds in the definition of a series of different passages – to which I totally agree – from culture to hegemony (and if there is an hegemonic culture, there is clearly a subculture) as well as the passages from sign to myth specifically with object that "become signs of forbidden identity" (p. 3).

Hebdige's speech finds, in this case, strong and clear support in the philosophy and thought by Marx, Gramsci and Althusser, but also in the works by Stuart Hall who exactly in the same decade was discussing the concepts and the practices of coding, encoding and decoding, as well as in some contributions by Umberto Eco who famously said "I speak through my clothes" (1973, in Hebdige 2002, p. 100). This is a perfect quote if applied to style and communication in a context like the one of hip-hop culture.

In all the evolution of Hip-Hop, it is possible to clearly see the different passages that already in 1979 Hebdige was only theoretically describing for other subcultures. In his book, cited also by Roy Shuker in the other seminal *Popular Music Culture. The Key Concepts* (2012), subcultures "are therefore expressive forms but what they express is, in the last instance, a fundamental tension between those in power and those condemned to subordinate positions and second class lives. This tension is figuratively expressed in the formed of subcultural style" (p. 132)

With Hip Hop, it is possible to see a clear subcultural original status at its beginning moving to be a global phenomenon in an hegemonic position: "Hip-hop music and other elements of hip-hop culture have transformed since the beginnings in the early 1970s in New York City as block party music played by African-American, Puerto Rican, and Jamaican party hosts"; and "by the early 1980s, hip-hop had gained commercial success, began to enter the musical mainstream in the U.S., and spread around the world." In other words: "Hip-hop has transformed from marginalised to mainstream in the United States, a circumstance that provides audiences and media access to those in other geographic locations in the early stage of a local hip-hop product lifecycle."

The definition of Hip-Hop as a subculture is evident considering what Hebdige defines as the elevation of crime or broken codes into art, following what Lipstitz states that some Hip-Hop artists used hip hop to "channel the anger of young people in the South Bronx away from gang fighting" (1994, p. 26). In the same way, we universally understand Hip Hop in terms of style and sign that, through objects, become elements of a forbidden identity.

The passage from being marginalised subculture to be mainstream and global implicitly involves some consideration. The community aspect of Hip Hop and its relation to identity is absolutely central. As stated by Grandmaster Flash, who represents the Holy Trinity of Hip-Hop together with DJ Kool Herc and Afrika Bambaataa: "Hip hop is the only genre of music that allows us to talk about almost anything. Musically, it allows us to sample and play and create poetry to the beat of music. It's highly controversial, but that's the way the game is" (Grandmaster Flash, in Light 1999, p. vii). Specifically, according to Osumare, quoted also in Motley and Henderson: "Rap's dense, poetic, lyric content [was] often underpinned by African-American messages about a historical marginalized status" (Osumare 2001, also in Motley-Henderson 2008, p. 245). Osumare (2001) and Keyes (2002), in different contributions, trace also a parallel between MCing and DJing and the practices of Western African story-telling.

Hip-Hop and Appropriation

The relation between marginalised communities and subculture and global culture automatically compelled us to define some concepts related to cultural appropriation.

First of all, it is needed to define the different understanding of 'appropriation' in appropriation art and cultural appropriation. Still connected to the concept of 'borrowing,' in appropriation art we have an almost overlapping with citation art, in terms of reinvention and reinterpretation of specific elements in order to create something new according to a new concept and intention. Fundamental in contemporary visual arts and it is enough to see the case of *After Walker Evans* by Sherrie Levine, this discussion results also in the understanding of the spread and the reinterpretation of some practices and processes in performing arts, including the passage of Hip Hop from local to global.

Secondly, appropriation as cultural appropriation should be investigated through a specific lens that can help to define if cultural appropriation is always a negative process. Cultural appropriation, as known, is the adoption of an element or elements of one culture or identity by members of another culture or identity. It can be divided according to what a specific culture is going to adopt – subject appropriation, object appropriation, content appropriation, as proposed by James O. Young (2005), and reprised by music and visual artist Cyan D'Anjou (2020) in a contribution specifically on Hip Hop – as well as for the degree of controversy of the appropriation process by a culture that is dominant. In that case, 'appropriation' almost acquires a neutral meaning and becomes an umbrella expression under which we may have: cultural denigration, with the adoptions of an element of a culture with the purpose of humiliating or putting down people of that culture; cultural appreciation as is the respectful borrowing of elements from another culture; cultural exchange as a process of reciprocal exchange between cultures with an equal level of power; cultural dominance, based on the use of elements of a dominant culture by members of a subordinated culture; cultural exploitation or the appropriation of elements of a subordinated culture by a dominant culture without substantive reciprocity; finally, transculturation that is the process in which cultural elements are created from and/or by multiple cultures.

In the context of hip-hop dance, interesting contributions to this debate are not necessarily published and released in academic contributions, but in media and publication oriented to a professional but wider audience compared to the academic one only. For example, Brian Schaefer openly questioned, in an article for 'Dance Magazine,' *At What Point Does Appreciation Become Cultural Appropriation?* (2020), commenting on the words and in dialogue with Michele Byrd-McPhee, founder and Executive Director of Ladies of Hip-Hop.

In the understanding of Schaefer, cultural appropriation is always negative – and in this way very close to the common meaning we give to the expression – using as a reference the definition given by Michelle Heffner Hayes in her books on flamenco and on dance and history of cultural appropriation as "taking the external trappings of cultural traditions and using them as decorations on your own history without developing mutually supporting relationships in the community that you're taking from" (Schaefer 2020, online).

Coming back to the dialogue with Michele Byrd-McPhee, it is interesting to underline the intrinsic contradictions when we discuss Hip-Hop in terms of appropriation and in the passage from a specific community into a global phenomenon, "a trajectory she views with both pride and caution" (Ibidem). In the global impact of Hip-Hop dance, Byrd-McPhee, indeed, notices that "it's provided a voice for so many people around the world" (Ibidem), but, at the same time, "it's used globally in ways that the people who made the culture don't benefit from it" (Ibidem).

Academic Insight

Implicitly, what both Byrd-McPhee and Schaefer is an appropriation that include subject, object and contents:

> "People think that all you have to do is have certain postures, wear certain clothes, dance to certain music" to make it Hip Hop, Byrd-McPhee says, pointing out that simply donning toe shoes and tutus and dancing to Tchaikovsky does not a ballerina make. "It's that kind of disconnect from the origins of the culture and the people who created it that's problematic."
>
> (Ibidem)

Adding that:

> In popular culture, more recent accusations of cultural appropriation have been aimed at Madonna's use of voguing in her famous "Vogue" video, Miley Cyrus' adoption of twerking as a way to rebrand herself, and the New Zealand choreographer Parris Goebel's use of Jamaican dancehall in Justin Bieber's "Sorry" video.
>
> (Ibidem)

In reality, and here the discussion become more intriguing, it is not really a matter of being based on forms of ethnic dances, because – reprising the above-mentioned positions of Michelle Heffner Hayes – "every dance form is an ethnic form," but in the power dynamic and, consequently, in the logic of cultural hegemony at the base of borrowing from a dance for from a marginalised community or culture.

On this point, and specifically on Hip-Hop, an interesting perspective comes from Lauren Michele Jackson, author of *White Negroes: When Cornrows Were in Vogue...and Other Thoughts on Cultural Appropriation* (2019). Jackson moves from a preliminary idea: cultural appropriation is not necessarily the big bad, but a process that cannot be stopped nor avoided, because it is almost an unconscious process that every individual and community is doing on a daily basis. So, the problem is not appropriation but the inequality that can be related or resulted from appropriation.

Hip Hop, as also underlined by Miss Rosen in her review to Jackson, is clearly cited as an enduring example of appropriation in many forms, already from its origin: "Born in the Bronx in the early 1970s, hip hop sprang forth as a new style of art, music, and dance invented by teens who blended shared elements of multi-ethnic Black and Latinx communities while remixing the past and present" (2020, online).

Is Global Hip-Hop-based on Appropriation?

In the above-mentioned *White Negroes: When Cornrows Were in Vogue...and Other Thoughts on Cultural Appropriation*, Jackson points out that Hip Hop emerged out of cross-generational, cross-cultural, cross-racial, and cross-national forms of cultural appropriation, mixing, and acculturation. In the chapter on "Rap Music and Hip Hop Culture," as part of *Cultures of Popular Music* (2001), Andy Bennet discusses Hip Hop as a global resource, Hip Hop in Western Europe, Hip Hop in Japan – and on that please see also Condry (2006) – and in Oceania as additional elements of interest to Hip Hop and the African Diaspora. In another contribution on *The struggle for ethnicity: Swedish youth styles and the construction of ethnic identities* (1977), Erling Bjurström talks about "Original Black Viking" as the marking of a new ethnic identity. In their complete contribution on *Hip-Hop & the Global Imprint of a Black Cultural Form* (2011), the earlier-mentioned Marcyliena Morgan and Dionne Bennett remember the growing study area on Hip Hop in a global perspectives: "Volumes have also been published in the emerging field of global hip-hop studies, including *Global Noise: Rap and Hip-Hop Outside the USA*; *The Vinyl Ain't Final: Hip Hop and the Globalization of Black Popular Culture*; *Tha Global Cipha: Hip Hop Culture and Consciousness*; *Global Linguistic Flows: Hip Hop Cultures, Youth Identities, and the Politics of Language*; and *The Languages of Global Hip Hop*" (p. 179). And they add: "We consider Hip-Hop to be the lingua franca for popular and political youth culture around the world" (Ibidem). Additionally, Osumare states that: "Global hip-hop youth culture has become a phenomenon in the truest sense of the word and has affected nearly every country on the map" (2001, p. 171. See also Osumare 2007).

It is clear that considering Hip Hop nowadays is something that evolved from a subculture to the condition of being a dominant one. However, according to which appropriation processes? Probably, and in this case, the proposed assumption may be considered provoking. There is a misunderstanding in considering the hegemonic relation today as the one of the 1970s. In my opinion, two are the possibilities among the one earlier investigated: cultural exploitation and transculturation. In the first case, the exploitation still considers a marginalised culture and a dominant culture, in a perspective that is quite binary and based on a dichotomy. As said, cultural exploitation is, indeed, the appropriation of elements of a subordinated culture by a dominant culture without substantive reciprocity. The other possibility is considering Hip-Hop nowadays as the result of transculturation, a hybrid form based on multiple cultural appropriations in the context of globalisation and transnational capitalism. It is not a case, from this point of view, that Carol M. Motley and Geraldine R. Henderson continuously refer to 'adaptation' in analysing Hip-Hop worldwide (2008, pp. 243–253).

Both possibilities seem plausible according to the industry system – and not only the cultural system – they are in. In a similar way to what happens in other contexts, such as the cinema industry (as admirably investigated by Laura Mulvey in her seminal work *Visual Pleasure and Narrative Cinema* on feminist approaches to film), the industry is an integral and essential part of the evolution and change in cultural perspective. Hip-Hop in a context of a white-based industry (dominant class) will assume the form of cultural exploitation, despite the ethnicity of the artist. On the other hand, in other contexts, the evolution of Hip-Hop may have the connotation of transculturation.

PROFESSIONAL INSIGHT – DEAN LEE

Location: London, New York, Los Angeles

Dean Lee has been Janet Jackson's choreographer since 2018. Working closely with her Creative Director, Gil Duldulao, Lee has created steps for all of Janet's recent international live performances. Originally from the UK, he began his career working for major artists as a dancer before graduating to associate choreographer and then to choreographer. He has also worked on projects such as X-Factor USA/UK and tours for Kylie Minogue, Beth Ditto and Leona Lewis.

Working with Janet is being with Family
It's not just a job, it's about who she is as a person, it's how the whole team functions and makes you feel. It's Family. I can say wholeheartedly it's the job where I feel like I'm using every single tool that I trained for – musicality, dynamics, pick up, stamina, creativity,

discipline.... I feel like I get to utilise every single one of those tools and I truly feel the most alive whenever I'm working with Janet.

She is the blueprint for so many after her, the impact Janet has had on pop culture is unparalleled, so to get to witness first hand her legacy, to be around that level of artistry, to be able to work alongside one of the greatest artists in the world is very humbling. We don't have many legends left, and no one is still doing it the way she does. It's a completely full circle moment in my life working with Janet. I'm beyond grateful to her for allowing me to do so.

Everyone wants to follow a trend.
Everyone right now wants to do what everyone else is doing, but I feel through impatience they have forgotten that actually you can create whatever you want. Maybe they haven't forgotten and just aren't brave enough to put in the hard work to explore their own authentic gift. There are literally no limits, no boundaries. Sure, there is a taste level that you have or you don't, but in reality there's no right or wrong to what we do because art is creative self-expression. If one does decide to explore that gift, I encourage them to ensure they're always pulling from the most authentic place possible.

I always wanted to be a choreographer. That was always the goal for me, but I don't think I was ready for it to happen as soon as it did.
There was this point in my life where I wasn't really getting the phone call to see if I was available as a dancer anymore. I don't know it's because I was always assisting choreographers at the same time as well as being a dancer, so from outside perception people just assume you've moved on from being dancer because of that you end up caught in no-man's land. A job came up with Brian Friedman. It was for a show in Berlin and he needed an assistant for a month so Jerry (Jerry Reeve, director of Kutes agency) suggested that he use me. So he did. After that, Brian for a period of time really became solely responsible for keeping me hired.

In 2016, I created a piece for my Boys Dance Company, Strike Boys Co. at Urdang called 'Eryka' for 'Move It' (a UK dance convention). I remember feeling I had found my formula – what I liked to create and how I liked to create it. Those numbers that I created for my dance company were my playground for what I wanted to do with artists. I put everything I had into that piece. Later on that year, Brian was coming back to London to do X Factor as Creative Director and I ended up booking the job as Head Choreographer because of that piece. X-Factor was the turning point. I felt like 'I'm a choreographer now.'

In terms of my style, I think it's quite hard to define because I'm influenced by so many different things.
I'm very old school. The people that I was trained by were some of the most incredible teachers who have truly lived Dance. Their ways of teaching were very old school which I'm so thankful for because those things have never really left me. I understand how important those qualities are. Even if you're doing commercial, you've still got to understand how to have technique alongside that. I still sit down and watch Bob Fosse, the old black and white movies, and the original West Side Story. There are so many different things that I just look at and I feel so inspired by because I, as an artist, am not one thing.

I am always thinking "how can you keep those elements of what's old school and has worked so well for so long but make it now?." That's the thing that I love to play with the most. My style is a bit of a blend of all different things – it's taking Jazz, it's taking Ballet, it's taking Contemporary, Musical Theatre but then putting it in that pot of Commercial Dance and then just letting it go and seeing what my body comes up with, my style is not one singular thing.

Academic Insight

I got a phone call from Gil Duldulao who is the creative director for Janet Jackson.
At the very beginning of 2019, I was working on the X Factor tour and I was on the tour bus. It must have been about 2 am and Gil called me and told me that Janet was doing a Las Vegas residency. He said, "I'm gonna send you a list of every song she's ever done or released and you just pick two and you do whatever you want. Just create…." I did my two songs and sent them off. 'Feedback' actually wasn't going to be in the show but Janet liked what I had done with it and decided to put it in the set-list. It ended up being the opening dance number in the show. The way everything happened was just really mind-blowing.

If I'm being paid to be a choreographer, I will do the work and I will make up the steps.
An assistant choreographer or an Assistant Creative, is almost like being a PA – being there to do the music, cleaning choreography if the choreographer needs to be somewhere else amongst many other things, but it should never involve actually making up steps. The minute you start making up any sort of choreography, you're an Associate Choreographer. Brian Friedman was very hot on that – he believed that if you've made up steps, then there's credit there for you. He really stuck to that distinction. Similarly, when I was working with Gil, if somebody was coming into the room, I'd introduce myself as Gil's assistant. Gil would correct me and say, "you are my associate – we are doing this together." He was very respectful and very clear on that.

I find it really hard to find a good assistant/associate, my brain doesn't stop thinking so I've always got creative options going on in my mind and sometimes when I have an assistant, I need them to understand I don't need them to come up with the steps. Not in the sense that I don't want them to, but it's about payroll. If I'm being paid to be a choreographer, then that's what I will do – be the choreographer.

Image 10.1 Dean with Janet Jackson in a break from rehearsals at Base Studios. In 2023, they began work on the choreography for Janet Jackson's 'Together Again' tour

Academic Insight

References

10a. Dancing on a Cliff Edge: Litza Bixler

Caves, R.E. (2000). *Creative Industries: Contracts between Art and Commerce*. London: Harvard University Press.

Decker, C. (2016). *Mindset: The New Psychology of Success* (Updated ed.). New York: Random House.

Parker, S.C. (2009). *The Economics of Entrepreneurship* (2nd ed.). Cambridge, UK: Cambridge University Press.

10b. Collaborations between Early 20th-Century European and American concert and Commercial Dance – Tamiris and Nagrin: Daria Lavrennikov

Au, S. (2012). *Ballet and Modern Dance* (pp. 148–153). London: Thames & Hudson Ltd.

Friscia, S. (2020). Is the Line between Concert and Commercial Dance Finally Fading?, *Dance Magazine*, June. https://www.dancemagazine.com/concert-dance-vs-commercial-dance/

Gottschild, B. (2001). Stripping the Emperor: The Africanist Presence in American Concert Dance. In A. Dils & A. C. Albright (Eds.), *Moving History/Dancing Culture* (pp. 332–241). Middletown: Wesleyan University Press.

Jowitt, D. (2012). Seven Strange Heroes. In C. Gitelman & B. Palfy (Eds.), *On Stage Alone: Soloists and the Modern Dance Canon* (p. 163–186). Tallahassee: University Press of Florida.

McPherson, E. and J. Tucker (2019). An Exploration of the Life and Work of Helen Tamiris, *Dance Today*, Issue No. 36, September.

Nagrin, D. (1994). *Dance and the Specific Image: Improvisation*. Pittsburgh/London: University of Pittsburgh Press.

Nagrin, D. (1997). *The Six Questions: Acting Technique for Dance Performance*. Pittsburgh: University of Pittsburgh Press.

Nagrin Foundation – Youtube channel. https://www.youtube.com/user/DanielNagrinFdn

Roses-Thema, C. (2003). Interview with Daniel Nagrin. *Journal for the Anthropological Study of Human Movement*, 12(3). https://jashm.press.uillinois.edu/12.3/12-3Interview_Roses-Therma114-119.pdf

Wawrejko, D. (2009). Helen Tamiris: Re-visioning Modernism in Modern Dance. Moving Naturally Conference, October, University of Surrey UK.

Wawrejko, D. (2009). A Tribute to Daniel Nagrin: Russian Jewish influences in American Modern Dance. *Dancing Voices*, November, Haifa Israel.

10c. Punkin' and Werkin' It: The Queer Roots of Commercial Dance: Joseph Mercier

Bragin, N. (2014). Techniques of Black Male Re/dress: Corporeal Drag and Kinaesthetic Politics in the Rebirth of Waacking/Punkin. *Women & Performance: A Journal of Feminist Theory*, 24(1), 61–78.

Chatzipapatheodoridis, C. (2017). Strike a Pose, Forever: The Legacy of Vogue and Its Re-Contextualization in Contemporary Camp Performances. *European Journal of American Studies*, 11(3), 1–15.

Davis, S. (2017). Trans Afro-Boricua Vogue Dancer On Signature Hair Flip That Inspired Beyoncé: "I Was Cheated", *VIBE*. https://www.vibe.com/features/viva/leiomy-maldonado-on-famous-hair-flip-482449/

Easter, M. (2020). Remembering Tyrone Proctor, a Pioneer of the 1970s L.A. Dance Style Waacking, *Los Angeles Times*, June 12. https://www.latimes.com/entertainment-arts/story/2020-06-12/tyrone-proctor-dies-dancer-waacking-soul-train

Garcia, L. (2014). An Alternate History of Sexuality in Club Culture. https://ra.co/features/1927.

Halberstam, J. (2005). *In a Queer Time and Place: Transgender Bodies, Subcultural Lives*. New York and London: New York Up.

Hylton, R. (2022). *Dancing in Time: A History of Moving and Shaking*. London: The British Library.

LaBeija (n.d.). Our History, *LaBeija*. https://www.royalhouseoflabeija.com/history.

Lawrence, T. (2006). In Defence of Disco (Again). *New Formations*, 58(Summer), 128–146.

Lawrence, T. (2011a). 'A History of Drag Balls, Houses and the Culture of Voguing'. *Voguing: Voguing and the House Ballroom Scene of New York City 1989–92*. London: Soul Jazz Books.

Lawrence, T. (2011b). Disco and the Queering of the Dance Floor. *Cultural Studies*, 25(2), 230–243.

Suraki, K. (2016). What Is Waacking?: Queer History of Punking, Whacking, Waacking 1970–2003. https://www.youtube.com/watch?v=l62XRkUym2Q&ab_channel=KumariSuraj

10d. A Reflection on Hip-Hop, Hegemony and Appropriation: Armando Rotondi

Alridge, D.P. and J.B. Stewart (2005). Introduction: Hip Hop in History: Past, Present, and Future, *The Journal of African American History*, 90(3), The History of Hip Hop (Summer), 190–195.

Basu, D. and S.J. Lemelle (2006). *The Vinyl Ain't Final: Hip Hop and the Globalization of Black Popular Culture*. London: Pluto Press.

Bennet, A. (2001). *Cultures of Popular Music*. Buckingham-Philadelphia: Open University Press.

Bjurström, E. (1997). The Struggle for Ethnicity – Swedish Youth Styles and the Construction of Ethnic Identities. *Young*, 5(3), 44–58. https://doi.org/10.1177/110330889700500304

Chang, J. (2006). Keeping It Real: Interpreting Hip-Hop. *College English*, 68(5), 545–554.

Condry, I. (2006). *Hip-Hop Japan: Rap and the Paths of Cultural Globalization*. Durham, NC: Duke University Press.

D'Anjou, C. (2020). Out of Line: On Hip Hop and Cultural Appropriation, *Medium*, 22nd June, online: https://medium.com/@cyandanjou/out-of-line-on-hip-hop-and-cultural-appropriation-1c060e6801e9 [accessed: 02/12/2022].

Eco, U. (1973). Social Life as a Sign System. In D. Robey (Ed.), *Structuralism: The Wolfson College Lectures, 1972* (pp. 57–72). Oxford: Oxford University Press.

Gramsci, A. (1992). *Prison Notebooks*, edited by Joseph A. Buttigieg. New York: Columbia University Press.

Hall, S. (2007). Encoding and Decoding in the Television Discourse. *CCCS Selected Working Papers*. London/New York: Routledge (originally 1973).

Hebdige, D. (2002). *Subculture. The Meaning of Style*. London/New York: Routledge (first edition Methuen, 1979).

Heffner Hayes, M. (2009). *Flamenco: Conflicting Histories of the Dance*. Jefferson: McFarland.

Jackson, L.M. (2019). *White Negroes: When Cornrows Were in Vogue…and Other Thoughts on Cultural Appropriation*. Boston, MA: Beacon.

Keyes, C.L. (2002). *Rap Music and Street Consciousness*. Urbana: University of Illinois Press.

Lifar, S. (2011). The Choreographer's Manifesto. *The Dance Thinker*, 9, July (originally 1935).

Light, A. (1999). *The Vibe History of Hip Ho*p. New York: Three Rivers Press.

Lipsitz, G. (1994). *Dangerous Crossroads. Popular Music, Postmodernism and the Poetics of Place*. London: Verso.

Mitchell, T. (Ed.). (2002). *Global Noise. Rap and Hip Hop Outside the USA*. Hanover: Wesleyan.

Morgan, M. and D. Bennett (2011). Hip-Hop & the Global Imprint of a Black Cultural Form. *Daedalus*, 140(2), *Race, Inequality & Culture*, 2(Spring), 176–196.

Motley, C.M. and G.R. Henderson (2008). The Global Hip-Hop Diaspora: Understanding the Culture. *The Journal of Business Research*, 61, 243–253.

Mulvey, L. (1975). Visual Pleasure and Narrative Cinema. *Screen*, 16(3), 6–18.

Nur Amin, T. (2010). Demystifying Hip Hop Dance? *Dance Chronicle*, 33(3), 490–493.

Nye, J. (2004). *Soft Power. The Means to Success in World Politics*. New York: Public Affairs.

Osumare, H. (2001). Beat Streets in the Global Hood: Connective Marginalities of the Hip Hop Globe. *Journal of American & Comparative Cultures*, 2(Spring/Summer), 171–181.

Osumare, H. (2007). *The African Aesthetic in Global Hip-Hop. Power Moves*. New York: Palgrave MacMillan.

Perry, I. (2004). *Prophets of the Hood. Politics and Poetics in Hip Hop*. Durham, NC: Duke University Press.

Potter, R.A. (1995). *Spectacular Vernaculars: Hip-Hop and the Politics of Postmodernism*. New York: State University of New York Press.

Rose, T. (1994). *Black Noise: Rap Music and Black Culture in Contemporary America*. Hanover: Wesleyan/University Press of New England.

Rosen, M. (2020). Cultural Appropriation Is Bad, But We Wouldn't Have Hip Hop Without It, *Document*, 6th March, online: https://www.documentjournal.com/2020/03/cultural-appropriation-is-bad-but-we-wouldnt-have-hip-hop-without-it/ [accessed: 02/12/2022].

Samy Alim, H., I. Awad, and A. Pennycook (Eds.). (2009). *Global Linguistic Flows. Hip Hop Cultures, Youth Identities, and the Politics of Language*. London/New York: Routledge.

Schaefer, B. (2020). At What Point Does Appreciation Become Cultural Appropriation?, *Dance Magazine*, 16th December, online: https://www.dancemagazine.com/cultural-appropriation/ [accessed: 02/12/2022].

Shuker, R. (2012). *Popular Music Culture. The Key Concepts* (3rd ed.). Oxon/New York: Routledge.

Spady, J., H. Samy Alim, and S. Meghelli (2006). *Tha Global Cipha: Hip Hop Culture and Consciousness*. Richmond: Black History Museum Press.

Stalling Huntington, C. (2007). *Hip Hop Dance: Meanings and Messages*. Jefferson: McFarland.

Terkourafi, M. (Ed.). (2010). *The Languages of Global Hip Hop*. New York: Continuum.

Young, J.O. (2005). Profound Offense and Cultural Appropriation. *Journal of Aesthetics and Art Criticism*, 63(2), 135–146.

Acknowledgements

When I first began writing and researching this book, I was worried that it may be difficult to persuade choreographers, dancers and creatives to contribute to a project they didn't know much about. It's been a relief that the responses I received were tremendous – very supportive and generous. The first contribution to this project was from one of Janet Jackson's original choreographers (Barry Lather) and the final interview I did was with Janet's current choreographer (Dean Lee), illustrating the breadth of support I have received from the dance community throughout the writing and research process. Many people, from the United States, Europe and the UK, have generously given their time, expertise and encouragement to this project and trusted me to deliver their stories and thoughts in these pages, whilst also understanding that the educational focus of this book is to inform the dance students of today and tomorrow.

In particular, I'd like to thank the following people:

My wife Evgeniya for her constant support and for designing the front cover, my family for their belief in me, my colleagues and the students at the Institute of the Arts Barcelona, Ben Piggot, Steph Hines and the team at Routledge for making this happen … *and* Alyssa Renard at MSA agency Los Angeles, JaQuel Knight, Steve Gaeto at Bloc Agency Los Angles, Mary Pelloni, Rich + Tone Talauega, Paul Roberts, Randall Watson, Reshma Gajjar, Dean Lee, Francis Yeoh, Robert Penman, Rebbi Rose, Callum Powell, John Graham, Xena Gusthart, Stefano Rosato, Joseph Mercier, Nathan Clarke, Karla Garcia, Litza Bixler, Kiel Tutin, Barry Lather, Kashika Arora, Claire and Jamie Karitzis, Jono Kitchens, Aaron Silas, Nuria Beltran, Shaun Earl, Armando Rotondi, Ida Paulsen, Kate Prince, Gary Lloyd, Adam Boland, Daria Lavrennikov, Ailish Oliver-Kerby, Nicole Guarino, Mirko D'Agostino, Graeme Pickering, Dax O'Callaghan, Kike Granero, Mark Summers, Andy Señor Jr, Natricia Bernard and anyone else who has been kind enough to support and contribute. I'm very grateful to all!

Keep up to date with news and features about this book at
www.commercial-dance.com

Index

Abdul, Paula 70, 73, 76, 145–146
African diaspora 27–29, 211
DJ Afrika Bambaataa 13, 212
Arora, Kashika 183

Base Dance studios 180
Basil, Toni 17, 75, 151–152
Beyoncé 94–95, 108–109, 131, 134, copyright 158–160; sexualisation 167
Bixler, Litza 56, 60, 189–197
Blankenbuehler, Andy 37, 89–90
Bourne, Matthew 88–89
Boy Blue dance company 24, 87, 90

Campbell, Don 17–19, 151
Chandelier music video 109–111
A Chorus Line film 25, 76
Clark, Nathan 184–186
contemporary dance 81, 88–89, 92, 110, 159, 198–203
copyright law 109, 157–162

dance class culture 162–165, 173, 179–182
Daniel, Jeffrey 43, 158, 169
disco 204–206
Durell, RJ 26, 112–113

employment 74–75

Falcon, Bruno 'Pop n Taco' 19, 152
Fenty fashion show Vol 2 117–119, 166
Flashdance 15–16, 167
Florez, Nick 26, 111–113

Fosse, Bob 27, 35–36, 58, 118, 216; Single Ladies music video 108–109, 158–160
freelance work 189–197
Friedman, Brian 26, 60, 80, 123–124, 217

Gajjar, Reshma 61–63
Garcia, Karla 96–98
Gatson, Frank 108–109, 130–131, 160
Gibson, Laurieann 135–138
Goebel, Parris 9, 46, 81, 117–119, 166, 184
Gusthart, Xena 174–175
Grant, Chris 94, 131
The Greatest Showman movie 114–115

Heffington, Ryan 109–111
In the Heights movie 127–128
Honey movie 136
Hip-Hop: appropriation 209–215; collective culture 11–17; music 78–79; social steps 21–22
Hornaday, Jeffrey 25, 76

inclusivity 165–166

Jackson, Janet 73–74, 145, 216–217; Rhythm Nation video 105–107; Velvet Rope Tour 150
Jackson, Michael 47–49, 68–73, 127, 148, 153; Beat It music video 72, 82; copyright 157; This Is It concert 93–94; Thriller music video 103–105
Jazz Dance 24–37; historical overview 27–29; music 29; in music video 73; in musical theatre 83–90; pioneers 29–37

Index

Keersmaeker, Anna Teresa de 158–159
Khan, Akram 92
Kidd, Michael 32–33, 158
King, Jamie 132
Kitchens, Jono 63–65
Knight, JaQuel 94, 108–109, 133–135, 159–160
K-Pop 44, 82, 98–99, 161
Krump 23–24
Kudelka, Marty 80, 138–139

Labanotation 161
La'Donna, Charm 95–97, 125–126
Landon, Tina 39, 74, 80, 149–151
Lane, William Henry 28
Lather, Barry 47–49, 61, 77
Lavrennikov, Daria 198–203
Lee, Dean 215–217
LGBTQ+ 41–42, 63–65, 91, 165–166, 203–208
live concerts 90–96
Lloyd, Gary 84
Locking 17–19, 152

Madonna 61, 149; Blonde Ambition Tour 90–91, 152; Vogue music video 42, 154, 208, 214
Madrid, Keone & Mari 120–121
Mattox, Matt 26, 33–34
Mercier, Joseph 203–209
Millennium Dance Complex 182
Minogue, Kylie; Showgirl Homecoming concert 91–93; video 141
MTV and music video: a history of 67–82, 154; MTV Video Music Awards 67–68, 72
musical theatre 82–90

Nappy Tabs 60
New Jack Swing 21–22

Paterson, Vincent 42, 72, 77, 91, 153–154, 158
Payne, Travis 93–94, 148, 150
Peters, Michael 1, 72–73, 103–105, 153
Phillips, Arlene 76
Pineapple dance studio 181–182
Popping 19–21

Prince 47, 133
Prince, Kate 87–89
Procter, Tyrone 43, 206

Rhythm Nation music video 74, 105–107
Roberts, Paul 143–145
Robinson, Fatima 128–130
Robson, Wade 124
Rooney, Michael 92, 140–142
Rose, Rebbi 49–51
Rotondi, Armando 209–215
Ruffin, Nadine 'Hi-Hat' 115–116, 142–143

Scott, Christopher 85, 126–128
Scott, Tanisha 45–46, 50
sexualisation 165–168
Single Ladies music video 108–109, 132, 134, 159–160
Smith Jnr, Lavelle 106–107, 133, 148
Steezy 172
street dance 169–172

Talauega, Rich +Tone 58, 80, 147–150
terminology: backing dancer/supporting dancer 168; street dance 169–172
Thomas, Anthony 105–107
Thriller music video 103–105
Timberlake, Justin 138–139
Tutin, Kiel 98–100

UK choreographers 80–81
unions 194–196
urban dance 169–172
Us Again short film 120–121

video recording in class 162–165
Vogue dance 40–43; Madonna Vogue video 42, 152, 201, 203–209

Waacking 43–45, 206–207
Wallen, Ashley 114–115
Watson, Randall 172–174
What About Us music video 111–113
Williams, Hype 78

Ziegler, Maddie 109–110
Zoonation: The Kate Prince Company 87–90